Violence and Thought
Essays on Social Tensions in Africa

Violence and Thought
Essays on Social Tensions in Africa

Ali A. Mazrui D.Phil.(Oxon)
Professor and Head of the Department
of Political Science,
Makerere University College,
Uganda

Longmans

Longmans, Green and Co Ltd
London and Harlow

*Associated companies, branches and representatives
throughout the world*

*Printed in Great Britain by
Western Printing Services Ltd, Bristol*

Contents

Acknowledgments

Three of the chapters in this book were written in collaboration with colleagues who were once at Makerere. 'The Soldier and the State in East Africa' was written jointly with Professor Donald S. Rothchild, who is now at the University of California, Davis. The sixth and seventh essays ('The Tensions of Crossing the Floor in East Africa' and 'Violent Constitutionalism in Uganda') were written in collaboration with Professor G. F. Engholm, who is now at Lakehead University in Canada. I am grateful to my co-authors for permission to use these essays in my book.

I am also indebted to all the journals which gave me permission to reprint essays which first appeared as articles in them. More precise acknowledgement is made in footnotes to each chapter.

Research assistance and secretarial support for most of these studies came from funds provided by the Rockefeller Foundation for political science research at Makerere University College. On behalf of myself, and of political science at Makerere, I would like to reaffirm our continuing gratitude to the Foundation.

To Mrs Gwen McIntosh, Mrs Winifred da Silva and Mrs Pamela Senabulya I am grateful for many hours of patient typing, proof-reading and sympathetic involvement in the work. To my fellow social scientists at Makerere I owe the atmosphere of sustained stimulation. To my wife I owe the intelligent companionship which makes reflection and meditation at home possible.

A.A.M.

Preface

The phenomenon of social violence has intrigued a number of thinkers. Georges Sorel linked it with the myth of a general strike as an instrument of proletarian assertion. Karl Marx before him had regarded revolutionary violence as something which must recur periodically to restore compatibility between the relatively stagnant social-legal structure of society and the relatively dynamic productive forces of the economy. More recently, in the period of decolonization in our own time, Franz Fanon, having first observed and then participated in the Algerian war of independence, came to the conclusion that violence of that kind was a purifying experience and a moral preparation for the freedom-fighters engaged in it.

The essays collected in this book are not concerned with putting forward any single thesis about the role of violence in society. On the contrary, the diversity of subjects covered here is itself an assertion that social violence has such a wide spectrum of relevance that it cannot be reduced to a single ray of theoretical illumination.

Some of the essays are empirical, others more theoretical; some of our claims are universalistic, while others are more area-bound. Each chapter can stand on its own as a separate study of an aspect of social experience. But the collection as a whole hopes to achieve a cumulative elucidation of some of the areas of contact between four kinds of phenomena. These are, first, the phenomenon of violence itself; secondly, the symbols of power in society; thirdly, the process of national development; and fourthly, the instincts of man in society. The focus of illustration is Africa, but many of the conclusions arrived at in the essays aspire to a broader human validity.

Makerere University College,   A.A.M.
Kampala, Uganda

SECTION A

INTERNATIONAL VIOLENCE AND THE MILITARY

1 The Soldier and the State in East Africa: Some Theoretical Conclusions on the Army Mutinies of 1964[1]

written in collaboration with

DONALD ROTHCHILD, *University of California, Davis*
(formerly of the University of East Africa, Nairobi)

'There is not the slightest chance that the forces of law and order in Tanganyika will mutiny.'[2] These were the words of Julius Nyerere. The occasion was mid-1960. Nyerere was about to become Chief Minister of an internally self-governing Tanganyika. Independence was not far off, and some people were seeking reassurance that events in the newly independent Congo would not be repeated in Tanganyika. Nyerere was emphatic in his answer: 'These things cannot happen here. First, we have a strong organization, TANU. The Congo did not have that kind of organization. . . . [And further] there is not the slightest chance that the forces of law and order in Tanganyika will mutiny.'[3]

Three-and-a-half years later Nyerere faced the worst crisis of his political career—a mutiny of his First Battalion, and then of his second. The interval since then has been an opportunity for renewed reflection on those events of early 1964.

From the records of the courts-martial held in East Africa following the mutinies one can compile evidence on immediate

[1] Reprinted with permission from *The Western Political Quarterly*, Vol. XX, No. 1, March, 1967.
[2] *Inside East Africa* (August/September 1960), 13–14.
[3] *Ibid.* Considering the nature of the analysis, it would help clarity if we referred to Tanganyika and Zanzibar as distinct entities and avoid the *joint* name of 'Tanzania' for our purposes.

causes.[1] But the purpose of this essay is not to establish immediate causes. What is of broader comparative interest is the complex of fundamental issues raised by such events. Army mutinies, even when concerned with pay, have an importance that extends beyond the mutinies themselves. They have repercussions which always exceed the intentions of the mutineers. And they raise questions about power and legitimacy in the political systems in which they occur.

Among the issues which were raised by the army mutinies in East Africa were, first, the nature of military loyalty to a newly invented state; secondly, the place of the soldier in a governmental system involving popular leadership; and third, the doctrine of non-intervention in the kinds of situations presented by contemporary Africa. It is primarily these three broad issues which will be considered here.

PATRIOTISM IN UNIFORM

In most of the older countries of the world the armed forces are, in the final analysis, the ultimate repository of patriotism. The traditions of the services over generations amount to an accumulated loyalty, sometimes an exaggerated loyalty—to the state, to a supposed national interest or even a supposed national glory.

If we now turn to the place of the soldier in old tribal Africa a

---

[1] The actual chronology of events was of the following order: *January 12, 1964*, the Sultan's Government of Zanzibar was overthrown. *January 17*, Tanganyika police were sent to Zanzibar to help restore order. *January 20*, the men of the First Battalion of the Tanganyika Rifles stationed near Dar es Salaam mutinied—demanding higher pay and the complete Africanization of the officer corps; President Nyerere's whereabouts were unknown to the public at large. *January 21*, the Second Battalion of the Tanganyika Rifles stationed at Tabora also mutinied. Nyerere came out and broadcast to the nation. Order was temporarily restored. *January 23*, Uganda's Minister of Interior Felix Onama was reportedly manhandled by two companies of the First Battalion of the Uganda Rifles over the issue of increasing privates' pay. The Uganda Government requested British military assistance—and 450 British troops were sent from Nairobi. *January 24*, troops of Kenya's Eleventh Battalion mutinied at Lanet Camp near Nakuru. Units of the Third Royal Force Artillery were called to restore order. *January 25*, British troops broke up a sit-down strike of still-mutinous troops at Nakuru in Kenya. British troops descended near Dar es Salaam and at Tabora and disarmed the Tanganyika mutineers at the request of the Tanganyika Government. Three Africans were reported killed in the engagement near Dar es Salaam.

similar phenomenon is discernible. 'All young men between the ages of eighteen and forty should form a warrior class (*anake*), and be ready to defend the country, and that the country should respect them and have pride in them.' This was one of the principles of the traditional system of government of the Kikuyu as described by Jomo Kenyatta in his book in 1938.[1] As for the leaders of the warriors, these were 'men who had proved by their own actions their capability of leadership; had shown bravery in wars, impartiality in justice, self-sacrifice *and above all, discipline in the group*'.[2] In other words, the armed forces in tribal Africa tried to embody in their different ranks some of the highest values admired by the tribe. And we have already suggested that in a long-established developed state the armed forces try to embody at least the basic virtue of loyalty to their country.

The new states in Africa have virtually the same basis for military troubles as they have for political troubles—they are no longer adequately tribal and are not yet fully national. Their armed forces are inspired neither by the dedication of tribal warriors nor by the patriotism which comes with a long-established national consciousness.

Their role looks even more anomalous when it is remembered that the armed forces in a new state are often inherited from the colonial regime. On January 26, 1964, Jomo Kenyatta issued a public rebuke of Kenya's mutineers, firmly asserted his Government's authority, and went on to say: 'During the colonial days the men of the King's African Rifles served the British Government loyally. Now that we have our own African government the world and our own people are justified in expecting even greater loyalty from the Kenya Army.'[3]

If those soldiers had indeed been so loyal to the colonial regime there must have been times when the Kenya soldiers and the Kenya nationalists were in opposing camps. The immediate past history of the Kenya Army had certainly not prepared the men for the role of being some ultimate repository of Kenya nationalism before independence. It was truer to say of the military than of almost any other group of the population that in them a

---

1 *Facing Mount Kenya* (London: Secker and Warburg, 1959 reprint), p. 188. The book was first published in 1938.
2 *Ibid.*, p. 200 (emphasis supplied).
3 *East African Standard*, January 27, 1964. .

tradition of loyalty to Kenya as a national unit under indigneous rule had just not grown yet. And this simple factor was inevitably fraught with risk.

There is irony in this when we remember the role which ex-soldiers were supposed to have played in the very birth of African nationalism. It has been said, for example, that the 150,000 ex-servicemen throughout British West Africa after World War II contributed to the general feeling of unrest, which remained unassuaged, if it was not stimulated, by the mild constitutional reforms of the mid-1940's.[1] In a country like Nigeria it was 'not surprising to find ex-servicemen among the more militant leaders of the nationalist movement during the postwar period'.[2] Perhaps it was fitting that in 1964 it should have been Nigerian soldiers who took over from British troops in Tanganyika when Tanganyika's own army failed her.

In Kenya's history, too, a whole chapter stands out with the title, 'The Role of the Ex-Soldier in Kenya's Political History'. On one side we have the role of *European* ex-servicemen in the conversion of Kenya into a country with white settlers—with all the political repercussions which that entailed. As far back as the first world war the War Council of Kenya concerned itself not only with the war and problems of conscription—'in which East Africa led the way in the Empire'—but it sought to strengthen the European position in particular by devising a Soldier Settlement Scheme for the postwar period.[3]

And at the end of the second world war the Kenya Government and the British Government announced an agricultural settlement scheme for European ex-soldiers released from the armed forces—'men and women of pure European descent, who were thus eligible to farm in the area reserved for Europeans in Kenya, and whose war services a grateful country wished to recognize'.[4]

---

[1] See Dennis Austin, *West Africa and the Commonwealth* (London: Penguin African Series, 1957), p. 14.

[2] James S. Coleman, *Nigeria, Background to Nationalism* (Los Angeles: U. of California Press, 1958), p. 254.

[3] See George Bennett, *Kenya, A Political History: The Colonial Period* (New York: Oxford U. Press, 1963), p. 38. This earlier soldier scheme was ill conceived and badly organized. But it was not without significance for future developments.

[4] Sir Michael Blundell, *So Rough a Wind* (London: Weidenfeld and Nicolson, 1964), p. 63.

What emerges from this is the importance of 'soldier settlers' as a factor in the land question in Kenya's history.[1]

As for the role of the *African* ex-serviceman in East Africa's history, one Kenya settler who served with Africans abroad has suggested that the first signs of nationalism in East Africa were discernible in the African *askari* and the questions he had to ask after serving in South-East Asia. The *askari* was at last prompted to ask why only Europeans were officers in the East African Army and why the food scales were different between white and black soldiers. As in West Africa, though less dramatically, 'the first real seeds of African nationalism were sown in the later years of the war, when the African thus began to question the traditional differences between himself and the white man'.[2]

Actually, Jomo Kenyatta's own nationalism antedates the second world war. If Blundell sees the birth of African nationalism as being the effect of the second world war, Kenyatta sees the birth of acquisitive colonialism as being, in a sense, the effect of the first world war. Africa had already been colonized before World War I, but a new acquisitiveness now characterized imperial attitudes. As Kenyatta passionately said in 1938:

> Take the case of the Great War, 1914–18, in which tens of thousands of Africans lost their lives. The reward for this was taking away the best lands from the Africans, the introduction of *kipande* [the identity and employment card] with its diabolical system of finger-prints as though the Africans were criminals, imposition of heavy taxation and denial of freedom of speech, of the Press, and of forming political or social organizations. This is what 'democratic Britain' did in recognition of the services rendered by the Kenya Africans during 1914–18.[3]

[1] The phrase 'soldier settlers' is Blundell's. See his chapter on them in *ibid.*, pp. 61–71.

[2] *Ibid.*, pp. 58–60. See also Donald S. Rothchild, *The Effects of Mobilization in British Africa*, Duquesne University Institute of African Affairs Reprint Series No. 2. (Pittsburgh: Duquesne U. Press, 1961.)

[3] *Kenyatta, op. cit.*, p. 212. If soldiers in Africa were, in the early days, carriers of nationalism, soldiers elsewhere in underdeveloped countries were often carriers of 'the spirit of modernity'. See Daniel Lerner and R. D. Robinson, 'Swords and Plowshares: The Turkish Army as a Modernizing Force,' *World Politics*, 13 (October, 1960), 513–59; Manfred Halpern 'Middle Eastern Armies and the New Middle Class' and Lucian Pye, 'Armies in the

If we now take an abstraction like 'the African soldier' or
askari, and try to define its historical role, we can discern at least
three phases in the history of East Africa. When the African
soldier was sent abroad to fight, say, the Germans or the Italians
or the Japanese, he came back a carrier of ambitious and
nationalistic ideas. He was, in this case, one of the founding
fathers of the nationalism of discontent. When this nationalism
spread and exploded into riots or even insurrections, a new
African *askari* now served colonialism—and sought to stifle the
nationalism which former African *askaris* had helped to ignite.
This must have been what Kenyatta meant when, following the
army mutinies in January 1964, he observed how loyally the men
of the King's African Rifles had served the British Government
during the colonial days. Those men not only fought against the
Mau Mau but helped to maintain the colonial regime generally.

The third role which the African *askari* was now called upon
to play was to serve a government of African nationalists at long
last. It was this role which was nearly shattered by the mutinies.
And the irony was heightened when the new nationalist
governments in East Africa were driven to seek the aid of former
imperial troops—to force their own troops into submitting to
African rule.

DEMOCRACY, CHARISMA AND THE SOLDIER

Colin Legum, in analysing events in Africa following the
mutinies in January 1964, wrote as if those mutinies were just
one extra piece of evidence that what African countries needed
were 'strong governments'.[1] There is indeed a sense in which this
is true. But Legum contrasted 'strong government' with 'Western' forms of government. It is certainly not self-evident that
army revolts arise more easily in Western governments than in
others. Colin Legum's error in this analysis was that he unconsciously put an army mutiny into the same category as a tribal

---

Process of Political Modernization' in John L. Johnson (ed.) *The Role of the
Military in Underdeveloped Countries* (Princeton: Princeton U. Press, 1962),
pp. 279–315; and Dankwart Rustow, *Politics and Westernization in the Near
East* (Princeton: Princeton U. Press, 1956).

[1] *The Observer* (London), January 26, 1964.

revolt. Both types of revolts do need strong governments to put them down—but 'strong' governments in different, sometimes *opposite*, senses.

A situation which gives rise to a tribal revolt may compel government officials to resort to authoritarian ways. A situation which gives rise to an army revolt may, however, be one which requires popular support to frustrate the military. The government may not succeed in frustrating the military; but the least we can say is that it is surely easier for the military to shove aside a dictator than to replace a government with effective popular support. The difference may be marginal but it is usually there all the same.

This is not to underestimate the hazards of a politically minded military force in a well-established democracy. Eisenhower—himself a former military man—made it a point to warn his country of the growing political power of the military as he retired from the American Presidency. All the same it does remain true that the only safeguard a leader sometimes has against a military takeover is the amount of popular support he has in the country at large. And a democratic system of government helps to strengthen the principle of 'popular support' as a criterion of legitimacy and as something which can be measured at the polls, if only very roughly.[1]

In the East African countries the principle of legitimacy is still much less a matter of systems of government than of the

---

[1] President de Gaulle is an interesting case. Essentially he is a popular authoritarian. He was brought into power by the military but has been maintained in power substantially by the authority of his popular standing even in the face of an anti-Gaullist military revolt. S. E. Finer analyses that revolt of April 22, 1961, and sees it as a triumph of De Gaulle's 'moral authority'. See Finer's *The Man on Horseback: The Role of the Military in Politics* (London: Pall Mall, 1962), pp. 95–8. As for Eisenhower's foreboding about the power of the military in the United States, this does not seem to have been fully shared by Morris Janowitz. Janowitz argued in a book published in the very year in which Eisenhower sounded his warning: 'The military [in the United States] have accumulated considerable power and that power protrudes into the political fabric of contemporary society. It could not be otherwise. However, while they have no reluctance to press for larger budgets, they exercise their opinion on political matters with considerable restraint and unease. Civilian control of military affairs remains intact and fundamentally acceptable to the military; any imbalance in military contributions to politico-military affairs—domestic or international—is therefore often the result of default by civilian political leadership.' See M. Janowitz, *The Professional Soldier* (Glencoe: Free Press, 1960), p. viii.

personalities of the leaders. This is where that elusive quality of *charisma* comes into play. Of course, not every African leader is a charismatic leader. But Kenyatta and Nyerere surely are. Why were the personalities of these leaders inadequate to ensure loyalty in the soldiers? Why had the military camp failed to respond to political charisma?

One possible answer is that too much is taken for granted by the questioner. There is no evidence that the ordinary soldier in the camp *had* really been insensitive to the qualities of the country's leaders. One of the significant aspects of the mutinies on the East African mainland was that they seemed to be primarily non-political. The *askaris* did not challenge the legitimacy of Kenyatta's rule or Obote's rule—the mutineers were engaged in what the Uganda leaders described as a 'sit-down strike'. This was no more a case of being insensitive to charisma than a strike by railway workers would have been. A government leader could be popular and be denied the title of infallibility at the same time.

And yet this answer is not entirely convincing. The principles of discipline and obedience to superiors must remain more crucial for the soldier than for the railway worker. A 'strike' by the military is very nearly an insurrection—and is fraught with enormous risks for life, property, and stability. It cannot be treated as just another problem for the Labor Department.

But how can this kind of reasoning be instilled in the soldier? How can the soldier's loyalty be assured?

This is where we must distinguish between loyalty to a country and loyalty to a government in power. It is possible for the military to be loyal to the country and yet seek to overthrow a government in power at a particular time. Indeed, it is even possible for patriotism to consist in disobedience to a particular government. In such cases the military could overthrow a government on the ground that members of the government were unpatriotic—and were about to sacrifice, say, the territorial integrity of the country or even betray its independence.[1]

---

[1] The entry of the military into politics is often legitimized in terms of saving the nation from the politicians. Sometimes the legitimation sounds almost like defending the nation against the people. In 1961 the Argentine armed forces presented themselves in the capacity of having 'a sacred trust— that of supervising the democratic structure of the republic, of ensuring that

But who was to judge whether a government was being 'unpatriotic'? Faced with this problem, the ethic of Western democracies has tended at times to treat the word 'state' as meaning both the government and the country. And the whole idea of 'loyalty to the state' became, on fundamentals, something very near 'loyalty to the particular government in power'.

And yet, isn't the whole idea of a multiparty system a basis for distinguishing between loyalty to a government and loyalty to the country? Surely, it is pre-eminently the ethic of Western democracies which insists on such a distinction. This is in contrast to a doctrine which argued in terms like 'The CPP is Ghana and Ghana is the CPP'. It is in this latter case that 'treason' itself became definable in terms of disloyalty to the party in power. How then can the *Western* democratic ethic be accused of blurring the distinction?

This is certainly a counter-argument of some weight. And it can only be met by admitting that, insofar as party politics is concerned, it is the multiparty system which is most adamant in its refusal to equate *patriotism* with the *party line*. But this picture immediately changes as soon as we examine what is expected of the military in a Western democracy. Insofar as, say, the British Army is concerned, disloyalty to the government in power is nothing less than disloyalty to the state. The relationship between political parties in Britain may indeed differentiate opposition to the government from disloyalty to the state. But no such distinction is admissible in the relationship between the army and the Government. Public opposition to the Government by soldiers can all too easily degenerate into treason.

It is these assumptions which have led to the Western ethic of keeping the army out of politics. And Britain at least has succeeded in having military services which are as politically neutral as her civil service.

---

its destiny shall never fall into the hands of totalitarians—and especially of Perónists and Communists. When the electorate is seduced from the path of rectitude, or when democratically elected authorities betray their trust, it becomes the duty of the army to intervene and "save the nation" '. This interpretation of their posture occurs in *The Times* (London), April 6, 1961. Why North America and other *developed* countries have been more successful in insulating the military from politics is sometimes attributed to higher technology as well as to greater stability. See Samuel P. Huntington, *The Soldier and the State* (Cambridge: Harvard U. Press, 1956), pp. 20 and 32.

And yet it is precisely this ethic of political neutrality which Nyerere has now challenged. He started first by disputing the desirability of having a politically neutral civil service. And since the army mutiny he has apparently been disillusioned about a non-political military force, too. As soon as he got the British troops to disarm the Tanganyika mutineers, Nyerere turned to the active youth of his *party*. He said in a radio broadcast: 'I call on all members of the Tanu Youth League, wherever they are, to go to the local Tanu office and enroll themselves. From this group we shall try to build a nucleus of a new army for the Republic of Tanganyika.'[1] This did not mean that Nyerere had abandoned that part of the Western ethic which equated the military's disloyalty to the government with disloyalty to the state. On the contrary, Nyerere emphasized in his broadcast that 'no popular government can tolerate an army which disobeys its instructions. Any army which does not obey the laws and orders of the people's *government* is not an army of that *country*'.[2]

But whereas Britain believes it can best assure military loyalty to the Government by keeping the military politically neutral, Tanganyika seems to feel that it can best secure that loyalty by selecting an army which is politically *committed*—and is part of the party in power. This is where charisma looms into relevance again. The youth wing of an African political party is often the most sensitive and responsive to charismatic leadership. It

---

[1] See *Sunday News* (Dar es Salaam), January 26, 1964. The policy became more clearly defined later in the year. In June the Second Vice-President, Rashidi Kawawa, addressed a large group of new army recruits in these terms: 'You are just as much citizens of the country as are farmers or fishermen. There is no reason therefore of refusing any citizen of the country permission to have a say in the politics of the country.' Political discussions between officers and soldiers were to be encouraged, and the army was to be represented in the TANU national executive. See the *Nationalist* (Dar es Salaam), June 25, 1964, and the *Daily Nation* (Nairobi), June 25, 1964. There has been trouble with the military in Tanzania since then, including the arrest of a number of officers. But the idea of establishing institutional links between the military and the party is still upheld. The *Official Gazette* of Tanzania announced on January 29, 1965, the appointment of a Political Commissar for the Tanzania People's Defence Forces. No information as to his powers and duties was available. See also *East African Standard*, January 30, 1965.

[2] *Ibid*. The emphasis is ours. The mutinies in Tanganyika might not, in any case, have been as clearly non-political as their Kenyan and Ugandan counterparts. Some civilians, including trade unionists, were detained in Tanganyika following the mutinies. Nyerere's government was evidently of the opinion that the mutinies involved more than the soldiers.

therefore made sense for Nyerere to call on all members of the Tanu youth league to enroll themselves. In Britain the supremacy of the civilian leaders over the military is assured by tradition and long-established procedures of government. In Tanganyika, however, the supremacy of civilian leadership is more dependent on the quality of the leadership itself than on any long-established procedures. And if a state-conscious patriotism toward Tanganyika as a national unit has yet to be forged adequately, at least a leader-conscious loyalty can be cultivated for the time being. And the soldier must, as a policy, be no less exposed to charisma than any other party member. The party itself becomes a mechanism for the cultivation of responsiveness to leadership.

But all this makes better sense in a single-party country like Tanganyika than it does in those African countries which fall short of a one-party governmental structure. Even in Kenya the idea of an army which is politically committed in this way has yet to be accepted. On March 10, 1964, the then Leader of the Opposition, Ronald Ngala, asked for an assurance on precisely this point in the House of Representatives. The Minister of State in the Prime Minister's office, Joseph Murumbi, answered that recruitment was open to all citizens of Kenya, and the army had rules for recruitment which did not allow for political affiliations to be taken into consideration.[1]

Until Kenya decided to go the whole way in establishing a one-party system, Kenyatta's charisma could not fully be used as part of the process of loyalty-building in the Kenya army—at any rate, not with complete official sanction. Kenya's mutiny was, in any case, the least serious of them all—and it might not be necessary to indulge in novel experimentation in loyalty-building.

The idea of personalizing patriotism and focusing it on the head of the state is not by any means new. 'For King and Country' is

[1] 'Army Recruiting Non-Political', main headline story, *Mombasa Times*, March 11, 1964. Later in the year the Kenya African Democratic Union dissolved itself, and the country became a *de facto* one-party state for a while. But there was no official change in the recruitment policy. Uganda, too, opposed the politicization of the military. See the criticism made of Tanganyika's policy by the Minister for Internal Affairs, Mr. Felix Onama. 'If soldiers are allowed in politics', Mr. Onama said 'they may even challenge a Minister from a political platform.' *Daily Nation* (Nairobi), June 29, 1964. Mr. Onama was the minister who was reportedly manhandled by soldiers at the Barracks in Jinja—the event which constituted the Uganda mutiny.

an ancient battle cry. In traditional East Africa it was best illustrated in the Buganda Kingdom. As Audrey Richards has pointed out, command over the military in traditional Buganda was 'a favour granted by the king to a loyal follower . . . but any subject's refusal to fight was regarded as treachery to the king'.[1] And treachery to the *Kabaka* was indistinguishable from treason in Buganda.

But such cases of personalized patriotism disguise an important distinction—it is not the personality of a Mutesa but his position as *Kabaka* which is the basis of patriotism. In the case of the utilization of charisma as a base for patriotism, however, it is the personality of the individual leader which matters, rather than the office he fills. And yet this very use of personality to instill patriotism must lead to an institutionalization of charisma. This process was well under way in Ghana under Nkrumah. The dynamic and humble *Kwame* of former days developed into the awesome *Osagyefo*, and disloyalty to him became disloyalty to Ghana. It is not likely that Tanganyika would closely follow Ghana in this trend—although she has followed her in one or two other courses. But some resemblance is inevitable if the following prospects do in fact materialize—first, if the army is indeed linked to the party; second, if the party is identified with the state; and third, if the leader is deemed to personify the state.

But what happens when the leader goes? A state personified has always to contend with the problem of succession. The main thing in Tanganyika is to build an army loyal enough to resist the temptation of creating a problem of succession in the first place. The previous army had, at least indirectly, failed that test. For one anxious day the world wondered what had happened to Nyerere. But the only problem of succession which the mutineers finally managed to create was the problem of who was to succeed *them*—once they were disgracefully disbanded.

'I call on all members of the Tanu Youth League, wherever they are, to . . . enroll themselves.' Thus had the President of Tanganyika responded.

But where do we place 'Field-Marshal' John Okello in this

---

[1] A. I. Richards, 'Authority Patterns in Traditional Buganda', Chapter 6 in L. A. Fallers (ed.), *The King's Men* (published on behalf of the East African Institute of Social Research by Oxford U. Press, 1964), p. 277.

hypothesis about the relationship between the soldier and charismatic authority? In some ways John Okello, ostensibly a spearhead of the Zanzibar coup, is closer to Weber's conception of a charismatic leader than is Nyerere. This is particularly true if we remember that 'pure' charisma in Weberian terms has a strong element of irrationality about it. The charismatic leader tends to be almost messianic—and the compulsion of his personality on his followers is often psychic. 'In general, charisma rejects all rational economic conduct', Weber tells us. He also refers to a charismatic capacity for 'heroic frenzy'.[1]

All this refers to an archetype of the charismatic leader in 'pure' Weberian terms. And John Okello comes more readily to mind as an example than does either Julius Nyerere or Jomo Kenyatta. And while the issue with Nyerere and Kenyatta as civilian leaders has been how far their stock of charisma could command obedience from their soldiers, the issue with Okello was how far this apparently charismatic *soldier* could command the obedience of the civilian population at large.

And yet, can one talk of charisma at all unless the spontaneous obedience is already forthcoming from the following? Surely nothing in a leader can be deemed to be 'charismatic' without reference to the response it positively evokes. This should be as true as the statement that no person can be deemed to have an impressive personality unless he does, in fact, impress others.[2]

---

[1] 'The Sociology of Charismatic Authority.' See *From Max Weber: Essays in Sociology*, translated and edited by H. H. Gerth and C. Wright Mills (London: Routledge & Kegan Paul, 1957), pp. 245–52. See also Edward Shils, 'The Concentration and Dispersion of Charisma—Their Bearing on Economic Policy in Underdeveloped Countries', *World Politics*, Vol. II (1958–59); Hans Gerth, 'The Nazi Party: Its Leadership and Composition', *American Journal of Sociology*, Vol. XIV (January 1940); C. J. Friedrich, 'Political Leadership and the Problem of Charismatic Power', *The Journal of Politics*, Vol XXIII (1961); John T. Marcus, 'Transcendence and Charisma', *Western Political Quarterly* 14 (March 1961), 236; K. J. Ratnam, 'Charisma and Political Leadership', *Political Studies*, Vol. XII (October 1964).

[2] There might be a case for distinguishing between authoritative leadership and popular leadership. It can be argued that political leaders in East Africa, as indeed in many other new states, started by having more popularity and less authority than the colonial officials they had just replaced. In another context it has been said that 'authority . . . was a complex psychological bond unifying leader and followers through the different and mutually dependent attitudes of each. . . . Authority was a leader's credit fund stored in the soul of his followers which he could draw upon in those inevitable moments of common despair. It was distinguished from "popularity" as it implied a self-respect and

How much of an impact did John Okello make on the masses of Zanzibar? It seems reasonable to suppose that Okello was popular for a while in Zanzibar because, first, it was believed that he had been *the* military instrument of the coup; second, because he filled a kind of Pan-African void among these island people; and third, because the novelty of his colorful character momentarily appealed to the masses. He was later ousted with relative ease by Karume and Abdulrahman Babu. There was no evidence in Zanzibar that the masses were hankering for his return. On the contrary, the general impression was that Okello's hold over the ordinary people of Zanzibar had not been all that firm.

Why had it failed to be firm? One reason might have been that people had begun to be afraid of John Okello. It is true there have been leaders in history who have managed to command admiration as well as inspire fear. Indeed, what is 'awe' but a blend of reverence and timidity? Here then was John Okello—perhaps an adventurer in disguise, perhaps a visionary among Pan-Africanists with a confused mission of racialistic socialism. But he came to be dreaded on the island he ostensibly liberated. Why should such dread have neutralized popularity? Because John Okello was feared not because of his strength but because of his weird unpredictability. In other words, he was too eccentric even for a messianic character—and it had become difficult to be a consistent admirer of his.

Perhaps an even more significant reason for the apparent evaporation of Okello's popularity in Zanzibar was the fact that the revolution he ostensibly spearheaded was in Zanzibar instead of Lango, in Uganda. From a Pan-African standpoint, it may have been fitting that an African from Uganda should have actively helped to 'liberate' Zanzibar from non-African rule. But in spite of being an African, John Okello was just a little too different from the Zanzibaris whose hero he was supposed to be. His

---

a steadfastness which forbade ingratiation for minor personal advantages. When an officer had appropriate authority, his men complied with his directions, regarding him with a *mixture* of "reverence," "admiration" and "fear". ' This constitutes an interpretation of Justus Lipsius, *Six Bookes of Politickes of Civil Doctrine*, Trans. William Jones (London, 1594), Vol. III. See David C. Rapoport, 'Military and Civil Societies: The Contemporary Significance of a Traditional Subject in Political Theory', *Political Studies*, Vol. XII (June 1964).

language was different, as well as his tribe and religion. In any group of Zanzibaris John Okello was unmistakably a foreigner. Zanzibaris themselves were, admittedly, mixed—and a large proportion of them were of mainland origin. But it could not be easy for Zanzibaris to identify themselves with a mainlander who originated as far from the coast as Lango. It was like expecting Abeid Karume to be acclaimed as the Chief of Lango for any length of time—or expecting Dedan Kimathi to be long admired as a governing hero by the Baganda. It is not enough for a John Okello to have a charismatic mission.

In meaning and content the mission may be addressed to a group of men who are delimited locally, ethnically, socially, politically, occupationally, or in some other way. If the mission is thus addressed to a limited group of men, as is the rule, it finds its limits within their circle. . . . The holder of charisma seizes the task that is adequate for him and demands obedience and a following by virtue of his mission. His charismatic claim breaks down if his mission is not recognized by those to whom he feels he has been sent.[1]

John Okello's mission did not earn that recognition. Perhaps the story would have been different had Okello been a native of Tanganyika. Conceivably he might have been in the cabinet of the United Republic of Tanganyika and Zanzibar.

What all this suggests is that there is, indeed, a sense of national identity within each East African country after all. Nyerere could be accepted as leader by the Wachagga of Tanganyika and even the Watumbatu of Zanzibar. Kenyatta could be accepted as leader by the Luo of Kenya. But if either migrated to Uganda he would have a much harder time persuading the people of Uganda to accept either as their leader. In other words, the sense of a Uganda identity is now sufficiently well established to preclude a successful bid for power within Uganda by a Tanganyikan even of Nyerere's calibre or a Kenyan of Kenyatta's stature. What that sense of identity is still not strong enough to preclude is, of course, internal rebellion.

[1] *From Max Weber, op. cit.*

WHEN IS INTERVENTION 'FOREIGN'?

But if Kenyatta and Nyerere are, in practical terms, 'foreigners' in Uganda, what does that make the British troops? This is where it is necessary to point out that there are not only degrees of foreignness but also types of foreignness. There are, at any rate, two levels of sovereignty operating within African political thought—state sovereignty (as, for example, the sovereignty of Kenya when distinguished from Uganda) and racial sovereignty (the sovereignty of those who are African by race). Okello might have been a foreigner in Zanzibar according to the principle of state sovereignty—but his *racial* identity as an African seemed to vindicate his intervention against 'Arab rule' on the island.[1] By the criterion of state sovereignty, the Sultan Jamshid was a native of Zanzibar while Okello was a foreigner. But by the criterion of racial sovereignty, it was the other way around.

But were not British troops 'foreign' troops by either criterion in post-colonial East Africa? What could possibly legitimize their own intervention in any of the East African countries? 'A government which needs foreign support to enforce obedience from its own citizens is one which ought not to exist.' This was said by a British philosopher in the nineteenth century.[2] In January 1964 the British Government seemed to agree with their old philosopher in regard to Zanzibar. The Sultan's Prime Minister asked for British help but Britain declined to intervene. And yet Britain responded swiftly in the other crises in East Africa. Why?

There were, indeed, important differences between what happened in Zanzibar and what happened on the mainland. Yet each was a case of utilizing foreign troops 'to enforce obedience from the citizens'. In the case of the mutinous local troops, submission was *directly* exacted. But the British presence on the mainland also indirectly encouraged a law-abiding spirit among

[1] For a fuller discussion of the two levels of sovereignty in African nationalistic thought see Ali A. Mazrui, 'Consent, Colonialism and Sovereignty,' *Political Studies*, Vol. XI, February 1963.

[2] J. S. Mill, *Dissertations and Discussions*, Vol. III. It can even be argued that a government that has to use its military forces, and not merely its police forces, for any length of time has dubious credentials for legitimacy. For this distinction between police coercion and military coercion see Peter Calvocoressi, *World Order and New States* (London: Chatto and Windus for the Institute of Strategic Studies, 1962). See also W. Gutteridge, *Armed Forces in New States* (New York: Oxford U. Press, 1962).

citizens who might otherwise have quickly degenerated into looting or racialistic mobs. It is too early to be certain about what happened in Zanzibar. Revolutions tend to conceal their more hideous aspects until at least a generation after the event. It is nevertheless a good guess that the worst excesses in Zanzibar were committed by looting or racialistic mobs—who bursts out in a frenzy as soon as it became obvious that the normal law-enforcing agencies were not there to stop them.

Indeed, both Zanzibar after the coup and Dar es Salaam on January 20 following the first mutiny presented what political philosophers might describe as Hobbesian situations—a disintegration of order in the armed forces leading to a disintegration of order in society. To use Obote's description of a similar situation in Uganda, 'The nation was faced with a considerable danger, not only from these disobedient elements in the Army, but also by the likelihood of unruly elements in our society who might have cashed in on the situation'.[1]

If we interpret relationships between individual citizens as being partly based on 'a covenant' promising mutual respect of each other's person and property, it could be maintained that such promises of mutual respect are useless without a sword to enforce them. The 'sword' may be taken to be the armed forces. And the person who is supposed to use the sword is the sovereign.

This Hobbesian analysis, however, postulates a further covenant—this time between the sovereign and his sword. By the second covenant the sword undertakes to be a willing instrument of the sovereign. But who is going to enforce this second covenant? It is easy enough to see how the sovereign can enforce covenants between citizens—if he can use his sword. But how can he force the sword to be loyal to this duty—and be a willing implement of sovereignty?

This was one dilemma which each East African government had to face in January 1964. To use Hobbes's language, the problem for each government appeared to be, if not 'solitary', certainly 'nasty'. But the solution which was finally invoked was, at any rate, 'British and short'. What was supposed to be an implement of East African sovereignty could only be disciplined

---

[1] See *East African Standard*, January 28, 1964. In the same issue of the *Standard* is Nyerere's declaration that 'the disgraceful conduct of the Tanganyika Rifles has led to a situation of fear with a possibility of much bloodshed'.

by a partial East African retreat from sovereignty itself. It could only be disciplined by calling in foreign troops. But which level of sovereignty was involved here? This takes us back to the distinction between state sovereignty and racial sovereignty. Dependence on troops of another race would seem to be a detraction from racial sovereignty. And yet this might well be a case of detracting from racial sovereignty in order to consolidate state sovereignty.

However, there is one thing which must be borne in mind. In the military field there had all along been a dilution of racial sovereignty—British officers having been in command in Tanganyika, Uganda, and Kenya well before the mutinies. British officers are indeed still in command in some parts of Commonwealth Africa. A nationalism which refused to tolerate for very long expatriates in top administrative jobs was nevertheless pragmatic enough to tolerate expatriates in top military jobs.

In Tanganyika the situation was changed in January 1964 as a direct result of the mutiny. British officers were replaced at the insistence of the mutineers. But the impact of this change was softened when one of the expelled British officers returned later at the head of British troops to subdue the mutineers. In any case, the important point to grasp is that the use of British troops to make East African troops behave themselves was, in a sense, just an extension of the previous use of British *commanders* to make African troops behave themselves.

But under what circumstances should Britain respond to requests for troops from African governments in jeopardy? What sort of considerations could have justified differentiating between Sheikh Muhammad Shamte's appeal for British help in Zanzibar and Prime Minister Obote's request for similar help in Uganda?

The simple answer is that all depended on the assessment of the British Government as to where British national interests lay. But commitment to the British national interest does not preclude other considerations provided these are compatible with that interest or can be reconciled with it.

One thing which should be noted first of all is a simple point— that the principle of 'not interfering in the internal affairs of another country' does not normally mean not interfering in *any* internal affairs at all. If it did, then Britain was in error when she interfered in an internal quarrel between the Tanganyika Army and the Tanganyika Government. That quarrel, in its nakedness, was as much an internal affair between Tanganyikans as anything else could be.

What, then, does the principle of noninterference signify? It would seem that what the principle encompasses is noninterference in domestic *political* affairs, rather than internal affairs generally. But what are political affairs? Surely an army mutiny is pregnant with all sorts of political implications and consequences. This is true. But a mutiny only becomes political if the mutineers can legitimately claim political asylum elsewhere in case of failure. In other words, it is not enough that a mutiny should have political consequences before we call it political. What is needed to make it political is that the mutiny should have *conscious political aims*.

The nearest thing to a conscious political aim which the Tanganyika mutiny had was—as far as our knowledge extends—the quasi-racialistic aim to replace British officers with African ones. And yet kicking the British officers out of the old Tanganyika Rifles was the one aim of the mutineers which British troops could not specifically be used to frustrate.

As a generalization we can say that a mutiny can only immunize itself against intervention by British troops if it politicizes its aims while at the same time remaining internally oriented. If the mutineers just want to extract a few more shillings from the government the aim is sufficiently non-political to justify outside intervention on the side of the government in power. But if the mutineers should raise their ambitions and proceed toward overthrowing the government altogether the aim would then look sufficiently political to make foreign intervention morally dubious. In other words, there is a level at which it becomes true to say that the greater the danger which a mutiny poses to its own government the safer is the mutiny from blatant foreign intervention. With certain modifications this is perhaps *one* of the factors which distinguished the armed rebels of Zanzibar from the armed mutineers of Tanganyika and elsewhere on the mainland—and made British help forthcoming in the latter cases and withheld in the Zanzibar case.

Another way of defining the frontiers of legitimate intervention is to say that British troops may indeed be called to maintain law and order; but they may *not* be called to maintain in power

the supposed constitutional maintainers of law and order. To put
it in a slightly different way, British troops may maintain law
and order but not the government that is normally supposed
to maintain it.

It is, in part, this distinction which make British intervention
in East Africa tolerable in Pan-African eyes but French intervention in Gabon much less so. In the one case Britain was frustrating
mutinous demands for more pay. In the other case France was
frustrating an actual coup.

But was this problem of the frontiers of legitimate intervention
an important factor at all in the calculations of either Britain or
France? After all, it was Sir Alec Douglas-Home who later said
in a statement to the House of Commons: 'In Kenya, Tanganyika
and Uganda, we are there in response to requests from their
governments to prevent takeovers by mutinous elements who
would overthrow the elected governments only a few months or
a few weeks old.'[1]

Here it would seem that Britain, far from avoiding political
intervention, actually decided to intervene on the ground that
the aim of the mutineers was the *political* one of overthrowing
the government. And yet we should remember that Sir Alec's
interpretation of the East African situation involved two postulates—(1) that the aim of the mutineers was indeed political, but
also (2) that the aim was not internally oriented in the first place.
In that same statement to the Commons Sir Alec quoted Chou
En-lai's remark that revolutionary prospects were excellent
throughout Africa. The British Prime Minister was at the time
convinced that events in East Africa were, at least partly,
communist-inspired. And what was communist-inspired was to
him necessarily externally instigated. Such instigation, if true,
must itself shift the boundaries of legitimate intervention by
others.

But was it true? Was there external influence behind the
mutinies on the East African mainland? All three governments
concerned have denied any such influence. If their denial be
genuine, the only conclusion which can be drawn is that Sir
Alec's government responded to appeals for British troops on the
basis of a misreading of the East African situation. The Marxists
in the ranks of the Zanzibar revolutionaries had created a fear

[1] *East African Standard*, February 7, 1964.

that there were other plotting Marxists on the mainland. In helping the East African governments in their hour of mutinous peril Sir Alec might indeed have done the right thing—but seemingly on the basis of an error of judgment.

The moral of all this is perhaps the fact that there is less rationality behind momentous decisions than political analysts sometimes assume. But that does not make the decisions any less important. And what is important keeps on *demanding* to be rationally understood in all its varied implications—be it a decision by a British Prime Minister or a mutiny in some barracks at Jinja.

2 Anti-Militarism and Political Militancy in Tanzania[1]

Two dialectical tendencies in military affairs have characterized the ethos of Tanzania under Julius Nyerere. One is a marked distrust of men professionally under arms at home and involved in inter-African relations. The other is a faith in military or quasi-military solutions to some of the remaining colonial problems in Africa. The distrust of 'pure soldiers' has, in part, resulted in Tanzania's experimentation with new forms of civic-military relations. The faith in quasi-military solutions to the remaining colonial problems was symbolized by Tanzania's role as the 'headquarters' of African liberation movements, as well as by Tanzania's position on the Rhodesian issue. These two paradoxical tendencies have then interacted with Tanzania's own self-conception as a revolutionary country and affected the tone of her development activities as well as other aspects of policy.

In this essay we hope first to demonstrate that there has been a tradition of anti-militarism in Tanganyika, going back well into the days before the union with Zanzibar. Involved in this is the story of East African integration at large. We shall then examine the growth of militancy in African liberation movements and how this affected the nature of Tanganyika's involvement in such movements. We shall finally explore how these tendencies have influenced the pace and tone of Tanzania's domestic policies in recent times. In this last part of the essay we shall particularly note the growing 'militarization' of the political rhetoric of the country and its influence on the ethic of political integration and economic development.

[1] This essay was originally written for the panel on 'Militarism and the Professional Military Man', working group of the International Sociological Association, London, September 1967. It was later published in *Journal of Conflict Resolution*, September 1968.

ANTI-MILITARY TRADITION IN TANGANYIKA

Tanganyika attained internal self-government in the same year in which the Congo attained her independence. Tanganyika also shares a border with the Congo. This double-nearness to the Congo's experience caused speculation about Tanganyika's future as she approached independence. To the question whether the events of the Congo could happen in his country too, Julius Nyerere in 1960 was emphatic:

> These things cannot happen here. First, we have a very strong organization, TANU. The Congo did not have that kind of organization. . . . [And further] there is not the slightest chance that the forces of law and order in Tanganyika will mutiny.[1]

Dr. Nyerere was wrong in his conviction that the forces of law and order in Tanganyika would not mutiny. When they finally did mutiny this started a new era of suspicion of the military in Tanganyika. Nyerere was right in describing the organization of the Tanganyika African National Union (TANU) as a major difference between his country and the Congo. What Nyerere did not mention was the essentially pacific record of the people of Tanganyika as compared with some of their neighbours. The people that had sacrificed 120,000 lives in the Maji Maji rebellion against the Germans in 1905–6 came to develop a form of nationalism that was at once shrewd and placid. Tanganyika's neighbours speculated as to the reasons for the peacefulness of her progress to independence. Kenya's Tom Mboya attributed it to the relative absence of white settlers. In this regard he placed Tanganyika in the same category as Uganda and contrasted it with those African countries that had experienced a significant settler presence. Mboya said:

> If one can draw a general rule, it is that in any colony where there has been considerable white settlement, violence has become inevitable, although it was not the original policy of the nationalist party. Uganda and Tanganyika escaped this form

[1] *Inside East Africa*, Vol. II, No. 3, Aug./Sept., 1960, p. 13.

of violence on their paths to independence, but Nyasaland and Northern Rhodesia had to pass through it in 1959 and 1961.[1]

Mboya should perhaps have made it a little clearer that what was crucial in Nyasaland was not a white-settler presence within the territory itself—which was limited—but control from the white federal government under Sir Roy Welensky. It might also be pointed out that although Uganda had even fewer settlers than Tanganyika, its path to independence had had much more tension. Yet, when these allowances have been made, Mboya is basically right in asserting some kind of correlation between white settler presence and a potential for violence. This is one factor which distinguished Tanganyika from Kenya. But the factor which distinguished Tanganyika from Uganda concerned conflict situations between tribes rather than between races. Both these factors contributed to the relatively placid nature of politics in Tanganyika until the union with Zanzibar. What is apt to be overlooked is that they also contributed to the apparent distrust of men professionally under arms that Nyerere's Tanganyika has often exhibited.

Nyerere's regime is perhaps the only nationalist regime in Africa that seems to have had a genuine crisis of conscience as to whether to have an army at all on attainment of independence. Suggestions were made that while Tanganyika's independence would mean the end of political trusteeship by the United Nations, there could still remain some kind of military trusteeship exercised by the world body. Tanganyika could set a precedent that would help to make the United Nations a greater instrument of world order. The chief spokesman for this point of view was the Tanu leader's brother, Joseph Nyerere. The younger Nyerere proposed to the National Assembly that the new independent Tanganyika should consider placing her army under the United Nations. After all, Tanganyika had been a trusteeship, and the Congo crisis had demonstrated that the world body was not unwilling to help out small countries in need of military assistance. In any case, Joseph Nyerere argued, Tanganyika could not really defend herself against a major power and might as well put herself under the protective umbrella of the world body.

[1] Mboya, *Freedom and After* (New York: Little, Brown & Co., 1963), p. 44.

What I am suggesting is that . . . as far as military operations against any other country is [*sic*] concerned, we would have no right to use our forces at all, except under the orders of the United Nations command.[1]

Julius Nyerere himself shared some of the premisses of his brother's advocacy, but his conclusions were somewhat different. In a speech addressed to a seminar of the World Assembly of Youth in August 1961, Tanganyika's national leader criticized the whole concept of each state in Africa arming itself separately. Given the discrepancies in power, it was unlikely that an African state armed itself in order to protect itself against attack by one of the great powers of the world. 'If an African state is armed, then realistically it can only be armed against another African state',[2] Nyerere asserted.

On his visit to the United States the previous month as a guest of the Kennedy Administration, Nyerere had expressed the hope that the United States would not sell arms to African countries. Nyerere said:

If a country has money to spare in helping others it should spend it fighting poverty, illiteracy and disease.[3]

At first glance this reasoning does not sound fundamentally different from the reasoning which made Houphouet-Boigny of the Ivory Coast rely on France for defence needs, at least for a while. The reasoning Houphouet-Boigny gave for this was: 'We wish to devote our modest means to economic and social development.' So earnest did the Ivory Coast appear in this policy that Henry Tanner of the *New York Times* was driven to observe in March 1962 that

The most striking anachronism [in the Ivory Coast] to radical African nationalists is that Mr. Houphouet-Boigny has practically abdicated sovereignty in the military field. The Ivory Coast has only a small force for internal security. And even

[1] Tanganyika, *Assembly Debates*, Thirty-Sixth Session (Sixth Meeting), November 30, 1961. Cols. 18, 20.
[2] 'The Second Scramble'—Speech delivered on August 5, 1961, to the Seminar. See *The Second Scramble* (Dar-es-Salaam : *Tanganyika Standard*, 1962).
[3] See *New York Times*, July 15, 1961.

this force has French officers. The French army assures the external defense of the country.[1]

Nyerere shared the view that African countries should limit their military expenditures to a small security force for internal use. In Nyerere's own words:

> All that we need within our national boundaries are sufficient forces for the purposes of maintaining law and order within those boundaries.[2]

But what about broader defence needs? This is where Houphouet-Boigny's answer differs from that of Julius Nyerere. To Houphouet-Boigny it was all right to rely, for a while, on the former colonial power. To Julius Nyerere such a solution was not all right. It is true that in January 1964 he was driven to ask for British troops to subdue his own mutinous soldiers. But for Nyerere's regime that expediency was a painful one. From the time she became independent Tanganyika has been reluctant to entrust her defence to the former colonial power even indirectly. One indirect method of relying on Britain would have been to link Tanganyika's defences with those of the other two countries of East Africa at a time when the other two were still colonies. But Tanganyika shrunk from such ties. The same Nyerere who in 1960 had seemed prepared to delay Tanganyika's political independence for the sake of an East African federation did not seem prepared to delay Tanganyika's military autonomy for the same goal.[3]

In a sense, Tanganyika's desire to be militarily 'autonomous' went back well before independence. Even as a non-self-governing territory Tanganyika seemed to yearn for defence arrangements that were 'independent' of those made for Kenya and Uganda. In a Legislative Council debate in February 1957 Paul Bomani—who later became Minister of Finance after independence—argued that since Tanganyika was a 'trusteeship country' he could not 'see any reason why it should have military

---

[1] Henry Tanner's dispatch, *New York Times*, March 25, 1962.

[2] *The Second Scramble*, op. cit.

[3] The text of Nyerere's statement in 1960 on readiness to delay independence for the sake of federation is now available under the title of 'Freedom and Unity', *Transition*, Vol. IV No. 14, 1964. See especially p. 48.

amalgamation with colonies and protectorates. I think we should stand on our own'.[1]

As Tanganyika approached independence the grounds for military autonomy began to change. In April 1960, in a debate in the East African Legislative Assembly, Francis Khamisi of Kenya asked the East Africa High Commission

> to develop the Royal East African Navy in order to make it a permanent defence service for the East African territories.[2]

The Tanganyika members of the Assembly opposed the motion on the general grounds that the whole future of the Commission was in doubt in view of Tanganyika's impending independence.[3]

In February 1961 a special study group reported that the three governments of Kenya, Uganda and Tanganyika were

> unanimously of the view that the Navy should be maintained as a common service financed through the [East Africa] High Commission.[4]

Yet in December that same year, within a week of attaining independence, Tanganyika announced its withdrawal from the navy. Tanganyika's yearning for military autonomy had taken yet another form.

Kenya's Mboya complained that Tanganyika had consulted neither Kenya nor Uganda. He argued that an independent East Africa would, sooner or later, need a significant navy. The break-up of the small navy was bound to be 'a very bad omen for the East African Federation we all hope for.' Mboya warned his fellow East Africans about the dangers of regional disintegration.

[1] Tanganyika, *Council Debates*, Thirty-First Session (February 5, 1957), pp. 891–6.
[2] See East Africa High Commission, *Proceedings of the Central Legislative Assembly*, Vol. XIII, No. 1 (April 8, 1960) cols. 220–39.
[3] I am grateful to Dr. David Johns of San Diego State College for our discussions on some of these matters and for bibliographical guidance.
[4] United Kingdom, Colonial Office, *East Africa: Report of the Economic and Fiscal Commission*, Cmnd. 1279 (London: Her Majesty's Stationery Office, 1961) p. 57.

He urged a closer look at the lessons of West Africa's experience. In his own words,

> A study of the trends in former British West Africa shows that after Ghana's independence one by one the Common Services was [sic] scrapped on the basis of one excuse or another until the talk for West African Federation was reduced to nothing.[1]

In spite of the protests, however, the East African Navy as a nucleus defence service came to an end in June 1962. Any future maritime experiment on a regional basis was to be strictly non-military.

But in what way was Tanganyika's desire for military autonomy related to her distrust of armed forces? Part of the explanation hinges on Nyerere's fears that, apart from internal needs, an African army could only be used against another African army. The real safeguard for Nyerere was not a unified East African army but a unified army of the African continent as a whole. A purely East African army could, after all, still be used against another African country. It might be involved in Kenya's dispute with Somalia, for example. It might have been considerations such as these which made Nyerere insist that

> All that we need within our national boundaries are sufficient police forces; . . . as far as the larger commitments are concerned, these should be on an African basis.[2]

But how could Nyerere ensure such a division of labour? The creation of a continental army was beyond his powers. What was within his powers was a policy to keep Tanganyika's military capacity as low as possible. One pre-requisite for such a policy was to retain an exclusive right of deciding Tanganyika's own military affairs. And this in turn meant autonomy in defence matters.

As independence approached Tanganyika began to contemplate military secessionism from joint East African defence arrangements. The reasons given amounted to a simple case of

[1] 'Why East Africa Needs its Navy', *East African Standard* (Nairobi), January 4, 1962.
[2] *The Second Scramble*, op. cit.

newly acquired sovereign sensitivity. As a Tanganyika Minister put it to the East African Legislative Assembly,

> we had to decide, on the question of policy, whether we would be responsible for defence or not . . . and you cannot approach any other powers . . . to be responsible for your defence.[1]

But against the background of Nyerere's views, as expressed in that year of independence at home and abroad, this was not perhaps a simple case of sovereign pride. The quest for military autonomy seemed to be just another manifestation of the underlying anti-militarism of Nyerere's regime. To renounce the principle of national autonomy in military affairs was, it was rightly assumed, to reduce Tanganyika's control over her own soldiers. It was also to run the risk of being 'dealt with' by soldiers other than one's own in case of an internal security breakdown in Tanganyika.

TANGANYIKA AND THE NEW STYLE ARMY

But when the security breakdown finally came it was, in fact, caused by the behaviour of Tanganyika's own troops. In January 1964 the men of the first Battalion of the Tanganyika Army mutinied. Tanganyika had only one other battalion. It was not long before this too mutinied. That old uneasy feeling that Nyerere had had was now vindicated. For a short period Nyerere was now forced to go into hiding. Sensitive as he was, the humiliation of it all affected him deeply. 'This week has been a week of the most grievous shame for our nation', he said in a broadcast to the nation after emerging from hiding. It was not merely the dignity of his government which had been compromised. It was the dignity of the country itself. And there was of course no doubt as to who was to blame for those ominous hours of instability. In Nyerere's words,

> those who brought this shame upon us are those who tried to intimidate our nation at the point of the gun.[2]

[1] East African Common Services Organization, *Proceedings of the Central Legislative Assembly, Debates*, Vol. 1, No. 1 (May 24, 1962), Cols. 156–7.
[2] Nyerere, broadcast to the nation, January 26, 1964.

Nyerere had become convinced that the restoration of national honour could only be accomplished if those armed Tanganyikans were first relieved of their weapons. But, as he himself put it,

> It is not easy to disarm an army, especially one which is already intoxicated with the poison of disloyalty and disobedience.[1]

And so a further national humiliation had to be invoked before national self-respect could be restored. Tanganyika—like the other two countries in East Africa—was forced to invite British troops to come and disarm her own mutinous soldiers. The use of British troops for such a purpose was an acute embarrassment for a nationalist regime. It reinforced Nyerere's desire to explore new ways of handling the problem of civic-military relations at home. But in the meantime he took the ruthless decision of disbanding the entire Tanganyika army—and relied on borrowed Nigerian troops as soon as the British troops withdrew.

Tanganyika's leaders might, for a moment, have been tempted to discard entirely the idea of having an army in addition to their police force. But, in the words of Janowitz, 'it appears to be a universal political conception that a new state requires an army'.[2]

It could, however, be asked whether a new state required a *'pure army'*, designed only to serve military needs. On this Nyerere's policy was now in the agony of reappraisal. He still believed that the military should be subordinate to the civil authorities. As he put it at the time, 'an army which does not obey the laws and orders of the people's Government is not an army of that country, and it is a danger to the whole nation'.[3]

Yet at the same time Nyerere now distrusted the inherited British principle that an army must be politically 'neutral'. After all, an army which was politically neutral was indeed an army which consisted of *pure soldiers*, with little experience beyond the barracks and the battlefield. Soldiers who were trained only in the arts of warfare had their horizons too narrowly restricted. Warfare is an exercise in physical power—and pure soldiers tended to be too dangerously preoccupied with those arts of

---

[1] *Ibid.*

[2] See Janowitz, *The Military in the Political Development of New Nations* (Chicago University Press, 1964), p. 100. Janowitz is himself sceptical about such a need, but the myth is widespread.

[3] See *Tanganyika Standard*, January 27, 1964.

physical force. Therefore, while Nyerere remained a believer in civilian supremacy, he was now also becoming a convert to the concept of a *developmental militia*—people trained not merely in the use of guns but also for participation in certain sectors of nation-building at large.

At first this concept was still rather vague in Nyerere's mind. All he apparently knew for certain was that he wanted not a politically neutral army, but a politically committed one. As soon as he got the British troops to disarm the Tanganyika mutineers, Nyerere turned to the active youth of his party—and said in a radio broadcast:

> I call on all members of the Tanu Youth League, wherever they are, to go to the local Tanu office and enroll themselves. From this group we shall try to build a nucleus of a new army for the Republic of Tanganyika.[1]

The policy became more clearly defined later that year. In June 1964 the Second Vice-President of the new United Republic of Tanganyika and Zanzibar addressed a large group of new army recruits. He said:

> You are just as much citizens of the country as are farmers or fishermen. There is no reason therefore of refusing any citizen of the country permission to have a say in the politics of the country.

Political discussions between officers and soldiers were to be encouraged, and the army was to be represented on the national executive of the Tanganyika African National Union.[2]

The problem of moving from a pure army to a developmental militia still bedevils Tanzania. There have been troubles occasionally, including the experience of having to arrest and detain officers of the new military experiment. But the policy of forging meaningful links between the soldiers and the party is still being pursued. On January 29, 1965, the *Official Gazette* of Tanzania announced the appointment of a Political Commissar

[1] See *Sunday News* (Dar es Salaam), January 26, 1964.
[2] See *The Nationalist* (Dar es Salaam) June 25, 1964 and *The Daily Nation* (Nairobi), June 25, 1964. See also Chapter 1 above.

for the Tanzania People's Defence Forces. No information as to his powers and duties was made available. The reason was simple —the Government itself was apparently not as yet sure what these should be. It was simply part of the effort to escape the tradition of 'pure soldiers'. And since then, with the help of Canadians, Israelis and others, Tanzania has continued the precarious experiment of a developmental militia. It is still very modest. But the tradition of distrusting 'pure militarism' in Tanganyika might yet culminate into an innovation of genuinely creative dimensions in the years ahead.

LIBERATION MOVEMENTS AND FORCE

But while the distrust of pure militarism was characteristic of Tanzania's domestic scene, Tanzania's foreign policy displayed an increasing faith in military solutions to some international problems.

Much of the neo-militaristic militancy of Tanzania's foreign policy is connected with her bid for leadership in certain sectors of Pan-African activities. And this question has a distinct history in its own right. The first important inter-territorial movement which old Tanganyika captured was the Pan-African Freedom Movement of East and Central Africa (PAFMECA), which came into being on September 17, 1958. The aim of the organization was to co-ordinate nationalistic movements mainly in British East and Central Africa and ensure periodic consultations on strategy and methods of agitation for self-government. But at that time nationalism in British Africa at large was still under the influence of Gandhism. The year of the birth of PAFMECA was also the year of the first All African Peoples Conference in Accra. At that conference the Algerians, then engaged in an armed struggle against the French, had to make an effort to get their black African colleagues to discuss the question of resorting to arms in the colonial struggle. The Algerians wanted unambiguous moral support from black Africa in their insurrection, but this was slow in coming at the conference. The whole issue of violence was debated with heat. In the end, the conference did pledge support to those who 'in order to meet the violent means by which they are subjected and exploited, are obliged to retaliate'. Yet as a general principle 'the conference rejected violence as a means of struggle'.[1]

The host of that conference was President Kwame Nkrumah. Nkrumah at that time was still basically Gandhian in his attitude to colonial liberation. His own ideal method for a nationalist struggle was what he had called 'positive action', and this he had already defined as:

> legitimate political agitation, newspaper and educational campaigns and, as a last resort, the constitutional application of strikes, boycotts and non-cooperation based on the principle of absolute non-violence, as used by Gandhi in India.[2]

At its birth the Pan-African Freedom Movement of East and Central Africa was firmly within this Gandhian tradition. Its Constitution included among its aims not only a commitment to avoid violence in its own approach but also a positive ambition to 'champion non-violence in the African nationalist struggles for freedom and prosperity'.[3]

It was the leadership of this movement which Tanganyika came to capture. Her credentials for leadership included the qualities of Julius Nyerere himself, geographical contiguity to many of the countries yet to be liberated, and the increasing likelihood that Tanganyika might well be the first country in British East and Central Africa to emerge into independence. And when in 1961 she did become the first to be de-colonized, her credentials for leadership were significantly reinforced.

But in the meantime black nationalism in South Africa, in Southern Rhodesia and in the Portuguese territories was beginning to doubt the need even to pay lip-service to the principle of non-violence. Such militant nationalist movements from further south became more directly affiliated to the organization when PAFMECA finally became PAFMECSA—when it became the Pan-African Movement of East, Central and *Southern* Africa.

[1] See Colin Legum, *Pan-Africanism: A Short Political Guide* (London: Pall Mall, 1962), pp. 42–3; 228–9.
[2] See *Ghana: The Autobiography of Kwame Nkrumah* (Edinburgh: Thomas Nelson & Sons, 1959), p. 92.
[3] PAFMECA's Constitution is reproduced as Appendix B in Richard Cox, *Pan-Africanism in Practice, PAFMECSA 1958–1964* (London: Oxford University Press, 1964), pp. 83–5.

This was a major change. Before long neo-militaristic liberation movements from further south assumed great influence within the organization. In the words of Richard Cox:

> The Liberation Movements, in addition to swelling PAF-MECSA, changed its policy fundamentally. The use of violence was a recurrent theme . . . Nelson Mandela . . . of South Africa made an unexpected appearance and, to great applause, spoke of sabotage, of people turning their faces from the paths of peace and non-violence.[1]

Nor was Mandela among the extremists. He at least *regretted* that violence was becoming 'inevitable'. Other delegates at the conference which transformed PAFMECA into PAFMECSA were less apologetic about resort to violence. One Malawi militant asserted: 'Force is bound to be used because it is the only language imperialists can hear. No country ever became free without some sort of violence.'[2]

This was a radical departure from the neo-Gandhism which had inspired the movement in its early days. In an important sense, it was also the beginning of the neo-militaristic tendencies of Tanzania's own foreign policy in African affairs. To some extent, Tanzania's diplomatic break with Britain over Rhodesia in 1965 can be traced back to Tanganyika's involvement with liberation movements under the original banner of PAFMECSA. As Dar es Salaam developed into the headquarters of such movements, and into a place of general political refuge and asylum for fiery rebels from Southern Africa, the Government of Tanganyika was soon caught up in a rising tide of militancy. As Harvey Glickman came to put it,

> Among the predictable corollaries of revolution is the proliferation of refugees and exiles. For the representatives and followers of the banned or exiled revolutionary parties of Central and Southern Africa, Dar es Salaam has become the political Mecca of the 1960's . . . Tanganyika's role in this

[1] *Ibid.*, p. 54.
[2] *Ibid.*, p. 54. According to some reports, Kaunda was the only delegate at that conference who did not applaud these remarks.

revolutionary decade is rendered unique by its proximity to the areas where frustration is greatest.[1]

The formation of the Organization of African Unity in 1963 confirmed the role that destiny had thrust upon Tanganyika. That African Gandhism was now nearly dead was amply demonstrated by the general tone of the Addis Ababa conference in May 1963. Milton Obote of Uganda spoke out strongly on the need for 'liberation forces' and offered his country as a training ground.[2]

Kenya's Oginga Odinga advocated the establishment of an 'African liberation bureau', entrusted with the co-ordination of liberation movements in all dependencies, with receiving and distributing funds and aids 'including military equipment and personnel' on behalf of the liberation movements, and with the organization of 'training of personnel for administrative, military and diplomatic services'.[3]

The Heads of State at the conference had also received a joint memorandum from the national liberation movements of different territories. That memorandum too urged the formation of an 'African Liberation Bureau' whose functions were to include the following basic ones:

a. To co-ordinate the struggle for African liberation in all non-independent territories.
b. To receive, distribute and transport funds and other forms of aid, *including military equipment and personnel*, on behalf of the African liberation movements.[4]

The Heads of State responded positively. A number of resolutions were passed on this matter. It was resolution 11 which established a co-ordinating liberation committee of the Organization of African Unity. The Committee, which later became known as

[1] 'Dar-es-Salaam: Where Exiles Plan—And Wait', *Africa Report*, Vol. 8 No. 7, July 1963, p. 3.

[2] *East African Standard*, May 29, 1963.

[3] Speech reprinted in *Pan-Africa* (Nairobi), No. 5, June 14, 1963, pp. 8–9. See also Odinga's speech to the United Nations upon Kenya's admission, also reprinted in *Pan-Africa*, No. 19, December 27, 1963, pp. 7ff.

[4] See *The Addis Ababa Summit 1963*, Publications of the Government of Ethiopia, Ministry of Information, 1963 (?). The emphasis is mine.

'the Liberation Committee' or 'the Committee of Nine', was made 'responsible for harmonizing the assistance from the African States and for managing the Special Fund to be set up for that purpose'.[1]

The nine members of the Committee appointed were Algeria, Congo (then Leopoldville), Ethiopia, Guinea, Nigeria, Senegal, Tanganyika, Uganda and the United Arab Republic. As Tanganyika's destiny would have it, she was appointed Chairman of the liberation committee. And Dar es Salaam became the headquarters. Tanganyika had now moved more conclusively from being the leader of the neo-Gandhian movement of PAFMECA in its early days to being the co-ordinating point of neo-militaristic movements from different parts of Africa.

As we suggested, this development had long-term consequences on the foreign policy of Tanzania. The country became increasingly convinced that she had to be in the forefront of Pan-African militancy on any major problem of de-colonization. But, as we indicated, within less than a year of becoming the headquarters of the OAU Liberation Committee, Tanzania had to suffer the humiliation of having to invite British troops to subdue her own mutinous soldiers. This compromised Tanzania's image as co-ordinator of anti-colonial militancy. At the OAU Cairo conference later that year Tanzania had to defend herself against serious insinuations made about her honour as a nationalistic country. President Nyerere clashed publicly with President Nkrumah. Nkrumah had gone to the extent of questioning Dar es Salaam's credentials in terms like: 'What could be the result of entrusting the training of Freedom Fighters against imperialism into the hands of an imperialist agent?' Nyerere answered 'the Great Osagyefo' with sarcasm as well as counter-argument. But in addition Nyerere took the position of a leader who was disillusioned with the arts of persuasion in matters of liberation and now demanded vigorous action to expel Portugal from Africa. As he put it,

> I am convinced that the finer the words the greater the harm they do to the prestige of Africa if they are not followed by action. . . . Africa is strong enough to drive Portugal from

[1] *Ibid.*

our Continent. Let us resolve at this conference to take the necessary action.[1]

Not all African leaders shared Nyerere's militancy in such matters, and action did not readily materialize. But the Tanzanian government continued to urge more drastic policies against the remaining pockets of colonialism. Pressures for tougher action were put not only on the Organization of African Unity but also on the United Nations. By the middle of 1965 Tanzania's Second Vice-President, Rashidi Kawawa, was telling a United Nations committee in Dar es Salaam that its functions were the same as those of the Liberation Committee of the OAU. It was the UN Committee of twenty-four on Colonialism which Kawawa bracketed together with the OAU Committee of Nine—and called them 'two liberation committees of historic importance in the struggle against colonialism'.

The Chairman of the UN Committee, M. Coulibaly of Mali, appeared reluctant to see a UN Committee identified with a neo-military regional body. M. Coulibaly therefore said that he had always advocated peaceful means. And with a shrewd diplomatic touch, he went on to praise President Nyerere of Tanzania for supporting 'the peaceful achievement of independence in colonial territories'.[2]

By the end of that conference in Dar es Salaam, Chairman Coulibaly's tone was different. His Committee adopted a resolution on Portuguese territories on June 10, 1965. Commenting on the resolution the following day, Chairman Coulibaly said it would be legitimate for other states to give every form of aid to nationalistic movements in Portuguese African countries. Force could legitimately be used in those territories to prevent the Portuguese from using force to suppress nationalist movements. M. Coulibaly added that this was the first time that a UN Committee had directly called for such military support for the African people. What is significant from the point of view of this essay is the simple fact that such a UN clarion call should have been

---

[1] This speech was given by Nyerere on July 20, 1964.
[2] Radio Tanzania, May 31, 1965. See BBC Monitoring Records, ME/1874/B/3. These developments are also discussed in Ali A. Mazrui, *Towards a Pax-Africana* (Weidenfeld & Nicolson and University of Chicago Press, 1967), pp. 210–11.

sounded in the atmosphere of Dar es Salaam and under the influence apparently of the host government.

RHODESIA

On Rhodesia too the influence of Tanzania has been exerted on the United Nations and the Organization of African Unity in the direction of greater militancy. Here again there is a deep Tanzanian faith in a military solution to the problem. Tanzania virtually captured the leadership of those who were in favour of a strong stand against Britain on the Rhodesian issue. A meeting of the Organization of African Unity in November 1965 gave Britain until December 15 of that year to end the rebellion—or face a collective African diplomatic break with her. In the discussions at that meeting Tanzania was practically leading the 'toughs'. Indeed, even before that particular meeting, Tanzania's Oscar Kambona, then Chairman of the African Liberation Committee of the OAU, had called for more direct military action by African states themselves against Rhodesia. African states, he asserted, should use 'the greatest force' to meet that 'deliberate affront to the dignity of the African people by a gang of racists'.[1]

This was the spirit which Tanzania took to the OAU ministerial meeting shortly afterwards when it was decided to issue that fatal ultimatum to Harold Wilson—'Break Ian Smith or Africa will break with you!'[2]

Tanzania maintained the leadership of the 'tough states' against Rhodesia. She was the first Commonwealth country to break diplomatic relations with Britain—beating even Nkrumah to the diplomatic draw. Nkrumah followed suit—but when he fell Tanzania was, until 1968, the only Commonwealth country without relations with Britain. Moreover, unlike Nkrumah's Ghana, Tanzania sustained a direct loss in aid as a result of breaking off relations with Britain—Britain suspended aid in the form of direct grants, though some had been agreed to before the break. Nyerere's Government knew about some of the losses

[1] *Daily Nation* (Nairobi), November 20, 1965.
[2] For a discussion of other implications of the ultimatum see also Ali A. Mazrui, *The Anglo-African Commonwealth: Political Friction and Cultural Fusion* (Oxford: Pergamon Press, 1967), esp. ch. III.

which would have to be incurred as a result of the diplomatic severance—but 'a moral stand is worth a sacrifice'. From then on the Tanzanian Government continued to use international platforms to urge the case for military action in Rhodesia.

But it was not merely military action by Britain or by African states that Tanzania urged. Nyerere also repeatedly called upon black Rhodesians themselves to take up arms against Ian Smith. 'We will give them guns. That is the only medicine left for Smith.'[1]

In April 1967 Tanzania was one of the five radical African countries which met in Cairo to take stock of the Rhodesian situation. Nyerere's theme was still a call to arms by black Rhodesians, to be supported elaborately by African states. He also once again denounced British policy on Rhodesia and British reluctance to use ultimate force.[2]

A few days after the Cairo conference the Second Vice-President, Mr. Rashidi Kawawa, announced that all able-bodied men in Tanzanian villages bordering Mozambique were being 'trained in the art of defending themselves'. Mr. Kawawa was describing the extended measures to the Standing Committee on Defence of the OAU African Liberation Committee. The policy of arming villagers was only indirectly connected with Tanzania's role as the co-ordinator of some of the activities of liberation movements in the Portuguese colonies. The immediate cause of equipping some villagers with arms seems to have been incidents on the border involving Portuguese military action. In the ultimate analysis, however, even the arming and training of villagers on hostile borders was part of the total picture of Tanzania's militancy in some of her African policies.[3]

MILITARISM AND THE ONE PARTY STATE

These then are the two themes in Tanzania's behaviour in military matters over the years—the marked distrust of men under arms at home combined with a faith in military or quasi-military solutions to some of the remaining colonial problems in Africa.

[1] See, for example, *East African Standard*, October 21, 1966.
[2] See *East African Standard*, April 5, 8 and 13, 1967.
[3] See 'Tanzania villagers armed', *East African Standard*, April 19, 1967.

But attitudes to military matters have non-military implications as well. They interact with other aspects of national life.
In Tanzania the whole style and rhetoric of political behaviour
has, to some extent, been affected.

We have already mentioned that, in order to avoid having
'pure soldiers' in the barracks, Tanzania has sought to establish
institutional links between the armed forces and the ruling party.
This was a case of politicizing the military as a direct act of policy.
But concurrently with the politicization of the military has been
a policy of militarizing the political style of the country with
appeals for discipline and mobilization. The crowning scheme
in this latter policy of militarizing the political ethos is the
compulsory National Service scheme which the Government
launched in October 1966. All sixth-form school leavers, university graduates and graduates of vocational and professional
institutions, were liable to two years in the National Service. The
scheme aimed at

> teaching the country's youths bravery, toughness, obedience
> and perseverance and this could not be done in the classroom
> alone.[1]

This militarization of the political ethos has in turn its roots
in the interaction between two aspects of the national self-image.
One aspect views Tanganyika as a country 'at war with poverty';
the other aspect conceives the country as one which must
purposefully be saved from conditions of potential *civil* war. The
conception of itself of being at war with poverty dominates the
Tanzanian ethos of economic development. The fear of a 'civil
war situation' is the ultimate impulse for policies of national
integration.

The latter fear has been part of Tanzania's case for a one-party
state for some years now. The mainland part of the country,
Tanganyika, emerged into independence virtually as a one-party
state by popular vote. For Julius Nyerere that was not surprising
—'a struggle for freedom from colonialism is a patriotic struggle
which leaves no room for differences'.[2]

[1] Mr. Rashidi Kawawa, the Second Vice-President, laid the White Paper
on the scheme before Parliament on October 3, 1966.
[2] See, for example, Nyerere, 'One Party Government', *Transition*, Vol. I,
No. 2, December 1961.

But what was to happen once the struggle against the colonial power had been brought to a victorious conclusion? For Nyerere the unity which had been forged by the colonial struggle should be jealously preserved in the service of other national 'battles' after independence. And the organizational expression of that unity was to be the single party—the Tanganyika African National Union.

The distrust of organized factionalism in Nyerere's political thought got stronger with the years. At first Nyerere was almost apologetic about the *de facto* one-party state—arguing that he could not help it if the people wished to support only one major movement. He thought that a genuine and responsible opposition might arise in time and would be 'no less welcome than it is in Europe or America'. Indeed, Nyerere added in 1961, 'I would be the first to defend its rights'.[1]

But it was not long before reservations crept in. As he came to put it a few years later,

Our Union has neither the long tradition of nationhood, nor the strong physical means of national security, which older countries take for granted. While the vast mass of the people give full and active support to their country and its government, a handful of individuals can still put our nation in jeopardy, and reduce to ashes the effort of millions.[2]

If a handful of individuals can be so dangerous, an *organized* faction might be an even greater risk. From this premise springs Nyerere's increasing suspicion of having more than one party in the country contesting for power. The two-party system became suspect not just within the conditions of Tanzania but *inherently*. Nyerere had begun to feel that the two-party system, by its very nature, reduced politics either into an argument about trivialities or into 'a state of potential civil war'. Where the differences between the parties were fundamental, the two party system promoted 'a spirit of purely artificial rivalry, like that

---

[1] *Ibid.*

[2] Address at the opening of the University College campus, Dar es Salaam, August 21, 1964. See Nyerere, *Freedom and Unity* (Dar es Salaam: Oxford University Press, 1966), p. 312.

which exists between a couple of soccer teams'. But where the differences *were* 'fundamental', Nyerere could see all the signs of Disraeli's 'Two Nations', with all the potential for internal conflict.[1]

And so the same Nyerere who, in 1961, had declared his readiness to defend the rights of a responsible opposition party, was by January 1963 announcing the intention of his party to inaugurate a system of government in which an opposition party would no longer be permitted. One year later he announced the appointment and terms of reference of a special Presidential Commission on the Establishment of a Democratic One-Party state. In his instructions to the Commission, President Nyerere said:

> I think I should emphasize that it is not the task of the Commission to consider whether Tanganyika should be a one party state. That decision has already been taken. Their task is to say what kind of a one party state we should have in the context of our national ethic. . . .[2]

The Presidential Commission submitted its Report in March 1965, and its recommendations were substantially accepted. As the Commission was not arguing the desirability of a one party state but had taken that for granted, there is little in their report about the dangers of having alternative parties. This too seems to have been taken for granted. Yet the Commission's Report still betrayed a deep consciousness that 'for a young nation, public order is precious but it is also fragile'. And the report went on to quote Nyerere's apprehension that 'a handful of individuals can put our nation into jeopardy'.[3]

It turned out that, in the case of Tanzania, this was no mere rhetoric to rationalize a self-prolonged tenure of service for those in authority. Tanzania turned out to be the most sincere of all African champions of the one-party state. In September 1965 a genuinely competitive general election under a one-party umbrella was held. Several Ministers were defeated in the election, including the influential Minister of Finance, Paul Bomani.

---

[1] See Nyerere, *Democracy and the Party System* (Dar es Salaam: Tanganyika Standard, 1962), pp. 7–10.

[2] See *Report of the Presidential Commission on the Establishment of a Democratic one Party State* (Dar es Salaam: The Government Printer, 1965), p. 2.

[3] *Ibid.*, p. 31.

The electors were indeed free to vote for the candidate of their choice, but the candidates had not been free to raise the issues of their choice. The Tanzanian election of 1965, though an admirable experiment in competitive elections under a one-party umbrella, was nevertheless dominated precisely by that old fear of creating conditions for civil disorder, if not civil war. Certain topics were simply 'taboo' in the campaign. These were in fact the most fundamental. They included tribal differences, religious suspicions, the fragile union between Zanzibar and Tanganyika and the whole basis of the one-party structure. Nyerere had once criticized the two-party system as tending to become either an argument about trivialities or a catalyst for potential civil war. In the 1965 election under a one-party system in his own country, Nyerere's government was so apprehensive of creating a state of potential civil war that the election was perhaps reduced to an argument about trivialities.

This does not suggest that the election was valueless. On the contrary, it remains an historic experiment in East Africa. And in any case the electors could vote on the basis of what they silently regarded as the fundamental issues, even if these could not explicitly be raised in the electioneering campaigns as such. But the taboos which did surround the 1965 election were one more indication of the *civil war complex* which, even in relatively homogeneous Tanzania, has pervaded the national ethic as a whole.[1]

PATRIOTISM AND POVERTY

If the civil war complex animates the policies of national integration, the self-image of being 'at war with poverty' is, as we intimated, at the root of the Tanzanian ethos of economic development. In his Inaugural Address President Nyerere said:

I know there are still a few people who think we are joking when they hear us using the word 'war'. Let me assure them that we are not. . . . Even if one were to take, for example,

[1] For brief accounts of the elections see Ruth Schachter Morgenthau, 'African Elections: Tanzania's Contribution', *Africa Report*, Vol. X, No. 11, December, 1965; William Tordoff, 'The General Election of Tanzania',

the Maji Maji Rebellion and the Slave Wars, one would find
no parallel to the slaughter of our people which has stemmed
from poverty, ignorance and disease. . . . In the same way
the famine last year, if it had caught us unprepared, could have
killed many more of our people than ever died in battle during
the Maji Maji Rebellion.[1]

This neo-militaristic conception of Tanzania's problems of
development was again an established part of Nyerere's ideology.
It went back to the day of independence and before. In terms of
policy it resulted in two inter-related guiding principles—social
discipline and mobilization of human resources for hard tasks in
the countryside.

The issue of discipline was also behind the single-party structure and the refusal to emulate liberalism's free interplay
between anatagonistic factions. To use Nyerere's own words in
1961, *This is our time of emergency*, and until our war against
poverty, ignorance and disease has been won, we should not let
our unity be destroyed by somebody's else's book of rules'.[2]

In this case the idea of a 'united war against poverty' is
partly intended to avert the danger of 'internal conflicts between
groups'. The joint endeavours in the tasks of economic development are partly intended to reinforce the task of national
integration. There is an obvious interplay here between the civil
war complex and the self-image of being at war with poverty.

There is of course also an inter-relationship between notions
of social discipline and of the mobilization of human resources for
developmental tasks. An early policy-outcome of this were the
self-help schemes. Self-help was first considered during discussions
on the Three-Year Plan envisaged for 1961–64. People were to
participate in projects which they could accomplish themselves
without governmental finance, such as roads, the building of
schools and wells and little dams in rural areas.

Journal of Commonwealth Political Studies, Vol IV, No. 1, March 1, 1966. A more
comprehensive coverage of the election is to be found in Lionel Cliffe (ed.)
One Party Democracy in Tanzania (Nairobi: East African Publishing House,
1967).

[1] The address was given on December 10, 1962. See *Freedom and Unity*,
op. cit., p. 177.

[2] 'One Party Government', *Transition, op. cit.* The italics are original.

Self-help was conceived mainly in terms of economic develop-ment and the war against poverty. In effect it had perhaps greater significance in relation to national integration. In the words of one academic observer,

> Self-help by no means solved the problem of rural services. What it did do was . . . to increase the number involved in the political process. With ten million people from 120 tribes scattered about the perimeter of the country at the ends of an infrastructure that is bad even by African terms, Tanganyika faces formidable problems of involving her people in a common political process. . . . While no figures are available, it is a generally accepted impression that a greater part of the population has been involved in self-help, and it might be called their first contact with 'the Tanganyikan Nation'.[1]

These were the policies which developed ultimately into the policy of *Self-Reliance* more systematically inaugurated by the Arusha Declaration in February 1967. By that time self-help was verging on becoming semi-autarky—as Tanzania nationalized the banks and other industries and declared her readiness drastically to curtail her reliance on foreign funds in the struggle against poverty. 'We have made a mistake to choose money, something which we do not have, to be our major instrument of development. . . . The development of a country is brought about by people, not by money. . . . Let us go to the villages and talk to our people and see whether or not it is possible for them to work harder.'[2]

This semi-renunciation of 'money' was put in militaristic imagery. Indeed, the essence of self-reliance was defined in the Arusha Declaration in a quasi-military idiom. The definition of self-reliance in the Declaration started with the sub-heading '*We are at War*'. It then went on to suggest that the new policy being promulgated was, in the ultimate analysis, an attempt to resolve a basic *contradiction of weaponry*. In the past Tanzanians had chosen 'the wrong weapon' in their 'war against poverty and

---

[1] Joseph S. Nye, Jr., 'Tanganyika's Self-Help', *Transition*, Vol. III, No. 11, November 1963, p. 37.

[2] See *The Arusha Declaration and Tanu's Policy on Socialism and Self-Reliance* (Dar es Salaam: Publicity Section, TANU, 1967), pp. 11–14.

oppression'. To rely on money in a war against poverty was to
pre-suppose a pre-existent victory over poverty. It was like asking
a poor man to use his wealth as a way of overcoming his
indigence. If he had the wealth with which to cure his poverty he
would not be poor. In the words of the Arusha Declaration, 'We
are trying to overcome our weakness by using the weapons of the
economically strong—weapons which in fact we do not possess'.[1]

This was the basic contradiction of weaponry which the new
Tanzanian policies were designed to resolve. The substitute
approach to the war against poverty was a simple mobilization
of the masses for specific tasks. This was the weaponry of labour
in its primitive efficacy.

CONCLUSION

It is not in her use of a quasi-military idiom that Tanzania is
distinctive. Warfare still remains the highest test of man's
loyalty to his group. It has therefore often called forth some of
the finest traits of heroism and sacrifice. It is not surprising that
the analogy of a country at war should be invoked metaphorically
by a government which is demanding sacrifice and discipline
from its citizens.[2]

What is distinctive about Tanzania is the earnest interplay
between this quasi-military idiom and the policies which emanate
from genuine ideological commitment. The militarization of
Tanzania's political rhetoric is almost an echo of the theme of
discipline and exertion in the country's domestic programme.
There is a basic congruence between rhetoric and strategy, idiom
and ethos. The National Service, the idea of 'Green Guards', the
one-party state itself and its rationalization, the insistence on
'economic conscription' of the unemployed in Dar es Salaam, the
ethic of ideological toil and 'mobilization of human resources'—
all these are factors which, added together, provide an intellectual meeting point between political ideas and the imagery of
military organization.

[1] The *Arusha Declaration and TANU's Policy on Socialism and Self-Reliance*
op. cit., pp. 4–5.

[2] The United States has sometimes deemed it inspirational to give quasi-
militaristic names to explicitly peaceful endeavours. The Alliance for Progress
and the Peace Corps are two examples.

Behind it all is that other aspect of Tanzania's national life—the politicization of the armed forces in the sense of establishing links between them and the Party. 'I call on all members of the Tanu Youth League, wherever they are, to go . . . and enroll themselves', President Nyerere had appealed soon after the army mutiny of 1964. The country's distrust of 'pure soldiers' had found a new vindication—and the President therefore turned to the younger members of the Party and asked them to build the nucleus of the country's new security force from their own ranks. It is a policy which, on the whole, has been followed ever since. Even on its own this kind of anti-militarism—in the sense of a distrust of 'pure soldiers'—is itself a form of political militancy, particularly if the point of reference is an ideology like Tanu's. But the Party's militancy in foreign policy took other forms, including a faith in the efficacy of force as a solution to the remaining colonial and racial problems of Africa.

The soldier, the state and the socialist have had to devise a new inter-relationship in the political personality of Tanzania.

3 Numerical Strength and Nuclear Status[1]

On April 18, 1965, a celebration took place in a town in Indonesia. The celebration was to commemorate the tenth anniversary of the first Afro-Asian conference held in Bandung in 1955. A number of changes had taken place in the world in those ten years. Opening the commemorative conference President Sukarno drew attention to one change that had occurred since the first Bandung conference. 'Now, one of us has an atomic bomb', Sukarno pointed out.[2]

While 'Afro-Asianism' entered its second decade of formal but unstable existence, the United Nations Organization entered its third. The United Nations did so amid renewed demands for the seating of Communist China in the Organization. China, the most populous country in the world, had just become the first non-white country to develop its own nuclear weapon. It is true that her image of internal cohesion was soon to be shattered by a worsening cultural revolution. But perhaps China's status as an emerging world power could not be diminished for long by internal shocks—any more than the global status of the United States since 1963 has been seriously diminished either by the increasing incidence of civil disobedience or by the single shock of a presidential assassination.

Moreover, whatever China's own domestic difficulties, her atomic achievement had given an added impetus to the whole

[1] This essay was first published in *The Journal of Politics*, Vol. XXIX, No. 4, November, 1967. It was written when I was on a grant from the Rockefeller Foundation. Research for it was done at the University of California, Los Angeles, and at the Centre for International Affairs, Harvard University. I am grateful to colleagues at both places. I am also indebted to Dr. Donald S. Rothchild of the University of California, Davis, Mr. T. V. Sathyamurthy and Dr. Yash Tandon for their valuable comments on the manuscript.

[2] See *New York Times*, April 19, 1965.

quest for a non-proliferation treaty in the world—a treaty which could hopefully rescue mankind from the hazards of an expanding nuclear club. A number of countries were particularly careful in their scrutiny of proposals for non-proliferation. Among such countries was India, the second most populous nation in the world, and one which had had a history of tragic disenchantment in her relations with China. As the ideal of non-proliferation was pursued in earnest, the old ideal of non-alignment came under a shadow—and the Indian general elections of 1967 emphasized the mood of disillusion.

What we should now proceed to note is that touching such developments in the world are problems not only of defence but also of demography and of race consciousness. It is the interconnections between these that this essay proposes to examine. The politics of the Third World in this analysis will include matters which affect the Third World even if they are external to it, as well as matters which arise within its chambers.

The concept of the Third World in the sense of the economically under-privileged sector of mankind must include Latin America. In a sense, this might well be the important meaning of the future.[1] But in this essay we use the word in a more restrictive sense. For us in this essay 'the Third World' will be the world of the new states. And the newness of sovereignty here must exclude Latin America. It is true that China is not a 'new state' in the normal sense either. But three things make it inevitable that we include her in our concept of the Third World as here defined. She was a vital part of the Bandung Afro-Asian movement; she is the most powerful non-white country in the world; and she had a revolution in 1949 radical enough to make her, if not a new state, certainly a *renewed* one.[2]

As a great arena of Afro-Asian participation in world politics, the United Nations will be a central element in our analysis. Yet this arena of Afro-Asian participation has excluded the most powerful Asian country from its membership. This paradox will be a continuing theme in our discussion. Behind it all is the issue of nuclear power and of race relations in the world.

---

[1] I use the term in this other sense in my paper 'Africa and the Third World', *On Heroes and Uhuru Worship* (London: Longmans, 1967).
[2] Cuba might also be regarded as a renewed state in this sense.

An important aspect of this latter factor of race relations is the impact on group consciousness of what we might for convenience call 'numericalism'. The varied repercussions of this factor in international politics are of significance to the other matters that we propose to analyse. We might define numericalism in inter-group relations to be that collection of attitudes or general principles which put a moral premium on numerical advantage. The range of forms which numericalism takes is from the moral complexities of 'majority rule' to the simple adage that 'there is strength in numbers'. The two ideas do not necessarily amount to the same thing, though they could indeed overlap. The liberal principle of majority rule asserts that those who prevail in numbers ought also to prevail in politics. But the adage of inner 'strength in numbers' might be invoked even in situations in which majority rule as an elaborate system of government is not in favour. The 'strength' that is meant in the adage could be physical. Yet even when the power of numbers is thought of in physical terms, numericalism remains, in the ultimate analysis, a belief in the dignity of being numerous.

What manifestations has numericalism had in international relations? And with what practical effects? It is to these questions that we must now turn.

NUMERICALISM AND WORLD ORDER

The ethic of numerical supremacy has played an important part in multiplying the number of sovereign states in the international community since the end of World War II. We know that in the history of colonial liberation the principle of 'One Man, One Vote' was often crucial. And the appeal of this principle for the colonized lay in the assumption that if 'One Man, One Vote' was conceded, power would inevitably pass to the majority of the people. In practice two concepts of 'majority rule' have tended to operate. One concept postulated that the rulers should be responsive and institutionally answerable to at least a majority of those they ruled. This was the normal liberal concept. The other concept of 'majority rule' simply required that the rulers should broadly be of the same ethnic or racial stock as the majority of those they ruled. In this latter sense the rulers were still 'representative'

—but more in the sense of being ethnically 'typical' rather than democratically accountable.

In the history of colonial liberation movements in the Third World it was the ethnic conception of 'majority rule', rather than the orthodox liberal one, which was particularly crucial. And yet for as long as the nationalist movements had the support of the general populace as a whole, this distinction was merely academic. The nationalist leaders were 'representative' by the canons of both liberalism and ethnic typicality.

The importance of numbers for the dignity of coloured people is not, however, limited to situations in which the coloured people are in a majority. The position of the Negro in the United States is as much a part of the total picture of race relations in the world as are the liberation movements in Angola. In the latter the Africans are in the majority; in the former the Negroes are in a minority. Yet the American Negro has been no less conscious of the liberating potential of numbers than has the Afro-Asian nationalist in colonial situations. There was a time when the more militant of American Negroes saw the significance of their numbers in quasi-militaristic terms. Even as far back as the slave days Negro numerical superiority in individual situations occasionally turned the Negro's thoughts towards a possible rebellion. And where it did not lead to rebellion this was sometimes interpreted by Negro militants themselves as a sign of their inherent servility. As the defiant Negro David Walker put it in 1829 in his *Appeal to the Coloured Citizens of the World:*

> Here now, in the Southern and Western sections of this country [the United States] there are at least three coloured persons for one white, why is it that those few weak, good-for-nothing whites are able to keep so many able men . . . in wretchedness and misery? It shows what the blacks are, we are ignorant, abject, servile and mean—and the whites know it—they know that we are too servile to assert our rights as men—or they would not fool with us as they do.[1]

---

[1] *The Appeal* is an important document in the history of Negro protest in the United States. It is reproduced in *'One Continual Cry' David Walker's Appeal to the Coloured Citizens of the World (1829–1830): Its Setting and its Meaning* by Herbert Aptheker (New York: Humanities Press, 1965). For the above excerpt, see p. 129.

In more recent times the American Negro has seen the significance of population figures in more realistic and less revolutionary
terms. While the Afro-Asian nationalist has linked numerical
power to the ethic of self-determination the American Negro has
linked it with the liberating potential of the franchise. As
Herbert Aptheker, the Negro historian, recently put it:

> It never was right 'for the Administration' to 'postpone'
> effective action on the Negro question because of so-called
> political expediency; today it is not wrong, it is unwise. This
> is shown . . . in the fact that President Kennedy would have
> remained a United States Senator if but 75% of the Negro
> vote went his way in 1960 rather than the 85% cast for
> him.[1]

This situation constituted a significant advance in the position of
the Negro since Abraham Lincoln liberated the slaves a hundred
years previously, though the pace of change towards permitting
the Negro population its due weight in national politics might
have been much faster than it was. Lincoln himself also romanticized numbers—and his views on this came to influence
nationalists in British colonies many years later. It was, for
example, from Abraham Lincoln, as well as from John Stuart Mill,
that Julius Nyerere says he learned of Western notions of
institutionalized democracy.[2]

In 1958 Nyerere was quoting from Lincoln's romanticization
of numbers to rebut those who shared Cecil Rhodes' dictum of
'equal rights for all civilized men'. He quarrelled especially with
the 'undignified assertion' of the colonial Tanganyika government
that in the special circumstances of East and Central Africa
universal suffrage would put the common good in jeopardy. He
defended the idea of allowing 'the common people' to have their

[1] Herbert Aptheker, *Soul of the Republic: The Negro Today* (New York:
Marzani and Munsell, 1964), p. 109.
[2] '. . . the idea of government as an institution began to take hold of some
African "agitators" such as myself, who had been reading Abraham Lincoln
and John Stuart Mill . . .'—Nyerere, 'The African and Democracy', *Africa
Speaks*, (eds.) James Duffy and Robert A. Manners (Princeton: Princeton
University Press, 1961), p. 33. The implications of this point are discussed
more fully in my article 'On the Concept of "We are all Africans"'. *The
American Political Science Review*, Vol. LVII, No. 1 (March, 1963), pp. 94–7.

own way—and quoted Lincoln's statement that 'God must love the common people because he made so many of them'.[1]

But, as we have indicated, it is not only to democracy that demography is linked. It is also to defence in a more physical sense. Yet from the point of view of race relations the demographic aspect of defence needs to be placed in a broader context. We need first to examine the basic connection between military power and the quest for mutual esteem between races. That the distribution of military power affects the state of race relations in the world is something which is all too easily underestimated. And yet some of the human sensitivities involved are not difficult to recognize in more modest political situations. The whole concept of military capacity has points of contact with normative notions like equality and self-confidence. Historically the dignity of the individual citizen, for example, has some times been conceived in quasi-militaristic terms. For some societies there was something rather effeminate or infantile in being 'defenceless'. Manliness postulated a capacity to defend oneself physically. On this point the Constitution of the United States and the tribal ways of the Kikuyu people have been in accord. The Second Amendment of the American Constitution guarantees 'the right of the people to keep and bear arms'. And Jomo Kenyatta tells us of the paramount resolution of young Kikuyu boys on being initiated by ancient custom—'We brandish our spear, which is the symbol of our courageous and fighting spirit, never to retreat or abandon our hope, or run away from our comrades.'[2]

Such equation of manliness with capacity for self-defence is then extended from the individual to the group, from the head of a household to the ruler of a people. In other words, the concept of manliness in the individual comes to affect notions of *national* honour.

In the context of imperial history Afro-Asian 'defencelessness' might be deemed to have militated against racial dignity as well. In 1941, against a background of what came to be World War II, a distinguished British friend of Africa reminded Africans of

---

[1] Julius Nyerere, 'The Entrenchment of Privilege', *Africa South*, Vol. II, No. 2 (January–March, 1958), pp. 86–9.

[2] Jomo Kenyatta, *Facing Mount Kenya* (first published in 1938), (London: Secker and Warburg, 1939), p. 199. The initiation ceremonies have been simplified since then.

Europe's might and its role in Europe's expansion. In a book addressed to Africans, Margery Perham said: 'Let it, therefore, be admitted upon both sides that the British Empire, like others, was obtained mainly by force. Even where there was no serious fighting, news of victories near by, or the fear of stronger weapons, was often enough to persuade tribes to accept the rule of the white strangers. . . . African tribes, backward, disunited, weak, were helpless before Europe, especially since the perfection of the machine-gun.'[1]

To Margery Perham the Imperial experience was nevertheless necessary for Africa's own good. But Africa's conception of her own humiliation has continued to be disturbed by the implications of military weakness. As Sékou Touré put it more recently: 'It was because of the inferiority of Africa's means of self-defence that it was subjected to foreign domination.'[2]

In the meantime Africans had established some links of identification with Asians. Afro-Asianism had become a solidarity based on a vague sense of shared humiliation as coloured people. But what defences do the coloured people now have against the technologically more advanced white people? Almost the only measurable military factor in which the coloured races have a superiority over the white ones is that of numbers. It seemed at first that the advent of nuclear weapons had made the numerical factor virtually irrelevant. If war remained conventional a numerical superiority of soldiers under arms would remain an asset. But in a conflict of massive nuclear destruction the size of a conventional army appeared to be of dubious military significance.

And yet this whole line of reasoning is itself tied to conventional assumptions about 'victory' and 'defeat' at the end of a war. In a nuclear war numbers are indeed irrelevant in determining a conventional 'victory', but that is mainly because a full-scale nuclear holocaust could not have an orthodox victory. As soon as one starts to assess the consequences of a nuclear war less in terms of 'victories' and more in terms of the balance of survival, population figures once again become admissible in the calculations. As Mao Tse-tung is reported to have said to a visting Yugoslav

[1] Margery Perham, *Africans and British Rule* (London: Oxford University Press, 1941), pp. 53–4, 60.
[2] Conakry home broadcasting service, June 7, 1965. See BBC Monitoring Service Records of Broadcasts in Non-Arab Africa.

official in 1957, 'We aren't afraid of atomic bombs. We have a large territory and a big population. Bombs could not kill all of us. What if they killed over even 300,000,000? We would still have plenty more. China would be the last country to die.'[1]

It is not certain that Mao ever made such a statement. A specialist on Chinese studies at an American university has even suggested in a conversation that the statement was probably propagated by the Russians in their anti-Chinese strategy for the specific purpose of gaining concessions from the West. But, as Edgar Snow put it, 'Even if Mao did not say that, someone would have had to invent it.'[2] The statement is certainly consistent with Mao's general philosophy on the role of population in warfare. In April 1960, for example, the *Peking Review* had the following to say in this connection:

> The U.S. imperialists and their partners use weapons like atom bombs to threaten war and blackmail the whole world . . . Marxists-Leninists have always maintained that in world history it is not technique but man, the masses of the people, that determine the fate of mankind. There was a theory current for a time among some people in China before and during the War of Resistance to Japanese Aggression, which was known as the 'weapons-mean-everything theory'; from this theory they concluded that since Japan's weapons were new and its techniques advanced while China's weapons were old and its techniques backward, 'China would inevitably be subjugated'. Comrade Mao Tse-tung in his work *On the Protracted War* published at that time refuted such nonsense. . . . Comrade Mao Tse-tung pointed out that the most abundant source of strength in war lay in the masses, and that a people's army organized by awakened and united masses of people would be invincible throughout the world.[3]

This view continued to be emphasized even after China's successful testing of a nuclear weapon. An article in the *Peking*

[1] Cited by, among others, Edgar Snow in his *China, Russia and the U.S.A.: Changing Relations in a Changing World* (New York; Marzani and Munsell, 1962), pp. 631–2.

[2] *Ibid.*, p. 632.

[3] 'Long Live Leninism!', *Peking Review*, April 1960. See Arthur P. Mendel (ed.) *Essential Works of Marxism* (Library of New York: Basic Ideas (Bantam Classic), 1961), pp. 532–3.

Review in February 1965 argued that precisely because modern warfare kills too many people resources of manpower have become extra-important. In the words of the article, 'Once a war breaks out, we have to have powerful reserves which can ensure a continuous supply of manpower and materials to meet our needs. The existence of a large-scale people's militia provides an inexhaustible source of replacements for the army.'[1]

What is important here is not whether Chinese reasoning is sound, but how far it affects their outlook on world affairs. There seems little doubt that China's conception of her role in the world is affected by her consciousness of the massive size of her population. As K. S. Karon reported to a British weekly in February 1965, 'in all their diplomatic notes, as in their public speeches, Chinese leaders insist on their numbers: "We are 650 million and we are one." '[2]

These then are some of the ways in which numericalism conditions people's conceptions of their place in the political universe. And such conceptions in turn have their consequences for world order at large.

PEACE VERSUS HUMAN RIGHTS

But how do these factors impinge on the world organization? What repercussions have the politics of numericalism had on the fortunes of the United Nations?

In an important sense, the world body has been fundamentally transformed by the triumph of numericalism in certain sectors of world politics. We can best comprehend this phenomenon if we place it in the context of the historical evolution of the United Nations. And in that context the first factor which needs to be grasped is that the United Nations was intended to be a peace-keeping body with a military aristocracy. The tradition of a bi-cameral legislature in the history of Western political institutions came to be reflected in the organizational structure of the world body. There was an Upper House with five permanent members;

[1] See Liu Yun-Cheng, 'People's Militia in China', *Peking Review*, Vol. VIII, No. 6 (February 5, 1965), pp. 19–20.
[2] See *New Statesman* (February 19, 1965), p. 267.

and a Lower House called the General Assembly.[1] In its original
conception the Upper House was supposed to be the only decision-
making body—the prerogative of the Lower House being at best
to 'consult, advise and warn'. The élite of the Upper House, the
five permanent members, had the power to veto each other and
to veto the wishes of the rest of mankind on certain matters.

This élite of the peace-making body was not chosen from among
the most peace-loving countries in the world. On the whole it
was chosen on the basis of military strength, actual or presump-
tive, rather than by consideration of pacific intentions. There were
perhaps good, solid reasons why a peace-making body should
have a military aristocracy. It was arguable that peace could best
be assured only by entrusting it to those with the greatest military
capacity.

One point of relevance which this military aristocracy had for
race relations was that it was an aristocracy which also happened
to be primarily white. China had been intended to be the non-
white Permanent Member of the Security Council, and Chinese
the only non-European official language of the world body. But
the subsequent exclusion of mainland China from that privileged
seat made it difficult for the Security Council to shed itself of the
image of a white man's club. Taiwan was too controversial, too
weak and too dependent on the United States to be a convincing
'representative' of the coloured races among the ultimate veto-
holding decision-makers of the world body.

The inadequacy of Taiwan for this role was complicated by
one further factor—a deceptively simple matter of census figures.
Involved in this is a dichotomy which has been important in race
relations on a global scale. And that dichotomy is between
numerical strength and total military capability. In military
terms almost the only superiority that the coloured races have
had over the white races has been, as we have noted, that of
population figures. In this connection the original choice of China
to 'represent' the coloured faces within the military aristocracy
of the world body was an apt choice. Merely by being the most
populous country in the world China had a unique stature

[1] In formal legal structure the Security Council is supposed to be in a co-
ordinate relationship more with the Economic and Social Council than with
the General Assembly. But political realities dictate a different interpretation
of the workings of the UN.

within the increasingly self-conscious community of coloured faces.

In due course the ultimate symbol of military capability became the testing and possession of a nuclear weapon. Here again the original choice of the élite within the Security Council was vindicated. The first five countries to become 'nuclear powers' in this sense were precisely the five original permanent members of the Council. But the seat of the non-white member was occupied by Taiwan, which was neither numerically impressive nor as yet distinguished with nuclear status.

In the meantime the balance of influence as between the Security Council and the General Assembly had been changing. The nature of the change was in keeping with the history of bicameral legislatures within individual national traditions in the West—traditions after which the whole institutional structure of the world body was originally modelled. The tendency in individual Western nations had been for the Upper House to become progressively less powerful than it was at the time of inception. The ideal type of this tendency is perhaps the British experience, with the gradual emergence of the supremacy of the Commons over the Lords. In the United States the Senate remains, in some important ways, the more powerful of the two houses. But even in the American experience can be discerned a progressive rise in power and influence of the more popularly based House of Representatives—a narrowing of the difference between it and the Upper House.

As between the two houses of the world body itself what crucially tilted the balance in the first instance was a device which was used to commit the United Nations to what, ironically, became a military confrontation with China. The confrontation was that of the Korean War. And the device which affected the proportion of power as between the two Houses of the world body was the 'Uniting for Peace' resolution by the General Assembly. It virtually became a method of circumventing the veto in the Security Council in times of crisis.[1]

[1] It was in November 1950 that the General Assembly passed the 'Uniting for Peace' Resolution. Among its main features was a provision that the Assembly could meet in twenty-four hours if the Security Council was prevented by the veto from fulfilling its primary function of keeping the peace. On such occasions the General Assembly could recommend collective measures, including the use of armed forces. A Collective Measures Committee was set

But a deeper and more enduring change in the General Assembly and its powers came as a consequence of decolonization in Asia and Africa in the last decade. Here again an analogy demands to be made between lower houses in the experience of individual nations and the fortunes of the General Assembly of the United Nations. To the extent that lower houses have tended to be more popularly-based in composition than upper houses any strengthening of the lower house is *ipso facto* a process of democratization in this popular sense. But the strengthening of the Lower House has in turn tended to be a consequence of democratization. The broadening of political consciousness in the society as a whole gradually comes to be reflected in the composition of the law-making body. In individual Western countries this process of democratization took the form of demands for the extension of the franchise. In the international community it came to take the form of demands for self-determination by Asians and Africans. And just as the House of Commons in England was fundamentally affected when the franchise was broadened, so was the General Assembly of the United Nations transformed when colonial self-determination was permitted to prevail.

But it is not merely the functions of constituent units of the world body that have been affected by the triumph of numericalism abroad. It is also the whole conception of the purposes of the world organization. The political values of the new states, fresh from their victories over European colonial rule, have constituted a significant departure from the dominant mores at the San Francisco conference of 1945. For these newly liberated members of the world organization, the ultimate purpose of the United Nations has become the promotion of human rights. This is in contrast to the original conception of the older members, who had seen the United Nations' role primarily in terms of securing peace in the world. As I have argued elsewhere, this is

---

up to study and report on ways and means of securing and maintaining peace between nations in accordance with the Charter of the United Nations. The Committee started to report periodically to the General Assembly.

For an early discussion of the implications of the 'Uniting for Peace' Resolution see Hans J. Morgenthau, *Politics Among Nations: The Struggle for Power and Peace* (Second edition, revised and enlarged) (New York: Alfred A. Knopf, 1956), pp. 284–6; 456–9.

not to deny the importance which some of the major powers attach to human rights. Nor is it to suggest that the new states are so preoccupied with demands for such rights that they have no time to worry about the problem of peace. On the contrary, these states revel in seeing themselves as peacemakers in the disputes of the giants. Nevertheless, there does remain a fundamental difference in emphasis as between the newer and older states. The actual framers of the Charter in 1945 first declared their determination to 'save succeeding generations from the scourge of war' and then only secondly to 'reaffirm faith in fundamental human rights, in the dignity and worth of the human person, in the equal rights of men and women and of nations large and small'.[1]

But judging by their record and general attitudes so far, it seems likely that the new states of the Third World would have reversed the order of affirmation: they would have reaffirmed first 'faith in fundamental human rights [and] in the dignity and worth of the human person' and only secondly their determination 'to save succeeding generations from the scourge of war'. Nor is their stand unreasonable, given the derivative nature of the very importance of peace. In the ultimate analysis peace is important because 'the dignity and worth of the human person' are important.[2]

The dichotomy between peace and human rights has a complex but direct relationship with the two roles of numerical strength that we have discussed so far. Numerical strength as a military or quasi-military factor touches the issue of peace; numerical supremacy as a component of democratic theory touches the issue of human rights—while the denial of the right of numerical supremacy to people of colour in places like South Africa is deemed to be both a negation of human rights and a danger to peace.

But now an additional variable in global race relations needs to be linked to these others—the issue of distribution of wealth. As in a number of other issues, South Africa itself is an exaggerated symbol of this global problem. The wealth of the richest

---

[1] From the lines of reaffirmation opening the Charter.
[2] This dichotomy between peace and human rights within the politics of the United Nations is discussed more fully in my article 'The United Nations and Some African Political Attitudes', *International Organization*, Vol. XVIII, No. 3 (1964), and in my book *Towards a Pax Africana*, ch. 8.

country in Africa is shared in a glaring disproportion as between the white and non-white. It epitomizes the interconnections which coloured people sometimes see between their colonial and racial subjugation, their poverty, and the enrichment of the white countries. As W. E. B. du Bois put it in a grotesque but poetic way in 1935:

> Immediately in Africa a black back runs red with the blood of the lash; in India, a brown girl is raped; in China a coolie starves; in Alabama seven darkies are more than lynched; while in London the white limbs of a prostitute are hung with jewels and silk.[1]

The whole idea of a community of coloured races is a fellowship as much of 'underdevelopment' and poverty as it is of shared racial humiliation. And the sensitivity which new states sometimes show when they are described as 'under-developed' underlines the connection between indignity and indigence. Julius Nyerere articulated a widely-shared view when he said in September 1963 that although Tanganyikans had won the right to international equality when the country became independent, yet a man who was ignorant, who could not produce enough food for himself, or who suffered from disfiguring diseases could not really stand on terms of equality with all others.[2]

Two years earlier Nyerere had linked the international distribution of wealth to a Marxist analysis of class. He had argued in these terms:

> Karl Marx felt there was an inevitable clash between the rich of one society and the poor of that society. In that, I believe, Karl Marx was right. But today it is the international scene which is going to have a greater impact on the lives of individuals. . . . And when you look at the international scene, you must admit that the world is divided between the 'haves' and

[1] See the general conclusion in W. E. B. du Bois, *Black Reconstruction in America 1860–1880* (first published in 1935) (New York: The World Publishing Company, 1964), p. 728.

[2] See 'The Stress is Now on Dignity', *Sunday News* (Dar es Salaam: September 8, 1963), p. 9.

the 'have-nots'. . . . And don't forget the rich countries of
the world today may be found on both sides of the division
between 'Capitalist' and 'Socialist' countries.[1]

Nyerere himself was not a Marxist, but a variant formulation of
his thesis has been discerned in analyses of world situations by
Chinese communists. And in the case of the Chinese a sensitivity
has persisted to the implications of the balance of population.
In November 1957 Mao Tse-tung was already discerning a
'turning point' in the balance of power in the world in numerical
terms. At a conference in Moscow he said:

The whole world now has a population of 2.7 billion, of which
the various socialist countries have nearly one billion; the
independent, former colonial territories have more than 700
million; the countries now struggling for independence or for
complete independence, 600 million; and the imperialist camp
only about 400 million . . .[2]

Elsewhere, as we have indicated, Mao has discussed more specifically the clash between wealth and poverty at the international
level and the significance of colonial liberation in this regard.
He has argued that 'man is more important than the weapon'—
and that the 'preponderant poor' would triumph over 'the
imperialist forces'. His conviction as to the ultimate victory of the
poor has in part his own immediate national experience as its
foundation. He himself had, after all, led one quarter of the
world's poor to victory.[3]

In the meantime Westerners too had become vaguely disturbed about the implications both of the distribution of wealth
in the world and of the relative coincidence between this distribution and racial differences. Radical opinion in the West

[1] Speech at the opening of the World Assembly of Youth Seminar in
Dar es Salaam in August, 1961. See *The Second Scramble* (pamphlet) (Dar es
Salaam: Tanganyika Standard Limited, 1962).
[2] New China News Agency, November 18, 1957.
[3] See Mao Tse-tung's essay 'A Single Spark May Start a Prairie Fire', and
his *Imperialism and All Reactionaries are Paper Tigers* (Peking: Foreign Languages
Press, 1958). See also Edgar Snow, *China, Russia and the U.S.A. Changing
Relations in a Changing World* (New York: Marzan and Munsell, 1962), pp.
667–8.

sometimes saw the problem in terms of blind economic forces dividing the world into a white bourgeoisie and a coloured proletariat.[1] This is not completely accurate. Much of Latin America must, as we indicated, be included in the poorer sector of the world. What is true is that almost all the rich countries of the world are white, and almost all the non-white countries are poor. It is therefore possible for nationalists in Africa, for example, to think of their continent as 'a proletarian continent' with all the connotations of revolutionary potential.[2]

But even non-radical opinion in the West has had its own way of responding to the implications of racial disparities. Writing for the *New York Times* in December 1961 James Reston claimed that Britain believed in a continuing dialogue between the West and Russia for considerations of future protection against the pressure of races far more numerous than the white races. And looking at the same long-range future a French official, talking to Reston, had forecast that 'the great conflict at the end of the century will not be ideological, but racial'.[3]

This French prediction of a racial conflict in the years ahead is similar to what was predicted by W. E. B. du Bois in an article in *Foreign Affairs* much earlier in the century. The main difference was that Du Bois had regarded the racial problem as

[1] For a fuller discussion of this see my article 'African Attitudes to the EEC', *International Affairs* (London) Vol. XXXVIII, No. 1, (January, 1963). The 'blind economic forces' which were stratifying the world in this way included the falling prices of primary commodities and the imbalance in the terms of trade at large. In 1964 the United Nations Conference on Trade and Development was held in Geneva to examine what might be done about this. For a discussion of the conference as seen by a representative of a developed nation see Richard N. Gardner, 'GATT and the United Nations Conference on Trade and Development', *International Organization*, Vol. XVIII, No. 4 (Autumn, 1964), pp. 685–704.

[2] See, for example, Touré, 'Africa's Destiny', *Africa Speaks*, (eds.) James Duffy and Robert A. Manners (Princeton: D. Van Nostrand, 1961).

[3] James Reston, 'The Problem of Race in World Politics', *New York Times* (December 13, 1961).

Arnold Smith, the Canadian diplomat who became the first Secretary-General of the Commonwealth of Nations in June 1965, had this to say: 'The division of humanity between the white and the other races, which coincides too closely for comfort with the division between the affluent industrialized peoples and the poor underdeveloped peoples is, I think, the most difficult and potentially dangerous problem in the world.' See *Manchester Guardian Weekly* (July 1, 1965), p. 5.

the dominant theme of the century as a whole, and not a mere closing conflict at the end of it.[1]

As for the connection between poverty and nuclear war, this is sometimes discussed on an assumption similar to that made by Hans Morgenthau in his concept of 'the *status quo* power'[2]. The assumption is that a vested interest in the international *status quo* is a child of satisfied needs. It is therefore to be expected that developed states, to the extent that they have satisfied many of their domestic needs, would be reluctant to risk a change in the prevailing situation. On the other hand, the very concept of a 'revolution of rising expectations' in the underdeveloped countries implies that those countries are keenly dissatisfied with matters as they stand—as they have numerous new expectations which are still far from being met.

From this kind of reasoning is an easy transition to the belief that rich countries are more concerned about peace than poor ones. To a certain extent this belief is vindicated by the very dichotomy in scale of values which we attributed to politics in the United Nations. The prevailing view of the purpose of the United Nations among the richer countries is, as we argued, the maintenance of peace; the prevailing view among poorer countries, especially the new states of Asia and Africa, is of the UN as a global ombudsman, protective of the rights of man at large. And, as we have noted, many nationalist leaders feel that the very poverty of their countries is not adequately consistent with human dignity. All these factors would therefore seem to suggest that the fear of war is more characteristic of developed than of underdeveloped states. And this suggestion in turn has sometimes led to the conclusion in the West that China was so poor that she would have nothing to lose by engaging in a major military conflict.

In rebutting this kind of reasoning, Edgar Snow has first admitted that 'it is true that individual Chinese have nothing much to lose, but their lives'. He has then gone on to ask 'Is fear of losing the wealth in private property of some of us in the West a greater deterrent against war than fear of losing all our lives?'[3]

---

[1] Du Bois in 1925 was repeating something he had said even earlier. See W. E. B. du Bois, 'Worlds of Colour', *Foreign Affairs* (April 1925). Reprinted in *Africa: A Foreign Affairs Reader*, edited by Philip W. Quigg (New York: Frederick A. Praeger, 1964), pp. 32–52.

[2] Hans J. Morgenthau, *Politics Among Nations, op. cit.*, esp. pp. 35–40.

[3] Snow, *op. cit.*, p. 632.

To a certain extent Snow is unfair to the view he is combatting. It is true that poor people still have their lives to lose in a war—and the fear of losing one's life can be at least as effective a deterrent as the fear of losing one's wealth.

But the point here is that the rich countries have both fears operating instead of only one. Nor is the meaning of 'losing one's life' necessarily the same as between the rich and the poor. Cultural factors, frequency of death in the family, general life expectancy in the society, as well as the degree of ease or hardship encountered in the course of being alive should all have a bearing on a people's attitude to death.

Nevertheless, there remains a serious fallacy in the argument that rich countries value peace more than do poor ones. The argument takes for granted that to have a vested interest in the *status quo* is the same thing as to have a vested interest in peace. That does not follow. Having a vested interest in the *status quo* can sometimes impel a nation to disturb the peace—in a bid to prevent change. Students of international politics see this easily enough when they are looking at events within the conceptual framework of 'balance of power' theories. They can interpret the action of President Kennedy over Cuba in the autumn of 1962 as a case of risking war in a bid to prevent a major change in the *status quo*. But some of the same students of international politics might then proceed to take it for granted that a '*status quo* power' necessarily has a greater interest in peace than a country which has yet to 'arrive'.

But perhaps a more serious fallacy in this theory lies in the psychological hypothesis which underlies it. The theory assumes that the acquisitive instinct in man is more violent than the protective one; that the 'have-nots' in their bid to acquire would be more reckless than the 'haves' in their bid to protect what they already possess.

And yet this psychological theory is contrary to all human experience at the level of the individual. Readiness to use force in order to protect one's property is (almost *a priori*) more widespread than readiness to use force in order to acquire new property. To put it in another way, there are more people who would use violence to avert losing what is already theirs than there are people who would use it to acquire new possessions.

If the same tendency is to be expected of human behaviour at the international level the theory that the poor are more likely to risk war than the rich would need serious reconsideration. Indeed, the reverse would now be implied. The potential for violence would be greater in the wealthy who were insecure than in the poor who were ambitious. Either might indeed precipitate conflict but the balance of risk would now be seen to be leaning the other way.

But where would this leave our previous argument that in the politics of the United Nations it is the established powers rather than the new states which put peace above human rights in importance? No contradiction need, in fact, be involved. The great powers could care more for peace than for, say, self-determination—and still be no more peace-loving than the small powers. The two sets of countries might have the same amount of love for peace—the difference between them being solely in their attitude to self-determination. That alone might vary from one member of the United Nations to the next—the value of peace, were it measurable, remaining constant.

An alternative but more modest claim is to say that what is in question is not the relative value which different sets of countries in the United Nations might attach to peace and human rights, but merely their conceptions of the role of the world body itself. Hypothetically all members of the United Nations might be equal in their concern for both peace and human rights and still vary in their notions of the proper functions of the world body. One set of nations might say that, given the state of the world and the limitations of the Organization, the United Nations should put this ideal first as a function, and the other ideal only second. Another set of nations might reverse the order of priority of functions for the world body.

But in fact the differences between the newer and the older members is more than merely varying conceptions of the role of the United Nations. There is a difference in scale of values between them; and their views of the purposes of the UN are conditioned by this initial difference. The older powers of Europe and America are just less concerned about problems of 'human dignity', 'racial equality' and 'self-determination' than are the countries of the Third World in Asia and Africa.

THE CULT OF NUCLEAR PARTICIPATION

But now that Empires have disintegrated, what battles of dignity remain to be won? There is, of course, the difficult issue of Southern Africa and its defiant racial minorities. There has been increasing pressure on the world organization to help solve the intractable problem of arrogant white South Africans and their allies, the Portuguese and the Rhodesians. The white rulers of Southern Africa are putting up a spirited fight against numericalism in their part of the globe.

And yet, in spite of the enormity of the problem, one tends to regard the South African issue as an inheritance from the past. Until it is solved it is, of course, still very much part of the present, and might well be an ominous part of the future. There does persist, however, a certain sense of anachronism in this particular battle for 'human dignity'—almost as if it does not belong to our age, and ought to have been won a while ago.

The theoretical problem which this sense of anachronism raises is the generational relativity of what constitutes 'human dignity'. And so we must now ask ourselves these basic questions: what effect has nuclear power had on the nature of man's self-esteem? What constitutes 'human dignity' in the nuclear age?

For an increasing number of countries, national honour will be linked to the ambition of becoming a 'member of the nuclear club'. But exclusive clubs are a matter of élite status, rather than of human dignity. Man's dignity today is not a matter of membership of the nuclear club. It is a matter of membership of the nuclear age. The credentials for membership of the club are possession of nuclear weapons. But the criterion of being a member of the nuclear age is a more modest participation in the science of the age. As former President Kwame Nkrumah put it once, neither Ghana nor Africa could afford to lag behind other nations in this 'age of atomic revolution'. Nkrumah declared:

> We must ourselves take part in the pursuit of scientific and technological research as a means of providing the basis for our socialist society. Socialism without science is void. . . . We have therefore been compelled to enter the field of atomic energy because this already promises to yield the greatest economic source of power since the beginning of man.[1]

[1] See *Ghana Today*, Vol. VIII, No. 21 (December 16, 1964), p. 1.

Nkrumah was speaking at a ceremony at which he laid the foundation stone of Ghana's Atomic Reactor Centre at Kwambenya near Accra.

When we link this cult of nuclear participation with our original dichotomy between peace and human rights, more ominous dichotomies emerge. The problem of peace has increasingly become one of trying to keep to a minimum membership of the nuclear club. On the other hand, the problem of human dignity is increasingly becoming one of maximizing membership of the nuclear age. In both these issues the world organization has attempted to play a major role. And in at least some aspects of the venture the absence of Communist China from the world body has been a serious handicap.

We might start with an ominous quotation from 1946: 'We are here to make a choice between the quick and the dead. That is our business. . . . We must elect World Peace or World Destruction.' In these words did Bernard Baruch, United States Representative to the United Nations Atomic Energy Commission, introduce his American plan to the Commission on June 14, 1946. The United States proposed the creation of an International Atomic Energy Authority to which were to be entrusted all phases of development and use of atomic energy, starting with the raw material. The proposals came to nothing. The Soviet Union was not prepared either to permit the kind of mutual territorial inspection which the Baruch plan demanded or to relinquish its veto in the Security Council as a *quid pro quo* for America's renunciation of her sole possession of nuclear weapons.[1]

On May 17, 1948, the United Nations Atomic Energy Commission came to an end.

By 1953 the United States no longer had a monopoly of nuclear technology. That year, in a speech in the General Assembly, President Eisenhower made a new bid to get international cooperation in the utilization of atomic energy under specific safeguards. Out of this new American policy came the proposal to establish an International Atomic Energy Agency (I.A.E.A.)

[1] For a contemporary discussion by Louis N. Ridenour, J. Robert Oppenheimer, Edward A. Shils and Eugene Robinowitch on this early failure to achieve international control of atomic energy, see *The Atomic Age* (New York: Basic Books, Inc., 1963), pp. 45–98.

linked to the United Nations. There followed in 1955 the first United Nations International Conference on the Peaceful Uses of Atomic Energy at Geneva. Significant exchange of 'declassified' nuclear information at this conference raised hopes about increasing international collaboration in this field. The second Geneva conference was held in 1958 and the third in September 1964. The initial hopes of greater openness in the exchange of nuclear data, leading to the kind of international trust which might make military self-denial possible, were only modestly justified. Nuclear technology by the 1964 conference could be discussed with greater ease and scientific detachment than had been possible in 1955. And a treaty against tests in the atmosphere had at last appeared on the international scene. But it was a deficiency of the Geneva conferences that Communist China was not invited to participate, and it was an inadequacy of the test-ban treaty that China had not signed it.

In the meantime there had been serious dissension in the International Atomic Energy Agency. A major bone of contention came to be the system of safeguards adopted by the agency at its 1960 general conference. According to the system which was devised, safeguards were applicable to fissionable material and equipment supplied by the agency for use in certain nuclear reactors. The system of safeguards was adopted but only in the face of bitter and protracted protests from the Soviet Union and a number of neutralist countries led by India. Those who objected to the safeguards regarded them as discriminatory, disproportionate to the amount of support rendered by the agency and likely to reduce the pace of peaceful nuclear development in underdeveloped countries. On the other hand, the Western argument in support of the safeguards was that they 'would help prevent the proliferation of countries manufacturing nuclear weapons and would be a useful first step toward an arms control agreement'.[1]

By 1963 the Soviet Union showed signs of having veered to the Western position on this matter. At any rate it accepted the system of safeguards for the first time and supported the extension of safeguards to large-scale reactors of over 100 thermal mega-watts.[2]

---

[1] For a review of the arguments, see Alvin Z. Rubinstein, 'On IAEA's Future', *Bulletin of the Atomic Scientists*, January, 1965, pp. 25–7.

[2] Rubinstein, *ibid.*

But what prospects have these attempts at international co-
operation in nuclear technology had either on parity of esteem
between members or on prospects for peace?

To understand the full ideological implications of nuclear
power for nationalists in the Third World one has to take into
account the romanticism which is sometimes invested in science.
As David E. Apter put it in connection with at least the African
part of the underdeveloped world:

> The most venerated of the beliefs of the Western literary
> intellectuals are placed lower on the scale of values than are
> those of science. Faced with the immense problems of building
> new societies and preventing chaos, it is the political leaders of
> new nations who come closest to the scientific culture, since as
> social engineers they possess an optimism similar to that of
> science.[1]

But to be a participant in the science of the atomic age postulates,
as we have noted, some kind of participation in nuclear science
itself. Not every new country can as yet afford a reactor and many
are prepared to wait until they can justify the expense which
would be involved in acquiring one. But early participation in
nuclear technology remains an attractive goal for reasons which
are not unconnected with ideological egalitarianism.

To a certain extent, then, the ideals of I.A.E.A., and the kind
of bilateral agreements which were first announced to the
General Assembly by U.S. Ambassador Henry Cabot Lodge on
November 5, 1954, have contributed towards giving the less
developed countries that much-needed sense of membership in
the atomic age. But equality of treatment as between them and
even the small European countries has not as yet been adequately
established. For example, international safeguards are not
applicable to the European Atomic Energy Community as they
are supposed to be applicable to countries like India. At a meeting
of the Administrative and Legal Committee of I.A.E.A. on
September 27, 1963, Dr. Homi Bhabha, the Indian representative and head of the Indian Department of Atomic Energy,

---

[1] 'New Nations and the Scientific Revolution', *Bulletin of the Atomic Scientists*,
SVII (February, 1961), p. 62.

articulated a view that is widely shared among the smaller powers. He said that it was desirable for the international agency to recognize Euratom and make arrangements with it in regard to safeguards. At the moment power stations operating under the auspices of Euratom were not subject to inspection by the agency: Euratom had its own system of inspection under which one country could inspect the installation of other countries. Dr. Bhabha felt that this was 'a multi-national and not an international arrangement' and was something quite different. For his part he believed that only a truly international safeguards system could be effective.[1]

In her bilateral agreements with Euratom the United States too has treated that body on a basis which can more nearly be described as 'co-operation between equals' than could the scheme she devised for dealing with other parts of the world. Defending this position in an article in *Foreign Affairs* in 1965, John A. Hall, Assistant General Manager for the International Activities, U.S. Atomic Energy Commission, and formerly Deputy Director General of I.A.E.A. itself, thought it pertinent to assert that 'Euratom is unique'.[2] And so it is in important ways. But the very fact that it is made an exception has tended to emphasize that the nuclear age has a Euro-American élite, complete with certain exclusive mutual privileges. This became particularly manifest in that single year between the Russian acceptance of I.A.E.A. safeguards in 1963 and China's testing of her first nuclear bomb in 1964. By February 1965 the *Peking Review* was asserting that China's intention had been 'to break the nuclear monopoly'.[3] After her successful nuclear test she was certainly on the way towards success.

But could the Chinese nuclear triumph be divorced from the help she had previously got from the Soviet Union in other aspects of nuclear technology? It seems likely that participation in nuclear projects under Soviet tutelage contributed to China's own nuclear development but that factor was probably not crucial. As a comprehensive private American study pointed out in 1960:

[1] Cited by Alvin Z. Rubinstein. See *Survival* (May–June, 1965), p. 124.

[2] 'Atoms for Peace, or War', *Foreign Affairs*, Vol. XLIII, No. 4 (July, 1965), p. 612.

[3] See *Peking Review*, February 5, 1965, Vol. VIII, No. 6, p. 19.

China now [August 1960] has approximately 210,000 engineers and 44,000 scientists, and of the scientists about 10,000 are physicists and about 15,000 chemists. A programme aimed at the production of plutonium bombs would require about 1.15 per cent of the Chinese scientists, 1.5 per cent of the physicists and 2.16 per cent of the chemists. In the engineering field only about 0.65 per cent of the total engineering personnel would be required.[1]

The report went on to estimate that if there were no long delays in materials, and if the Chinese started their nuclear weapons programme in 1958 without Soviet aid, they would explode their first bomb in 1963 and become a nuclear power in 1966 or later.[2]

But even if we agreed that in the case of China peaceful nuclear aid from another country did not significantly contribute to the military nuclear potential which China had from the outset, there is still room to speculate over the effect of international co-operation on nuclear proliferation in general. In the words of William C. Foster, Director of the U.S. Arms Control and Disarmament Agency since 1961,

> One of the central facts with which we have to deal is the very great overlap between the technology for the peaceful exploitation of the atom and that needed for weapons programmes. In the enthusiasm of the late 1940s and early 1950s we and others were perhaps oversold on the potentialities of the peaceful atom. . . .[3]

[1] General Electric Report on Nuclear Power, p. 110. Cited by Edgar Snow, *The Other Side of the River: Red China Today* (New York: Random House, 1962), p. 643. For related studies consult F. Henry Michael, *The Role of Communist China in International Affairs, 1965–1970* and Lawrence Krader, *The Economic Status of Communist China 1965–1970* (Santa Barbara, California: General Electric Company; Technical Military Planning Operation, 1958). For the demographic aspects of the issues involved, consult Charles G. McClintock *The Demography of the Asian 'Big Three'* and his *World Population Pressures* (Santa Barbara, California: General Electric Company; Technical Military Planning Operation, 1958).

[2] Snow, *Ibid.*, p. 644. For a discussion of early changes in Chinese attitudes to nuclear weapons, see Alice Langley Hsieh, *Communist China's Strategy in the Nuclear Era* (Englewood Cliffs, N.J.: Prentice-Hall, 1962), esp. Chapters 1 and 2.

[3] 'New Directions in Arms Control and Disarmament', *Foreign Affairs*, Vol. XLIII, No. 4 (July, 1965), p. 592.

It might follow from this that the massive release of information which took place at the three Geneva conferences and through the co-operative activities of the I.A.E.A., the United States and of other countries, contributed to greater understanding of certain *military* uses of atomic energy.[1]

If that is the case, then the concept of 'international co-operation'—which could have become a bridge between the demands of peace and the demands of equal dignity between peoples—has conceivably militated against both ideals in the specific field of nuclear collaboration.[2] Perhaps in the attempt to maximize participating membership of the nuclear age, the cause of trying to minimize membership of the nuclear club has sustained a setback.

Yet such a conclusion has perhaps a serious element of exaggeration. The conclusion tends to take it too readily for granted that nuclear proliferation would have been averted simply by having a total ban on international collaboration in this field.

In any case, it is arguable that the cause of trying to give more and more countries the sense of belonging to the age of nuclear technology might be worth the marginal risk of aggravating nuclear proliferation. Scientific knowledge has always included a suicidal risk. Knowledge about the peaceful uses of atomic energy ought not to be converted into a forbidden fruit.

CHINA'S BOMB AND THE FUTURE

But what consequences is nuclear proliferation having on the United Nations and the politics of the Third World at

---

[1] See John A. Hall's arguments for and against the implications of this hypothesis in his 'Atoms for Peace, or War', *Foreign Affairs, op. cit.*, pp. 606–10.

[2] The concept '*International co-operation*' was perhaps a potential link between the two ideals all along. To the extent that such co-operation implied reciprocity it had the potential of creating mutual esteem between the participants from the very habit of collaborating in matters of common interest. It can therefore be said that the concept of international co-operation, in fostering a sense of sovereign equality, should serve the ideal of human dignity. That same conception of co-operation, by helping the growth of a collaborative routine, might reduce areas of conflict—and therefore serve the ideal of peace.

The question which might now be asked is whether international co-operation has succeeded in fostering either ideal in the all-important matter of the utilization of nuclear power in the world.

large? And how does it relate to problems of race and of relative population?

That the Chinese nuclear success had significant racial implications is something which could not but be noted. As Ralph L. Powell put it, 'All previous atomic testing has been carried out by industrial powers of the Occident; Communist China is non-Western, non-white and only semi-industrialized.'[1]

Powell goes on to point out that many officials and newspaper editorials not only in Africa and Asia, but also in Europe, reacted to the Chinese success by urging more strongly than ever that Communist China should be given greater participation in world councils, especially in disarmament negotiations, but also in the United Nations. And late in November 1964 the *People's Daily*, responding to suggestions that China should take part in the 18-nation disarmament discussions, said that now that China 'has nuclear weapons' the United States was seeking to 'drag' China into the affairs of the United Nations.[2]

This whole line of reasoning which China is here ridiculing has important if ironic implications for our original dichotomy between numerical strength and nuclear status in the United Nations. In her own territory at any rate China has been the most 'numerically strong' country in the world. And yet her case for admission into the world body and its affiliated disarmament branch had to wait until China acquired nuclear status before it assumed a sense of real urgency. It remains to be seen whether the price which China is demanding before she would accept a seat in the United Nations would, in fact, be paid. For Communist China says she would settle for nothing less than the ousting of Nationalist China.

If, as a result of her potentially growing nuclear status, mainland China is finally persuaded to come into the world body one way or another, nuclear proliferation would have served one useful purpose. It would have helped to make the United Nations more representative. And it would have permitted its nuclear élite to become more diversified racially.

But at the same time China's admission would mean the end of non-alignment in the United Nations as it has so far been

[1] 'China's Bomb: Exploitation and Reactions', *Foreign Affairs*, Vol. XLIII, No. 4 (July, 1965), p. 616.
[2] *Ibid.*, p. 620.

understood. It would in fact bring into the world body something which is already discernible outside—the varied implications for non-alignment of China's dispute with India and with the Soviet Union.

In 1923, writing on his death bed, Lenin linked these three countries together and assessed their impact in terms of population. Lenin said:

> In the last analysis the outcome of the struggle will be determined by the fact that Russia, India, China, etc. account for the overwhelming population of the globe. And it is precisely that majority that, during the past few years, has been drawn into the struggle for emancipation with extraordinary rapidity.[1]

Lenin saw in this fact an assurance for the complete victory of Socialism. For a while in the 1950s it did seem that the three most populous countries in the world intended to remain on sufficiently friendly terms to exert a shared influence on the rest of the world. But then alternative possibilities began to be discernible. If China and Russia remained together communism would retain a powerful alliance on its side. If India and China remained together something approaching 'Pan-Asianism' would continue to exert a shared influence on diplomatic events in the world— and could constitute a collective leadership of the coloured nations of Asia and Africa at large.

And yet for a while it was India rather than China which was the effective leader of the new states. And one factor which helped India to retain this leadership for a decade was the general diplomatic isolation of Communist China, including her exclusion from the United Nations. In the meantime India bequeathed to the new states the doctrine of 'non-alignment'. As Milton Obote said in his tribute to Nehru when he died,

> Nehru will be remembered as a founder of non-alignment. . . . The new nations of the world owe him a debt of gratitude in this respect.[2]

---

1 Cited by Snow, *The Other Side of the River*, op. cit., p. 646.
2 See *Uganda Argus*, May 29, 1964.

But even as Obote said that, non-alignment in the old sense had already been rendered impossible by Communist China. The two biggest members of the old community of Afro-Asian states had each played a crucial role in the history of that old version of non-alignment—one, India, had virtually invented it; the other, China, had virtually destroyed it.

But contrary to what many commentators in the West concluded, it was not the Chinese invasion of India which killed non-alignment. At the most what the Chinese invasion imperilled was India's non-alignment. And even if that invasion had eliminated non-alignment from the rest of Asia as well, it could conceivably still have left Africa and the Middle East as the last and defiantly enduring bastions of non-alignment in the world.[1]

What killed non-alignment of the old sense was then not China's conflict with India, but China's dispute with the Soviet Union. The old non-alignment that Nehru had bequeathed to fellow Afro-Asians had assumed a bi-polarized cold war. Its whole conceptual framework postulated a dichotomy between 'East and West'—and sometimes between 'communism' and 'capitalism'. China's dispute with Russia suddenly rendered such dichotomies a little too simple. Reluctantly, but with increasing tempo, African states saw themselves having to cope not only with archaic contests between Russians and Westerners, but also with competition and hostility between the Russians and the Chinese.

Perhaps only in the United Nations is the ghost of non-alignment in the old sense still to be seen at work. The admission of Communist China into the world body is what is needed to exorcise it.

The extent to which members of the United Nations vote *en bloc* as between the new coloured nations and the older members has always been grossly exaggerated by journalistic concepts like 'the Afro-Asian bloc'. The triumph of numericalism in the old colonies has indeed transformed the General Assembly and affected its relationship to the Security Council. But as UN Undersecretary Ralph J. Bunche said in July 1965, the Afro-Asian states vote as a bloc only 'in cases of overt racial discrimination'.[2] The admission of Communist China would make a neat

---

[1] This point is discussed more fully in my article 'The United Nations and Some African Political Attitudes', *On Heroes and Hero-Worship*, pp. 514–15.

[2] Bunche was answering Richard Nixon's charge that the United

division between Afro-Asians and others even more rare. China and India might divide the vote on one issue; China and Russia on another. And some of the old alignments might retain just enough life to add further complexities to the politics of the world organization and of the Third World at large.

The nuclear status of the most crucial coloured nation in world politics might therefore yet serve to reduce the chances of neat racial confrontations in the years ahead.

But in the meantime the quest for non-proliferation is itself posing new problems for the viability of even of the new poly-centric version of non-alignment. Can India sign a non-prolifera-tion treaty without abandoning even a pretence at being non-aligned? In the course of the second half of 1965 this dilemma became increasingly clear. If a non-proliferation treaty was to materialize, there was a need for giving adequate guarantees to the non-nuclear powers on their own security. But guarantees given to India by Western powers against China would amount to a nuclear alignment with the West. The only way out seemed to be nuclear guarantees to India given by both the Western powers and the Soviet Union. This would be a whole new version of positive neutralism. For Nehru non-alignment had signified having an alliance with neither bloc. But for his successors facing the current dilemma, positive neutralism could at best only be maintained by having an alliance with both blocs. Only joint assurance from both the Soviet Union and the Western powers could make India subscribe to non-proliferation without betraying 'non-alignment'.

By 1967 the three leading nuclear powers—the USA, the USSR and Great Britain—had made some progress towards devising a basis for the requisite treaty. Nevertheless, for India the ultimate guarantees had yet to be worked out and firmly made.[1]

Nations was controlled by 'weak and neutral nations'. Bunche said that there were no 'solid blocs' in the UN apart from the communist one. See *Los Angeles Times* (July 13, 1965), p. 4. Partly because of the need to get Com-munist China involved in future disarmament discussions, Bunche also said that China could not now be kept out of the UN for longer than two years. See *New York Times* (July 14, 1965), p. 4.

[1] See *The Observer* (London) and the *Sunday Times* (London), February 19, 1967. See also *The Times* (London), January 18, 1966, for an earlier phase of India's nuclear problem. W. Goldstein has argued that non-proliferation will

It is true that many in India had in any case got less purist in their non-alignment. As early as 1964 it had been observed that Indian intellectuals, though supporting non-alignment in principle, nonetheless now desired to see the formulation of 'specific understandings' with the United Kingdom and the United States as an extra safeguard for the nation's security.[1] But nothing compelled Indians to appraise more fully their place in the nuclear age than China's achievement with her nuclear test. By the election campaign of 1966–67 India's nuclear armament had become a significant political issue at home. The party which most vociferously championed the nuclearization of India was Jan Sangh, a movement of right-wing militancy. But the cause of making India a nuclear power had other champions well to the left of Jan Sangh.[2]

In all their divergent ways, these then are the multiple implications of that atomic tremor from China late in 1964 as the world's most populous country announced her new nuclear credentials. To many radicals in the non-European and non-Western world, the event had, as we indicated, important racial symbolism. Chinese visitors or diplomats in distant Afro-Asian lands might at times be reserved, or objectionable or even subversive. Chinese youth in their own land might, in their excessive domestic fervour, reduce the stature of China as an enviable model for the Third World. The country's arrogance towards her neighbours might often cost her the goodwill of others further afield. Her hostility to the United Nations might embarrass those who champion her admission. But when all is said and done, that

---

continue to be a non-starter unless convincing sacrifices are made by the nuclear 'Haves'. See his article 'Keeping the genie in the bottle: the feasibility of nuclear non-proliferation agreement', *Background*, Vol. IX, No. 2, August 1965, pp. 137–46. See also K. Younger, 'The Spectre of Nuclear Proliferation', *International Affairs* (London), Vol. XLII, No. 1, January 1966, pp. 14–23.

[1] 'Pundits and Panchscheela: Indian intellectuals and their foreign policy', *Background*, Vol. IX, No. 2, August 1965, pp. 127–36.

[2] For discussions of aspects of India's defence policy see Amalendu Das Gupta, 'A Nuclear Policy for India', *Conspectus*, Vol. I, No. 1, First Quarter, 1965, pp. 3–11; N. D. Palmer, 'The Defence of South Asia', *Orbis*, Vol. IX, No. 4, Winter 1966, pp. 898–929; S. K. Gupta, 'Asian Non-alignment', *Annals of the American Academy of Political and Social Science*, 362, November 1965, pp. 44–51; M. S. Rajan, 'The Future of Non-alignment', the *Annals*, 362, November 1965, pp. 121–8. See also *The Times* (London), February 23 and 24, 1967.

explosion from China in 1964 had a proud hopefulness for many in Asia and Africa—the sort of hopefulness and the sort of pride not very different from those which accompanied Japan's victory over Russia more than half a century earlier.[1] After all, China had now demonstrated that nuclear status was reachable even by those who, on other grounds, might still be termed 'under-developed'.

Even for India, in all her forebodings, China's atomic device was a reaffirmation that the nuclear age had now more decisively made its entry into the Asian continent. The two giants of the Third World were now perhaps on the verge of a new form of their historic competition. And in the very dimensions of such a competition the ethos of numericalism might find yet another relationship with the new mystique of nuclear status.

[1] Of interest in this connection is M. Freeberne, 'Racial Issues in the Sino-Soviet Dispute', *Asian Survey*, Vol. V, No. 8, August 1965, pp. 408–16. See also H. M. Vinacke, 'Communist China and the Uncommitted Zone', the *Annals*, 362, November 1965, pp. 113–20; and G. Pauker, 'The Rise and Fall of Afro-Asian Solidarity', *Asian Survey*, Vol. V, No. 9, September 1965, pp. 425–32.

SECTION B

NATIONHOOD AND CREATIVE INSTABILITY

4 From Social Darwinism to Current Theories of Modernization: A Tradition of Analysis[1]

Much of the most interesting work in political science in the last decade or so has been concerned with processes of modernization, institution-formation, and socio-political change at large. In fact, modernization and political development have been—alongside system analysis—the most important themes of the new political science. In this essay we are addressing ourselves to this developmental revolution in political science. We propose to argue that the idea of analysing and classifying nations on the basis of the stage of modernization reached has long-standing historical connections with a tradition which goes back to social Darwinism and beyond. But it must be emphasized from the outset that this is not intended as a criticism of the new political science. On the contrary, there might even be special strengths in a revolution of thought which finds strong antecedents in a dynamic, if somewhat mistaken, period of intellectual theorizing in the past. Much of intellectual history itself is indeed a history of wave-formation—each succeeding wave owing something to the strength of what went before.

In its earliest forms social Darwinism had a strong and perhaps inevitable biological bias. Differing stages in the evolution of human societies were sometimes attributed to biological distinctions between peoples. This was the influence of Charles Darwin on racism in Europe. The ideological repercussions were indeed long-term.

[1] This essay was first delivered to a plenary session of the Second International Congress of Africanists, held at Dakar, December 11 to 21, 1967. The author is a Vice-President of the Congress. It has since appeared in *World Politics*, Vol. XXI, No. 1, October 1968.

Then there was also in social Darwinism an optimistic strain, assuming a line of development which leads to greater sophistication and effectiveness in human organization. This, too, is a theme that has continued in different forms to the present day.

Thirdly, there was in Darwinism the beginnings of conflict theory in modern social analysis—a belief in functional *struggle* and compulsive *adaptation* with the challenges of environment within each society. Again, this is a theme which has come to affect later academic explanations of the process of development. We propose to examine each of these trends in the tradition of analysis which extends from social Darwinism to these latter-day theories.

FROM RACISM TO ETHNOCENTRISM

In 1859 Charles Darwin's *Origin of Species* was published. It was soon to have long-term repercussions both for the study of biology and for the study of social science. Racists could now proceed to demonstrate, by the utilization of the theory of natural selection, that major differences in human capacity and human organization were to be traced to biological distinctions between races. But to some extent this theory was much older than Darwin. What Darwin added to it was the dynamism converting mere classification of beings into a *process*. The static version of the theory goes back to the ancient idea that God had so organized the world that the universe and creation were arranged in a 'Great Chain of Being'—that all creatures could be classified and fitted into a hierarchy extending 'from man down to the smallest reptile, whose existence can be discovered by the microscope'.[1]

But it was not just the species who were so classified. Even within the highest species (that of human beings) there were in turn divisions within it. Theories of the Great Chain of Being assumed that the Almighty in His wisdom did not want a big gap between one type of creature and the next. And so there had to be intermediate categories between orang-outangs and white

[1] Charles White, *An Account of the Regular Graduations in Man* (London: 1799), I. See also A. O. Lovejoy, *The Great Chain of Being* (Cambridge, Mass.: 1936).

men. As early as 1713 naturalists began looking for the 'missing link' between men and apes and apparently speculated on the possibility that Hottentots and orang-outangs might be side by side in the 'scale of life', separated only by the fact that orang-outangs could not speak.[1]

What Darwinism helped to finalize into specific theoretical form was the element of motion in this process, the idea that the backward people might be on the move towards a higher phase, and those in front further still.

The link between racism and ethnocentrism is not difficult to see. Even for the earliest racist theories there had been no difficulty about deciding where to place the white man in the chain of being. As Philip D. Curtin puts it in discussing these early biological theorists,

> Since there is no strictly scientific or biological justification for stating that one race is 'higher' than another, the criteria of ranking has to come from non-scientific assumptions. All of the biologists . . . began by putting the European variety at the top of the scale. This was natural enough if only as an un-thinking reflection of cultural Chauvinism. It could be held to follow from the assessment of European achievements in art and science. . . . It was taken for granted that historical achievement was intimately connected with physical form—in short, that race and culture were closely related.[2]

The dynamic element in ethnocentric theories of evolution inevitably led to assumptions about white leadership in the whole process of historical change. And within the white races themselves specific leadership was assumed to come from the 'tougher' of the European stock. For example, in his inaugural lecture as Regius Professor of Modern History at Oxford in December 1841 Thomas Arnold gave a new lease of life to the ancient idea of moving centre of civilization. Arnold argued that the history of civilization was the history of a series of creative races, each of which made its impact and then sank into oblivion, leaving the

---

[1] Lovejoy, *ibid.*, pp. 233ff.; also Lovejoy, 'Some Eighteenth-Century Evolutionists', *Popular Science Monthly*, Vol. LXV, p. 327 (1904).

[2] Curtin, *The Image of Africa* (London: 1965), pp. 38–9. We are indebted to Curtin's book for bibliographical guidance and for some insights.

heritage of civilization to a greater successor. What the Greeks passed on to the Romans, the Romans bequeathed in turn to the Germanic race, and of that race the greatest civilizing nation was England.[1]

Notions of leadership very often led on to notions of the right to rule the less developed. Even that prophet of liberalism, John Stuart Mill, could still argue that despotism was 'a legitimate mode of government in dealing with barbarians, provided the end be their improvement . . .'[2]

In Mill also there began to emerge the notion that democratic institutions constitute the ultimate destination of much of socio-political development. And the capacity to operate democratic institutions was already being regarded as an index of political maturity and institutional stability. Mill even seemed to share some of the reservations held by current modernization theorists about the possibility of operating liberal institutions in multi-ethnic situations. To use the formulation of John Stuart Mill, 'Free institutions are next to impossible in a country made up of different nationalities'.[3] Here, then, is the essential assumption of some of the current theories of integration—a process towards the fusion of nationalities within a single territory into a new entity capable of sustaining the stresses of a more liberalized polity. At least one major approach in theorizing about political modernization in our own day has rested on what Robert A. Packenham describes as 'the idea that political development is primarily a function of a social system that facilitates popular

[1] See Arnold, *Introductory Lectures on Modern History* (New York: 1842), pp. 46–7; consult also Curtin, *op. cit.*, pp. 375–7. See also Arthur Penrhyn Stanley, *Life and Correspondence of Thomas Arnold* (London: 1845), esp. pp. 435, 438. This notion of a moving centre of civilization is also discussed in Mazrui, *Ancient Greece in African Political Thought* (Nairobi: 1967).

[2] *Utilitarianism, Liberty and Representative Government*, with Introduction by A. D. Lindsay (London and New York: 1964), pp. 198–201, pp. 382–3.

[3] *Ibid.*, p. 361. More recently Carl G. Rosberg, Jr., for example, makes a similar point when he argues that 'the dangers to stability presented by ethnic and other parochialisms are magnified in most African states by a lack of that fundament of common values and sidely shared principles of political behaviour generally termed "consensus". Typically, the terms of a consensus prescribe that the pursuit of group interests be conducted peaceably and within established institutions of the constitutional framework' ('Democracy and the New African States', in Kenneth Kirkwood, ed., *St. Antony's Papers on African Affairs*, No. 2 (London: 1963), p. 26). Comparable arguments abound in the literature on democracy in new states.

participation in governmental and political processes at all levels and the bridging of regional, religious, caste, linguistic, tribal or other cleavages'.

Packenham goes on to argue that one form which this particular approach has taken today is assessing the social correlates of democracy. These correlates are supposed to include relatively high 'scores' on such sociological variables as an open class system, literacy and or education, high participation in voluntary organizations, urbanization and communication system.[1] Much of this side of analysis assumes that the highest of modern institutions must inevitably be those which have been devised in the West. The Darwinian evolution toward modernity is evolution towards Western ways. Edward Shils seemed to be expressing as much his own view of the matter as of some members of Afro-Asian élites when he said, ' "Modern" means being Western without the onus of dependence on the West'. And much of the rest of Shils' theorizing on the process of development bears the stamp of ethnocentric preference for 'a regime of representative institutions' of the Western kind.[2]

There have been models of theorizing about developments which have gone so far as to classify political regimes in the world in terms of firstly, the Anglo-American type; secondly, the continental European types; thirdly, totalitarian types; and fourthly, the types that one found in Africa and Asia.[3]

Evidently, this is ethnocentrism which has strong links with

[1] See Packenham, 'Approaches to the Study of Political Development', *World Politics*, *XVII*, October 1964, p. 115. For subsequent additional insights we have benefited from conversations with Gwendolen Carter, William O. Brown and James S. Coleman.

[2] See esp. Shils, *Political Development in the New States* (The Hague, 1965), p. 10ff.

[3] Gabriel Almond has shared such a vision of political development, especially in his earlier work. A more cautious but related formulation is that of Eisenstadt who says: 'Historically, modernization is the process of change towards those types of social, economic, and political systems that have developed in Western Europe and North America from the seventeenth century to the nineteenth and have then spread to other European countries and in the nineteenth and twentieth centuries to the South American, Asian, and African continents.' (*Modernization: Protest and Change* (Englewood Cliffs: 1966), p. 1). Consult also the series of books entitled *Studies in Political Development* sponsored by the Committee on Comparative Politics of the Social Science Research Council of the United States. Of special interest as a study of value-systems is Lucian W. Pye and Sidney Verba, eds., *Political Culture and Political Development* (Princeton: 1965).

older theories of Anglo-Saxon leadership as a focus of a new wave of civilization. Again, theories of evolutionary change culminating in the pre-eminence of a single nation had major *philosophers* of the West among their disciples. Not least among these philosophers was Hegel, for whom the entire process of change in the universe had for its ultimate human culmination the emergence of the Prussian state and the Germanic genius. Hegel, too, was in a sense, a pre-Darwinian social Darwinist, both in his notion of a creative tension between thesis, antithesis and synthesis and his notion of a purposeful evolution towards the emergence of a high species.

More recently there have been *historians* who have seen human evolution in terms of a progressive rise to the pre-eminence of their own nation or group of nations. William H. McNeill in our own day, though by no means lacking in humility, has interpreted world history in such a way that he might easily belong to this tradition.[1] McNeill challenges in part the Spenglerian pessimism of a Western decline and the whole conception of history as a collection of separate civilizations, each pursuing an independent career. For McNeill, human cultures have had a basic inter-relationship—and their history has been leading to a global pre-eminence of Western civilization.

In the field of *sociology* Talcott Parsons has talked about 'evolutionary universals' in terms which do indicate a belief that ultimately development is in the direction of greater comparability with the political systems of the Western World. Parsons argues that the existence of a definitive link between popular participation and ultimate control of decision-making is so crucial for building and maintaining support for the political-legal system as a whole, and for its binding rules and decisions that, in so far as large-scale societies are concerned, the 'democratic association' is an 'evolutionary universal'. In defence of this proposition against anticipated criticism Parsons declares,

I realize that to take this position I must maintain that communist totalitarian organization will probably not fully match 'democracy' in political and integrative capacity in the long run. I do indeed predict that it will prove to be unstable and will either make adjustments in a general direction of

[1] See McNeill, *The Rise of the West* (Chicago and London: 1963).

elective democracy and a plural party system or 'regress' into generally less advanced and politically less effective forms of organization, failing to advance as rapidly or as far as might otherwise be expected.[1]

A similar ethnocentrism is evident in the approach of J. Roland Pennock to the study of political development. Pennock enumerates principles like 'justice according to law', 'the rule of law', and 'due process' as among the political goods which are delivered when a society attains a certain degree of political development. Pennock declares in a long footnote,

It might be objected that modern totalitarian dictatorships may not subscribe to the standards of justice according to law outlined above. Are we then to call them less 'developed' than modern constitutional regimes? . . . I would be quite happy to say that to this extent they are in fact less developed, less fitted to fulfil the needs of men and society.[2]

Later in the same article Pennock refers to other tendencies in the discussion of political development which bear the ethnocentric theme that the history of human evolution is towards the type of institutions and ideals cherished in the Western World. Pennock does not describe them as Western ideals. There is a tendency to refer to such things as 'world culture'. But the inclination to discern an upward movement of human evolution towards Westernism is recurrent in the literature. In the words of the concluding sentence of Pennock's article,

It is common today to compare or rank states by the degree of party competition, or their adoption and use of the major devices of representative government, or their social mobilization. It is my suggestion that, to see a more nearly complete picture and to make more highly discriminating judgements, anyone who is concerned with political development in any

[1] Parsons, 'Evolutionary Universals in Society', *American Sociological Review*, *XXIX*, June 1964, p. 356. See also in the same issue of the journal, S. N. Eisenstadt, 'Social Change, Differentiation, and Evolution'. pp. 375–86.
[2] Pennock, 'Political Development, Political Systems, and Political Goods', *World Politics*, *XVIII*, April 1966, p. 424.

way involving measurement of comparison should take full account of some of the measurable elements of the political goods of security, justice, liberty, and welfare.[1]

Of course by the time of our current theories of modernization the racialistic element in theories of human development had virtually disappeared, at least within the ranks of scholarship. The racial component was what had given social Darwinism a continuing biological feature borrowed from the Darwin of the *Origin of Species*. In fact in the heyday of racial theories it was by no means all that clear where biological Darwinism ended and social Darwinism began.

But in the modern theories of modernization Darwinism has been debiologized. It is no longer racial bigotry that is being invoked to explain stages of political growth. What is now invoked is at the most ethnocentric cultural pride.

EVOLUTION AND OPTIMISM

The shift from biological explanations of human backwardness to cultural explanations of that factor had important implications. Biological differences imply a slower rate of mutation of character. The African thus could not help lagging behind for many generations simply because he could not help the biological traits he had inherited from his own sub-species. There is a quality almost of immutability, of being retarded, when a lack of development is attributed to hereditary characteristics within the race. But as ideas on social evolution took a turn more toward cultural determinism, the notion of a backward people catching up with more advanced people was at last brought within the bounds of feasibility.

The shift from biological determinism to cultural determinism had its transitional moments. Let us take W. R. Greg as a case

[1] *Ibid.*, p. 434. Pennock cites an appendix to Gabriel A. Almond and James S. Coleman, eds., *The Politics of the Developing Areas* (Princeton: 1960); and Phillips Cutright, 'National Political Development: Measurement and Analysis', *American Sociological Review*, XXVII, April 1963, pp. 253–64. A more recent discussion by Almond of some of these issues is his article 'A Developmental Approach to Political Systems', *World Politics*, XVII, January 1965, pp. 183–214.

of intellectual transition in this field of theorizing. Greg inherited
the leadership of Anglo-Saxon ethnocentrism from Thomas
Arnold. At any rate upon Arnold's death, Greg speculated further
in the *Westminster Review* on the whole destiny of human
evolution. He discussed Africa specifically. He noted that some
backward races elsewhere were indeed becoming extinct. But the
Negro race seemed to retain a striking resilience. Figures from
North America indicated that Negroes could continue in healthy
persistence even when they were transplanted from Africa to the
very different environment of North America, and to the very
different experience of constant contact with Europeans. Greg
was indeed of the opinion that Africans were intellectually
devoid of the possibilities of ultimate originality. But they had the
one thing which was very important from the point of view of
successful acculturation: Africans were endowed with a significant imitative genius. They could therefore assimilate what the
West could bequeath to them. This had implications for the
whole notion of progress. Greg was in fact to some extent a pre-
cursor of theories of 'demonstration-effect'. Human progress was
possible because the more backward of the races had at least the
ability to imitate. European achievements could therefore be
grafted onto African stock.[1]

Some of these notions were to last well into the period of
colonial expansion in Africa, and of the legitimation of individual
colonial policies consequent upon annexation. To some extent
the whole paraphernalia of ideas of the French assimilationist
policies had direct intellectual contact with the kind of tradition
to which Greg belonged—the kind which permitted the African
a capacity to emulate without permitting him a capacity to create.
The policy of attempting to Gallicize Africans was firmly within
the flow of this historical stream. As independence came, theorists
in the Anglo-Saxon world discussed for a while the feasibility of
upholding some of the inherited institutions from colonialism.
The argument of whether Ghana could sustain the 'Westminster model' or not was also part of this argument on the
potential imitative capacity of African political man. But gradually theories of political development attained a sophistication
which differentiated them more sharply than ever from simple
biological explanations of whether or not there was an important

[1] Greg, 'Dr. Arnold', *Westminster Review*, XXX, January 1843.

emulative genius within the African sub-species. Ghanaian capacity to maintain the Westminster model, or the ability of Nigeria to cope with inherited federal and Westminster institutions, became now more firmly associated with varied constraints and pre-conditions which the Western World had already managed to cope with but which the rest of the universe had yet to evolve.

Nevertheless there was a firm conviction that the direction of change would be towards a greater approximation to Western achievements. In the meantime political science as a discipline had embraced more fully the comparative ethos—the idea that different cultures *could* be compared in terms of what was being accomplished in the political process. Almost any two political systems could be a subject of such comparison. There have indeed already been comparisons between Ghana and Spain, Mexico and Uganda, Tanzania and the Soviet Union.

The comparative dimension in political science has been both a manifestation and a further reinforcing factor for the acceptance of cultural relativism and toleration of major differences. To some extent, then, the Darwinian evolutionary tendency achieved a high level of cross-cultural accommodation when the structural-functionalists in political science began to discern comparable functions, performed by different structures, between varied societies.

But side by side with this toleration and indulgence was the conviction that progress was almost inevitable for the more backward societies. And the direction of that progress was towards greater similarity of values, norms, and structures of the Western World.

In discussing the processes of change examined in the varying contexts of the five geographical areas reviewed in *The Politics of the Developing Areas*, James S. Coleman asserted that the consequences were by no means uniform and yet 'in general the changes have brought the countries concerned nearer the model of a modern society'. And what is a modern society? Coleman's own view as expressed elsewhere is more detached and less ethnocentric. But in the particular book he edited with Almond, Coleman derived a definition of a 'modern society' from Almond's introduction to the book and from Shil's model of a 'political democracy'. The attributes of a 'modern system' had thus been enumerated. On the basis of these Coleman concluded that 'it is clear from this list of attributes that the Anglo-American qualities most closely approximate the model of the modern political system. . . .[1]

Frederick W. Fray has pointed out also that 'the most common notion of political development in intellectual American circles is that of movement towards democracy'. He finds this a congenial notion, combining pride in one's own cultural achievements with optimism that the rest of mankind is on its way in the same direction.[2]

Sometimes the movement is described not as one towards democracy but as one towards participation. Again the definition of participation verges on being the liberal democratic one. And again also there is a conviction that this is the ultimate destination of the progress of new nations. Almond and Sidney Verba assert that the 'new world political culture will be a political culture of participation. If there is a political revolution going on throughout the world, it is what might be called the participation explosion. In all the new nations of the world the belief that the ordinary man is politically relevant—that he ought to be an involved participant in the political system—is widespread. Large groups of people who have been outside politics have been demanding entrance into the political system'.[3]

This optimism has ancestral roots in Darwinism, both biological and social. Certainly in the biological ideas that Darwin brings together in the *Origin of Species* there is a conviction of a progressive evolution towards greater complexity and greater sophistication in the structure of beings. In Chapter 8 of the *Origin of Species* Darwin talks of the 'one general law leading to advancement of all organic beings'. The direction of change is toward greater flexibility to cope with environment and with needs. Those who cannot cope do indeed fall by the wayside and die. There is an element of pessimism implied in this expiry of

---

[1] *The Politics of the Developing Areas*, (eds.) Almond and Coleman, p. 533, p. 536. In his introduction to *Education and Political Development* (Princeton: 1965), Coleman defines political development more neutrally in terms of enhancing 'political capacity'. See esp., pp. 15–16.

[2] Fray, 'Political Development, Power and Communications in Turkey', in Lucian W. Pye, (ed.), *Communications and Political Development* (Princeton: 1963), p. 301.

[3] *The Civic Culture* (Princeton: 1963), p. 4.

those that are not so strong. And yet it is pessimism only for those who are soft and romantic about these matters. For the hard-headed this is a defiant optimism. In Darwin's declaration, 'Multiply, vary, let the strongest live and the weakest die'.[1]

Twelve years after the *Origin of Species* Darwin published *The Descent of Man and Selections in Relation to Sex*. In this Darwin's optimism extends beyond the purely biological to a vision of man's social and cultural destiny. In his vision of man he sees 'the standard of his morality rise higher and higher' and he looks forward to the day when 'the struggle between our higher and lower impulses will be less severe, and virtue will be triumphant'. Looking at history he concludes that,

> It is apparently a truer and more cheerful view that progress has been much more general than retrogression; that man has risen, though by slow and interrupted steps, from a lowly condition to the highest standard as yet attained by him in knowledge, morals and religion.[2]

This optimism about the future has certainly been inherited by many schools of theories of modernization in contemporary scholarship. That was why Samuel P. Huntington's essay, 'Political Development and Political Decay' was such an important landmark in the literature on political development. In his essay Huntington complained about the gap between theory and reality in many concepts of political development. He pointed out among other things that these concepts were usually one-way concepts; little or no provision was made for their reversibility. Like Darwin's creatures it is true that societies according to these theories became more complex as their structures became more differentiated. But the modernization theories were not making enough provision for social regression. Huntington points out that structural differentiation may indeed occur but so also might structural 'homogenization'. Huntington detects in many of the theories 'an underlying commitment to the theory of progress

---

[1] Darwin, *Origin of Species*, 1st ed. reprinted (London: 1950), chap. 8.

[2] Darwin, *The Descent of Man and Selections in Relation to Sex* (London: 1871). Stanley Edgar Hyman has rightly remarked, '*The Descent of Man* is wrongly titled, at least in that its dominant mood is onward and upward. Man fell into the savage state, but he is rising out of it and he will abolish it.' See Hyman, *The Tangled Bank* (New York: 1966), p. 56.

[which] is so overwhelming as to exclude political decay as a possible concept. Political decay like thermo-nuclear war becomes unthinkable.'[1]

He cites Almond again as an example of someone who measured not just political development but *political change* by 'the acquisition by a political system of some new capability'. The specific capabilities that Almond had in mind were those for national integration, international accommodation, political participation and welfare distribution. Before the rennaissance, Almond argues, political systems 'acquired and lost capabilities . . . in anything but a unilinear, evolutionary way'. Modernization however reduced 'the independence of man's political experiments'. Change was 'far from unilinear' but it was indeed towards 'the emergence of world culture'.[2]

But Huntington asserts that modern and modernizing states could change by losing capabilities as well as by gaining them. And a theory of political development needed therefore to be mated to a theory of political decay.[3]

EVOLUTION AND CREATIVE CONFLICT

Huntington goes on to suggest that theories of instability might tell us more about the 'developing areas' than their more

[1] Huntington, 'Political Development and Political Decay', *World Politics*, XVII, April 1965, pp. 392–3. But see also S. N. Eisenstadt, 'Breakdowns of Modernization', *Economic Development and Cultural Change*, XII, July 1964, pp. 345–67. For another 'hard-headed' analysis of unpredictable change see C. S. Whitaker, Jr., 'A Dysrhythmic Process of Political Change', *World Politics*, XIX, January 1967, pp. 190–217.

[2] 'Political Systems and Political Change', *American Behavioral Scientist*, VI, June 1963, p. 6.

[3] See 'Political Development and Political Decay', *op. cit.*, p. 393. Eric Dunning, a sociologist, makes a similar point when he appeals to fellow sociologists to feel less inhibited about using the term 'development'. Sociologists have been more aware than have political scientists that theories of development tend to echo social evolutionism. But Dunning argues that the concept of development is an improvement over the concept of 'social evolution'. ' "Development" avoids the taint of biological reductionism. Societies are *sui generis* and contain their own mechanisms of change. Social development, furthermore, is reversible; organic evolution is not.' Dunning goes on to point out that 'nineteenth-century errors are not unavoidable concomitants of the study of social development' ('The Concept of Development: Two Illustrative Case Studies', in Peter I. Rose, ed., *The Study of Society* (New York: 1967), pp. 891–2).

optimistic opposites. He seems to imply here that instability is an indication of political decay. But in fact there have been theories which postulated a degree of functionality in certain types of instability. And these theories have in turn some intellectual connection with Darwinian assumptions of earlier social speculation. One form of relevant instability in this regard is the kind which arises from intense competition and conflict. Darwinian postulates about a struggle for existence and the survival of the fittest affected movements of thought both in conservative and liberal circles on one side and in radical and Marxist circles on the other. The process of natural selection provided a means for explaining and legitimating certain directions of social process. The American political economist William Graham Sumner (1840–1910), for example, saw society as a context in which each individual struggled for his own good and had to encroach upon some interests of others in order to realize his own interests. Survival was for the imaginative, the ruthless, the industrious, the frugal. The indolent and extravagant lost in the struggle, incapable as they were of adapting to the realities of life. They were therefore eliminated by a process of 'social selection'. Sumner presents society with an alternative: either 'liberty, inequality, survival of the fittest' or 'not liberty, equality, survival of the unfittest'. Self-made millionaires were a model of the fittest. They were 'a product of natural selection, acting on the whole body of men to pick out those who can meet the requirements of certain work to be done'.[1]

Darwinism did seem to provide some kind of additional credibility to Adam Smith's theory that each individual pursuing his own interest might indeed gain at the expense of another, but somehow an 'invisible hand' guided this process of intensive individualistic competition towards a better capability of the species as a whole. Man's innate tendency to 'truct, barter, and trade', when given natural freedom to express itself free of encumbrances from the state, would automatically develop in the direction of the economic wellbeing of the society as a whole.

The left-wing side of social thought also experienced the

---

[1] See Richard Hofstadter, *Social Darwinism in American Thought 1860–1915* (Philadelphia: 1944). See also Herbert Schneider, 'The Influence of Darwin and Spencer on American Philosophical Theology', *Journal of the History of Ideas, VI,* 1945.

impact of Darwinism on its postulates. Karl Marx wanted to dedicate the first volume of *Das Capital* to Charles Darwin, but Darwin declined the honour. In 1860 Marx had written to Engels after a month spent nursing his sick wife: 'During my time of trial, these last four weeks, I have read all sorts of things. Among others Darwin's book on *Natural Selection*. Although it is developed in the crude English style, this is the book which contains the basis in natural history for our view.' Marx elaborates this point elsewhere, arguing that in place of war of nature he provided a theory of the 'fierce strife of classes'. And Engels in his funeral oration over Marx' grave in 1883 said, 'As Darwin discovered the law of evolution in organic nature, so Marx discovered the law of evolution in human history'.[1]

In all this there is a definite assumption that historical materialism as a process, though involving class struggle, is nevertheless in the direction of better times in the future. Superior classes triumph over those that have decayed or become less fit, leading ultimately to the triumph of the proletariat in the penultimate stage of human progress. The steps towards this destination may be painful—and the path towards austere proletarian happiness is littered with the broken bottles and broken glasses of more decadent ages. But out of the weariness and anguish, out of the tears and ashes of human experience, development *does* take place—and mankind staggers one more step forward.

A similar kind of belief in creative conflict has sometimes animated theories of modernization in our own day. Huntington finds this an incapacity to allow for the feasibility of several steps backwards. He complains 'Almost anything that happens in the "developing" countries—coups, ethnic struggles, revolutionary wars—becomes part of the process of development, however contradictory or retrogressive this may appear on the surface.'[2]

[1] Hyman has a perceptive discussion on Marx's enthusiasm for Darwin and of the relationship between historical materialism and the theory of natural selection. See *The Tangled Bank*, pp. 121–6.

[2] See 'Political Development and Political Decay', p. 390. Among more systematic and influential conflict theorists in related disciplines are George Simmel (see his *Conflict and the Web of Group-Affiliations*, trans. by Kurt H. Wolff and Reinhard Bendix [New York: 1964]) and Max Gluckman (see his *Custom and Conflict in Africa* [Oxford: 1963]). Within a related persuasion may be placed Mazrui's paper 'Pluralism and National Integration', *Proceedings of the Colloquium on Pluralism, University of California, Los Angeles, 1966*.

It may be true that sometimes it is merely a failure to distinguish that some directions of change are reversible. But there are occasions when the modern theorists are consciously asserting that behind those tensions and coups, behind that bitterness in new countries, is a creative process of nations in the making. And even the clash between modernity and traditionalism itself is sometimes seen not as something which delays the process of modernization, but as something which leads to its full realization. The idea of a thesis colliding with an antithesis, and resulting in the improvement of a synthesis, is sometimes taken for granted in current theories of modernization. David E. Apter seems to regard the very struggle between traditionalism and modernity as an exercise in preparation—a method of giving society some readiness to meet the challenges of modernized change. And Eisenstadt also discusses the functions of 'eruptions', the nature of protest and the process of developing change-absorbing institutions in a manner which again sometimes takes for granted the functionality of social conflict in the process of modernization.[1]

CONCLUSION

It is by no means rare for major schools of intellectual analysis to have significant antecedents in earlier traditions. As we have indicated, that perhaps is what intellectual history is all about—a succession of waves, or alternatively a long chain of moments of inspiration linked together into a tradition of thought. We have attempted to demonstrate in this paper that current theories of modernization have ancestral ties with earlier notions of social evolution and Darwinism. There have been drastic changes in many of the postulates of this line of intellectual analysis. In fact the change sometimes has been from racism to broad humanism. But it has often been a form of humanism which is animated by the self-confidence of ethno-centric achievement.

[1] See Eisenstadt, *Modernization*; and Apter, *The Politics of Modernization* (Chicago: 1965). See also Apter, 'The Role of Traditionalism in the Political Modernization of Ghana and Uganda', *World Politics*, XIII, October 1960, pp. 45–68. Consult also Charles W. Anderson, Fred R. Von der Mehden, and Crawford Young, *Issues of Political Development* (Englewood Cliffs: 1967).

In many of the current theories of modernization, as indeed in old theories of social Darwinism, there has persisted a certain optimism about the ultimate destination of human history. It is an optimism which believes that, although every birth leads on to death, there is a constant process of rebirth in the history of human societies. Hence the deep belief in creative friction. The new nations are sometimes in total social anguish. But out of upheavals, societies might indeed be uplifted, and out of the depths of despair, development might still be feasible. Darwin's ultimate gift to human knowledge might well be the gift of an incorrigible scientific optimism. The new political science is often inspired by this optimism.

5 Conflict and the Integrative Process[1]

Our definition of pluralism is comprehensive. In its diversity of tribal and racial groups, we would regard Uganda as a case of ethnic pluralism. In its variety of systems of life, we would regard it as an instance of cultural pluralism. In the competitive relationship between Catholicism, Protestantism and Islam in the life of the country, we would attribute religious pluralism to the total society. In its party system, however unstable, the country has so far maintained competitive pluralistic institutions—a framework for power-contests in the polity. In its quasi-federal structure while it lasted, the country had *constrictive* pluralistic institutions—an attempt to narrow the field of contest in advance by entrenching a certain division of powers prior to the scramble for other areas of political or social control. Pluralism is, in short, a complex of relationships between groups in a wider society.

Having given a rough working definition of pluralism by invoking the Ugandan example, our next task is the no less ambitious enterprise of trying to understand the nature of integration. We shall do this in the next section. We shall then go on to relate pluralism to nationalism, and analyse the inter-relationship with reference to the two 'Anglo-Saxon' cases of Britain and the United States. Our next preoccupation in the essay will be the role of the state in the integrative process. In this regard we shall utilize some of the insights afforded by Marxism. We shall finally examine political activity as an exercise in integration. Our example in this last section will be Nigeria. This is not, of course, because Nigeria is among the

[1] This essay was first presented, under the title of 'Pluralism and National Integration' at a colloquium on 'Pluralism' at the University of California, Los Angeles, organized by Professor Leo Kuper in 1966.

areas of the world the author knows most about. On the contrary, the author's knowledge of Nigeria is derived from the general literature of that country and not from direct research experience therein. We choose Nigeria to illustrate the integrative function of politics mainly because of an impression that it might well be the best example in Africa of the phenomenon we have in mind. The picture we draw of Nigeria itself might conceivably be inaccurate. But if a mythical Nigerian 'model' nevertheless enables us to explore new hypotheses about the nature of the integrative process, the exercise might still be worth it.

Our conclusion at the end of the essay will be both a summary of the rest of the analysis and an attempt to place our pre-occupations here within the context of political development at large.

THE INTEGRATIVE PROCESS

The process of national integration involves four stages of inter-relationship between the different ethnic or cultural groups in the country. The minimum degree of integration is a relationship of bare co-existence between distinct identities within the borders. These groups need not even know of each other's existence. There are a number of tribal communities in almost every African country which have no idea where the boundaries of their country end, which tribes are their compatriots and which are not. Their co-existence with a number of other groups in the same national entity is not always a conscious co-existence. But it is there all the same.

The second degree of relationship between groups is a relation-ship of *contact*. This means that the groups have at least some minimal dealings with each other or communication between each other. The groups need not be on friendly terms. Tribes at war are still in a relationship of contact. And by that very reason they are at a higher stage of integration in spite of the war.

A third degree of integration between groups is a relationship of *compromise*. By this time the dealings between the groups have become sufficiently complex, diverse and inter-dependent to require a climate of peaceful reconciliation between the con-flicting interests. The groups still have clearly distinct identities of their own, as well as distinct interests. But the process of national integration has now produced a capacity for a constant discovery of areas of compatibility.

The final stage of national integration is the stage of *coalescence*. This is a coalescence of identities, rather than a merger of interests. Diversity of interests would continue. Indeed, should the society get technically complex and functionally differentiated at the same time as it is getting nationally integrated, the diversity of interests would increase as the distinctiveness of group-identities gets blurred. Capacity for compromise would still be needed at the stage of coalescence. But the conflict of interests is no longer a conflict between total identities.

But what is a total identity? Illustration is in this instance the best definition. A tribe in a relationship of bare co-existence with other tribes has a total identity of its own. But the Hotel Workers Union in Uganda or the American Political Science Association is only a partial form of identity. The process of national integration is a partialization of group-identities—as the tribes or communities lose their coherence as distinct systems of life. But the process of national integration is not only a partialization of older affiliations. It is, of course, also a quest for a new kind of total identity. Success comes when partially eroded group-personalities coalesce to form a new national entity.

In practice the process of integration is not even. The same African country might have groups that are in a relationship of bare *co-existence* with the rest of the country, groups that have established *contact* with others on a broad scale, groups that have begun to develop politics of *compromise* and groups which show a tendency towards *coalescing* with each other.

But by what mechanism does the process of integration move from stage to stage? This is what introduces the place of *conflict* in the integrative process.[1] A relationship of bare co-existence has little conflict potential. Somehow contact has to be established with other groups before conflict situations can seriously arise. The move from co-existence to contact might be caused by a number of different factors. It might be caused by

[1] I realize that the term 'conflict' is a term which is sometimes carelessly used. But for our purposes here the term is useful for social analysis precisely because it is comprehensive. For us the term ranges from the American Civil War to the contest for the election of Mrs. Wallace as Governor of Alabama. For our purposes they are all different degrees of conflict.

migrant trade, or by movements of population, or by a newly
built road. By definition, conflict plays little part in converting
a relationship of separate co-existence into a relationship of
contact.

Where conflict plays a crucial part is in moving from a relationship of contact to a relationship of compromise, and then from
compromise to coalescence. It is the cumulative experience of
conflict-resolution which deepens the degree of integration in a
given society. Conversely, unresolved conflict creates a situation
of potential disintegration. The groups within the society could
then move backwards from a relationship of, say, compromise to
a relationship of hostile contact.

One could even argue that internal conflict within a country
is inherently disintegrative. Yet, paradoxically, no national
integration is possible without internal conflict. The paradox
arises because while conflict itself has a propensity to force a
dissolution, the *resolution* of conflict is an essential mechanism of
integration. The whole experience of jointly looking for a way
out of a crisis, of seeing your own mutual hostility subside to a
level of mutual tolerance, of being intensely conscious of each
other's positions and yet sensing the need to bridge the gulf—
these are experiences which, over a period of time, should help
two groups of people move forward into a relationship of deeper
integration. Conflict-resolution might not be a sufficient condition for national integration, but it is certainly a necessary one.

But what makes conflict-resolution itself possible? Sometimes
it is the cumulative power of precedent—of having overcome
other crises before. Experience of previous clashes sharpens the
capacity to discover areas of mutual compatibility on subsequent
occasions of tension. Another factor which makes conflict-
resolution possible is awareness of reciprocal dependence. It might
be true that, for purposes of economic development in a given
area, it is essential that two particular tribes in the region should
get along with each other. But this 'truth' would not help the
cause of conflict-resolution between the two groups unless they
realize, firstly, that economic development is an important common
need, and, secondly, that it is a need which can best be met if
the two groups stopped fighting each other.

A third factor which might ease conflict-resolution in a given
society is a shared ideology. And the most basic ideology for

national integration is, of course, the ideology of nationalism itself.
It is to this that we must now turn.

PLURALISM AND NATIONALISM

For our purposes here it might be meaningful to distinguish
nationalism from national consciousness. We may define
'national consciousness' here as a sense of a shared national
identity. We may define 'nationalism' as a more assertive or
more defensive degree of that consciousness. It has been argued
that 'modern nationalism, as we know it today, has its original
seat in England'.[1] It is true that England has had her moments
of militant nationalism. But on the whole she has come to take
her nationhood so much for granted that her philosophers have
spent relatively little time on it. Leading British philosophers
have seldom concerned themselves in depth with issues like the
definition of a 'nation', or the reality of 'the collective soul', or
the concept of 'fatherland'. And so when Hans Kohn comes
round to paying special attention to nineteenth century nationalism he finds himself choosing John Stuart Mill as the 'prophet' of
British nationalism.[2] Compared with Mazzini, Treitschke,
Michelet and Dostoevsky, John Stuart Mill is hardly a striking
example of a 'people's prophet'. Kohn might have done better
if he had looked for a British politician or statesman to symbolize
British patriotism. British political philosophers were simply not
adequately preoccupied with the 'fatherland'.

American political thought has had more of a nationalistic
component than is found in British thought. And this is what
brings us back to pluralism. It is possible that one important
reason why Americans are more nationalistic than Britons is
because the United States is more pluralistic than Great Britain.
It is easy to see why a country should become more nationalistic
if it has a sense of external insecurity. What is apt to be overlooked is that a country can also become more nationalistic if

[1] See Carlton J. H. Hayes, *Nationalism: A Religion* (New York: The Mac-
millan Company, 1960), pp. 38–9. Hans Kohn argues in similar terms in his
Idea of Nationalism, A Study of Its Origins and Background (New York: The
Macmillan Company, 1943), pp. 155–83.
[2] Kohn, *Prophets and Peoples: Studies in Nineteenth Century Nationalism* (New
York: The Macmillan Company, 1957).

it develops a sense of *internal* insecurity. The United States is significantly more heterogeneous than Britain. This might be precisely the factor that has helped to create a greater sense of internal insecurity in the United States than in Britain. Complex heterogeneity multiplies the number of possible conflict situations between groups. The need for devices which would help the resolution of those conflicts becomes greater than ever. National consciousness is indeed there. But the situation is such that the sense of a shared national identity cannot be taken completely for granted as a moderator in inter-group tensions. And so that national consciousness has to take the more militant form of assertive nationalism. The potential for violence between groups has to be 'qualified' by a diversionary consideration. George Simmel once said:

It is almost inevitable that an element of commonness injects itself into the enmity [between two groups] once the stage of open violence yields to any other relationship, even though this new relation may contain a completely undiminished sum of animosity between the two parties.[1]

In the case before us in this paper, we would need to alter Simmel's sequence of causation. For us it is the 'element of commonness' itself which makes 'the stage of open violence' yield to another relationship. The dangers of American heterogeneity need to be conquered by a highly developed sense of a shared Americanness. This inner sense of internal insecurity in the United States is perhaps what continues to make American national consciousness more *self*-conscious than British patriotism normally is.

In May 1965 *The Observer* of London described the United States and Communist China as 'the two most ideologically inspired states of the modern world'.[2] This was an exaggeration. But it still has relevance to the question before us. The United States might have looked 'most ideologically inspired' to a relatively ideological British newspaper precisely because the British themselves were less militant than Americans in their patriotism.

---

[1] George Simmel, *Conflict and the Web of Group-Affiliations*, trans. by Kurt H. Wolff and Reinhard Bendix (New York: Free Press of Glencoe, 1964), p. 26.

[2] *The Observer* (London), May 9, 1965.

In a sense, it is ironical that the most powerful country in the world should show signs of insecurity greater than those of her weaker ally. But the irony would only be striking if one thought of insecurity in terms of danger from outside.[1] Once we think of insecurity in terms both of external danger and of internalized fears of fragmentation, it becomes much less surprising that the more pluralistic of the Anglo-Saxon powers should also be the more assertively nationalistic.

PLURALISM AND THE STATE

On the basis of the stages of integration we have defined, we might now say that the United States has achieved a high degree of *compromise*-relationships between total identities within itself. But Great Britain has achieved a greater degree of *coalescence* between its groups. In the meantime, the cumulative experience of conflict-resolution in the United States is gradually leading towards less compromise and more coalescence. In terms of political arrangements, a federal structure is an institutionalization of compromise-relationships. But the American federal system is perhaps already feeling the strain of the integrative process moving towards national coalescence. The institutional expression of such coalescence will presumably be a more unitary form of democracy.

The idea that conflict leads ultimately to coalescence has some of the same assumptions as the Marxist concept of integration. But certain distinctions need to be made. The dialectic in Marxism is sometimes described as a process of 'reconciling opposites'. In effect, the Marxian synthesis is not a 'reconciliation'. The idea of reconciling opposites is implicit in *compromise*-relationships but less so in synthesizing ones. A proletarian dictatorship, for example, is not an exercise in compromise. As Engels put it, 'the proletariat uses the state not in the interests of freedom, but in order to hold down its adversaries. . . .'[2] Compromise with

---

[1] For a stimulating discussion of the proposition that 'conflict with out-groups increases internal cohension', see, for example, Lewis Coser, *The Functions of Social Conflict* (New York: Free Press of Glencoe, 1956), pp. 87–110. See also Max Gluckman, *Custom and Conflict in Africa* (Oxford: Basil Blackwell, 1963), esp. pp. 11–26.

[2] Letter to Bebel. Quoted by Lenin in *State and Revolution* (1917).

adversaries can, by the logic of Marxism, only be a tactical move. One compromises with the opposing forces only until such time as one can 'synthesize' them altogether. And the synthesis is achieved by the liquidation of the separate identity of the preceding thesis.

There are other differences, too, between the concept of compromise and the concept of synthesis. Compromise tends to be a position *below* the ideal—it is at best a '*second* best' to all concerned. A Hegelian or Marxian synthesis, however, is a step *nearer* perfection than the two opposites from which it emerged. A synthesis combines the best elements from each side. A compromise combines not what is best, but what is least objectionable to the contestants.

Applying the distinction to our own preoccupations in this essay, we note that while a quest for synthesis is essentially anti-pluralistic, a quest for compromise is an acceptance of pluralism. If we used *Rousseau's* terms, the General Will is a synthesis of interests. The will of all is a compromise between conflicting interests. The General Will is supposed to be a collective good that is independent of particular interests. The will of all is an arithmetical exercise—a balancing of particular interests.

Institutionally, a one-party state has a bias for synthesizing, while a multi-party system has propensity to compromise. The one-party system seeks to embody the General Will. The multi-party system wants to discern the will of all.

But for our purposes the big difference between Marx and Rousseau is that Marx has a theory of integration while Rousseau has not. For Marx society moves towards closer integration by the mechanism of struggle and contradiction. This is not very far removed from a theory which looks upon the integrative process as a response to a cumulative experience of conflict-resolution. One point of difference between the Marxist view of integration and ours here is that while Marx thinks of integration in terms of a coalescence of classes, our own theory here allows for the possibility of their being other and more important differences between groups than class differences. Indeed, the Marxist concept of the integrative process assumes a high degree of pre-existent ethnic and cultural integration. This is an assumption which cannot be made in analysing integration in, say, African countries. In fact, tribes and races are more total and distinct identities than are economic classes. The process of integrating tribes and races tends therefore to be more complex.

Another difference between the Marxist view of integration and the one we are putting forward here concerns the nature of conflict-resolution. Marx thinks of conflict-resolution in terms of absolute victories. The conflict between the proletariat and the bourgeoisie can only end in the victory of the proletariat. But conflict-resolution can be thought of in terms of *adjustments*, rather than victories. And it is the latter conception of conflict resolution which might perhaps offer the best insights into the process of integrating total identities.

A related point of theoretical divergence concerns the Marxist concept of the 'withering away' of the state. This is a concept which is often underestimated by Western commentators. Yet, as part of a theory of integration, the idea of an ultimate withering away of the state has a depth of insight which deserves greater recognition than it has had so far. The process of integration is, after all, a process of reducing the potential for internal violence in a given society. And the concept of the state is intimately connected with the concept of controlling violence and its causes. If social integration therefore reaches a stage when there is only a limited degree of latent violence in inter-group relations, the state loses the most fundamental of all its roles.

An alternative way of approaching the problem is through the Weberian definition of a state. Weber defined the state in terms of its 'monopoly of the legitimate use of physical force within a given territory'.[1] But if a country has deep internal cleavages, the state's monopoly of the use of force might often be challenged. Even the legitimacy of the state might itself be in question, let alone its claim to a monopoly of violence. Mutually hostile groups might feel that they each retain the right to resolve their differences by a test of physical strength. The paramount duty of the state might then be to try and stop private resort to violence.

But as the integrative process gets under way, the cleavages

---

[1] See Max Weber, 'Politics as a Vocation', in *From Max Weber: Essays in Sociology* (New York: Oxford University Press Galaxy Book, 1958), pp. 77–8. Gabriel A. Almond has broadened Weber's definition in order to include types of political organization other than the state. See Almond's 'Introduction' to Gabriel A. Almond and James S. Coleman (eds.), *The Politics of the Developing Areas* (Princeton: Princeton University Press, 1960), pp. 6–7.

in the society would get less acute. When a highly developed sense of compromise is achieved, latent violence would be much reduced. And when the stage of actual coalescence begins to take place, private resort to violence between groups would become even more rare. What then would the state become? For the first time the state might indeed now have a clear monopoly of the legitimate use of force. All the groups might at last agree that only the state should be permitted to invoke forceful sanctions against offenders in a given dispute. This is the stage when the different groups have at last been integrated into a suprafactional community. The integrative process might therefore be almost definable as a process towards the centralization of suppression of social violence. It is national integration which gradually gives the state a real monopoly of the legitimate use of physical force.

Yet, because the different groups are now less inclined to resort to private force in their own disputes, the state's role as an instrument of suppression is now drastically curtailed. Of course, there is still work to be done in such fields as social welfare, the building of roads, and general national planning. But a fundamental change takes place when a society achieves a stage of deep internal coalescence. 'State interference in social relations becomes, in one domain after another, superfluous, and then dies out of itself; the government of persons is replaced by the administration of things.' In saying this, Engels was indeed exaggerating.[1] So was Lenin in envisaging a time when people would 'become accustomed to observing the necessary rules of social intercourse' and when there would be 'nothing that evokes protest and revolt and creates the need for *suppression*'.[2] But they were both right in suggesting that ultimate integration must lead to the redundancy of the state as an instrument of suppression. Their notion of what divides groups against each other was too simple. But their grasp of the logic of the integrative process was profoundly sound.

Involved in all this is the integrative function of suppression itself in the pre-coalescent phases of development. For Marxism sustained oppression creates a class-consciousness among the oppressed. But for our purposes in this paper what should be

---

[1] See Engels, *Socialism, Utopian and Scientific* (1877).
[2] Lenin, *State and Revolution* (1917).

noted is that sustained oppression helps to create national consciousness itself. A study of the Royal Institute of International
Affairs argued in 1939 in the following terms:

> Every government which has ever been set up has done some-
> thing to increase the amount of homogeneity between its
> subjects, although it may at the same time have taken other
> steps which increased the differences of opinion among them
> and stimulated opposition to itself . . . the downfall of govern-
> ments may (with many exceptions) be attributed to the failure
> to produce cohesion among their subjects. . . . The fact
> remains that any collection of men which has ever been sub-
> jected for any length of time to the same government will
> continue indefinitely to bear the marks of that subjection,
> and will possess a common factor making for unity among
> subsequent generations.[1]

The most dramatic demonstration of this is the effect of colonial
governments on their subjects. Africans, for example, will
continue to bear indefinitely the mark of their subjection to
European colonial rule. But contrary to what the above quotation
argues, the downfall of colonial governments was not due to
'failure to produce cohesion among their subjects'. On the contrary, it was the success of colonial governments in creating such
cohesion which led to their own downfall.

PLURALISM AND POLITICS

But the fall of African governments after independence is a
more complicated phenomenon. How much did the *ancien
régime* of independent Nigeria contribute to the greater unification of Nigeria? It is too early to be sure. But we ought to be on
guard against assuming too readily that the Nigerian government
before the first coup of 1966 was a factor for disunity. It is possible
that it was precisely the worst excesses of the regime which were
the most integrative. Nothing had helped the movement for a

[1] Royal Institute of International Affairs, London, *Nationalism* (Oxford
University Press, 1939), p. 4.

unitary state in Nigeria more dramatically than the mess in which the previous regime up to 1966 left the federal structure. The unitary movement has not succeeded so far. Perhaps Nigeria is too pluralistic a country to be ruled on any basis other than that of quasi-federalism. But the very fact that there is now a quest for *tighter* integration was substantially attributable to the errors of the previous regime.

Another possible measurement of how far the previous regime helped to unify Nigeria lies in the initial reaction of the North to the assassination of two distinguished Northerners. Did the Northerners accept for a while the assassination of Sir Abubakar Tafawa Balewa and the Sardauna of Sokoto, Sir Ahmadu Bello, simply because they were faced with the military might of the South? Or had the excesses of the previous regime disillusioned Northerners too? If the answer was a simple fear of military might, this does not tell us much about the rate of integration in Nigeria at the time. But should by any chance the answer have included a Northern disenchantment with the era of Sir Abubakar and the Sardauna, this would be more significant. The peoples of Nigeria had never before been jointly disenchanted by the same government. While the people of other countries might have resented colonialism together, the peoples of Nigeria had not even shared a joint feeling of anti-colonialism together. The North especially had been too suspicious of the South, and too cautious in her assessment of independence, ever to get worked up into a strong feeling of nationalism. Perhaps there had also developed a basic Anglophilia within the Northern élite which refused to be transformed into an anti-British militancy for the sake of independence. Nigeria therefore approached independence without the unifying effect of a shared spirit of anti-colonialism.[1]

It is possible that disenchantment with the first independent government of Nigeria was the first centrally directed feeling of political opposition that Northerners had ever shared with

[1] James S. Coleman is a little more cautious than this in his assessment. See especially Coleman, *Nigeria: Background to Nationalism* (Berkeley and Los Angeles: University of California Press, 1958), pp. 353–68. See also Richard L. Sklar, *Nigerian Political Parties* (Princeton, N. J.: Princeton University Press, 1963). On the attitudes of the old Northern élite, consult especially C. S. Whitaker, Jr., 'Three Perspectives on Hierarchy: Political Thought and Leadership in Northern Nigeria', *Journal of Commonwealth Political Studies*, Vol. III, No. 1, March 1965.

Southerners in recent times. This factor was of direct integrative significance for the country as a whole. Would Northern reaction to the assassination of Sir Abubakar and Ahmadu Bello have been less placid had this taken place within the first year of independence? This is not certain. Yet it is conceivable that four years earlier Northern reaction would have been stronger from the start. That this should be conceivable is itself of significance.

The Northern acceptance of the changed situation was not, of course, to last for ever. Indeed, there were reports before long that the North is getting restive, and is beginning to demand the punishment of at least some of the individual assassins of Northerners.[1] This does not negate the proposition that the Balewa regime had, by some of its very excesses, served an integrative function. In terms of our more general theoretical position, the *coup* was one momentous kind of conflict-resolution in the slow unification of Nigeria. The aftermath of the first *coup* was bound to create sooner or later other types of conflict situations. And some of these latent conflicts might themselves have had their origins in the manner in which the last conflict was resolved.

A third factor about the pre-*coup* regime which might have been unifying was the fact that it was a *political* regime. It is tempting to look at a new military regime as a better instrument of national consolidation than a band of politicians. The whole idea of military rule implies discipline. And the principle of discipline has perhaps an inner aversion against 'factionalism'. We might therefore say that demands for unity and demands for discipline are almost logically inter-connected. When Lenin wanted to ensure that the Communist Party of the Soviet Union was fully united, he thought of its organization in quasi-militaristic terms. He was convinced that

> The Communist Party will be able to perform its duty only if it is organized in the most centralized manner, if iron discipline bordering on military discipline prevails in it, and if its Party centre is a powerful and authoritative organ, wielding wide powers . . .

[1] See, for example, Walter Schwarz's report, 'Nigerians Want More Than Bribery Trials', *The Observer* (London), May 8, 1966.

He was opposed to what he called 'factionalism'. He believed in

> the unity of will of the vanguard of the proletariat as the
> fundamental condition of the success of the dictatorship of the
> proletariat.[1]

It might therefore seem that the new military regime in Nigeria had, by bringing in the ethos of discipline from the barracks to the polity, started a new and more vigorous phase of national consolidation in the country.

Yet the fact that the previous regime was a regime of politicians was not necessarily a point against it in the assessment of integration. A militarized polity might avert disunity without achieving integration. There is more to the integrative process than militaristic discipline. The discipline of men under arms is ultimately designed to win victories. Integration, however, is a matter of resolving conflict in more diverse, and often more subtle ways. The concept of conflict animates both the military and the integrative process—but it does not affect them in the same way.

It is these considerations which should caution those who would dismiss the *pre*-military regime in Nigeria as altogether counter-cohesive. It is not always remembered that political activity, as a continual intrigue and search for agreement, has an integrative function in its own right.

Perhaps one factor which temporarily saved Nigeria from becoming another Congo was the widespread political activity in Nigeria well before independence. The fragmentation of the Congo on attainment of independence was, in part, directly attributable to Belgian prohibition of political activity during the colonial period. By its very nature, nationalistic activity before independence would have had a propensity to involve more and more of the general populace. Experience elsewhere demonstrated that anti-colonial sentiments fostered by a few 'agitators' in the capital city gradually spread outwards and increased a consciousness of the territorial unit in the population as a whole. To that extent political activity in British Africa especially was an important contributory factor towards national integration in each colony. The Congo was kept in a state of depolicization—and the

[1] Quoted by Stalin in *Foundations of Leninism* (1924).

consciousness of territorial identity was retarded for that very reason.

But do politics still serve an integrative function *after* independence? The answer is yes. In the case of the Congo, it has been that country's relative inexperience in the arts of national politics that has kept it in a state of actual or potential civil war. Where political activity seems to be so divisive as to result in a civil war, the reason is usually because there was an inadequate capacity for politics in the population in the first place. The resort to arms comes when politics has *failed*.

If a resort to arms is an indication that politics has failed, what about the resort to an army *coup*? The answer varies with each country. In Ghana political life under Nkrumah had, in the words of Dennis Austin, already been 'reduce[d] . . . to a barely discernible level of private conflict among his followers over the distribution of presidential favours'.[1] The army *coup* might therefore be regarded as the first step towards the re-nationalization of politics in Ghana.

In Nigeria, however, the army *coup* was essentially a retreat from politics. If the previous regime had achieved nothing, it had certainly achieved the spread of nation-minded political activity all over in Nigeria. The defence of the North against the South had previously taken the form of isolation away from the South. By the time of the coup the Northern strategy had become an *infiltration* of the South. The interest of the North in consolidating its Federal power was perhaps the most significant integrative event in Nigeria's history. Tribalism and regionalism in Nigeria had indeed become worse than ever. Yet, by a curious paradox, the nation-wide participation in politics, or the nationalization of politics, had been taking place in Nigeria at the same time. Contrary to most expectations of a few years previously, observers were already talking about single-party tendencies in Nigeria.[2] The federal system was indeed in jeopardy. But now the danger was not merely disintegration, though that was still there. There was the new danger of imposed unitarism. That the

[1] Austin, *Politics in Ghana 1946–1960* (London: Oxford University Press, 1964), p. 8.

[2] See, for example, John P. MacKintosh, 'Electoral Trends and the Tendency to a One Party System in Nigeria', *Journal of Commonwealth Political Studies*, Vol. 1, November 1962. See also Nnamdi Azikiwe, 'Essentials of Nigerian Survival', *Foreign Affairs*, Vol. XLIII, No. 3, April 1965.

latter danger should have become conceivable at all was perhaps the most dramatic feat of integration that the previous regime of Sir Abubakar had accomplished.

Yet, it was in part precisely that feat which precipitated the events that led to the army *coup*. In an important sense the crisis of Nigeria arose from the fact that politics had been integrating the country too rapidly. The new Northern desire for hegemony in the South was, in national terms, a significant improvement over the old Northern isolationism. But the nationalization of politics in Nigeria was growing faster than the country's capacity for compromise. To put it in another way, politics were penetrating to every part of the nation before techniques of conflict-resolution were adequately developed. After all, to spread political activity over a widening field of national activity is to increase the areas of possible conflict between groups. It is with these resultant conflicts that the Nigerian system could not cope, in spite of its expansion.

This was not, of course, all that was wrong with pre-military Nigeria. Nigerian politics as well as getting more national were more nasty. Yet the nastiness itself was often a bewildered response to the new conflicts that nationalized politics were creating. Occasionally one form of nastiness atoned for another. In a country plagued with nepotism, for example, bribery has sometimes a useful function to serve. A person from the 'wrong' tribe might be able to get his particular skill utilized only after paying the necessary 'dash'. It might be unfortunate that he should have to pay. But it might have been even more unfortunate if that skill had no way of getting itself utilized. To put it in another way, the person from the 'wrong' tribe needs a chance to compete for a particular prize. But he has to buy a ticket in order to get into the competing arena—whereas his rivals from the 'right' tribe have free access into the arena. To have to buy a ticket for admission might still be better than total exclusion from the arena. It is this consideration which sometimes converts bribery into an antidote to nepotism.

In East Africa bribery is at times an antidote to racialism. Indian traders competing with Africans for licences or other commercial favours have sometimes to atone with cash for their racial handicap. Racialistic nepotism would give priority to Africans. But bribery from the Indian trader might sometimes tip the scale back into a position of fairer competition. To use our previous metaphor, the Indian has to buy a ticket to get into the marketing compound—whereas his African rivals are sometimes given free access. But once the Indian is in the market, he might be sufficiently superior as a businessman to compensate for the ticket he was forced to buy.[1]

There are varied reasons why we might lament the phenomenon of bribery both in Nigeria before the *coups* and in East Africa. But we should be clear about the reasons. It might be true that tribal and familial nepotism is essentially disintegrative in its exclusive tendencies. But precisely because nepotism is disintegrative, bribery might often perform a function of *re*-integration. It might help to break down barriers of nepotic exclusiveness. It might, in short, ease the process of conflict-resolution in a competitive and pluralistic society.[2]

CONCLUSION

On their road towards national coalescence few of the developing areas have got much beyond the stage of *contact* and enforced submissiveness. Indeed, some of the groups are still in a relationship of bare *co-existence* with each other. But in some of the countries, and Nigeria might well have been one of them, the politics of *compromise* might have started to take root. The roots might not as yet be deep. Growth in such instances is a slow process. But it is important that the process has begun.

In the meantime students of political development at large

[1] This is an exaggeration of what happens in East Africa. The idea of Africanizing commerce at the expense of Asians is an open policy and does not always involve such underhand dealings. For some discussion of corruption in East Africa, see J. David Greenstone, 'Corruption and Self-Interest in Kampala and Nairobi', *Comparative Studies in Society and History*, Vol. VIII, January 1966, and Colin Leys, 'What is the Problem About Corruption?' *The Journal of Modern African Studies*, Vol. III, No. 2, 1965.

[2] For a stimulating discussion of forms of corruption in Northern Nigeria, see M. G. Smith, 'Historical and Cultural Conditions of Political Corruption Among the Hausa', *Comparative Studies in Society and History*, Vol. VI, January 1964. For more general analyses of corruption, see M. McMullan, 'A Theory of Corruption', *The Sociological Review* (Keele), Vol. IX, July 1961; Ronald Wraith and Edgar Simpkins, *Corruption in Developing Areas* (London, 1963); and Carl J. Friedrich, 'Political Pathology', *The Political Quarterly*, Vol. XXXVII, January–March, 1966.

should perhaps re-examine more fully some of their assumptions about the wider process. Many of the studies of political development after independence have implied that it is a process which is as it were mechanical or semi-consciously induced and brought about. The attention of scholars has tended to be drawn towards the role of political parties, or of the military, or of the bureaucracy at large, or the function of education in national integration. These are or can be crucial elements in the process of development. But their relevance for development can be made a little over-conspicuous and thus diversionary. They could command so much attention that scholars might overlook the integrative function of factors which are less obviously pertinent—but crucially pertinent all the same.

There is perhaps such a thing as *political development as a laissez-faire process*. Yet the principle of 'laissez faire' in the political aspect of development is not an injunction against government intervention in the *economy*. It is merely an assertion that while economic development can, under certain circumstances, be consciously induced, political development is much less responsive to conscious manipulation. The case for government intervention in the economy might still remain very strong. After all, people must not starve even if they are yet to be integrated or have yet to devise a stable political system. What should be remembered is that political development is, in the ultimate analysis, a cumulative accident. It is the accretion of side-effects of random factors—some of which might, in fact, be actual deficiencies in the soil of the country. It is possible for unemployment to be a positive contribution to the long-term political development of a country while some new road built at the wrong time militates against national cohesion. The total effect depends on a whole complex of factors.

The scholar should therefore be cautious in categorizing complete processes as being either developmental or counter-developmental, integrative or disintegrative. One might discern a propensity in one direction or the other, but still allow for modifying side-effects. One might regard corruption as counter-productive and still allow for its functioning for the good in certain key areas.

National integration is, of course, only one aspect of political development. But it is perhaps the most fundamental. The crucial capacity which is to be cultivated in the integrative process is, as we have indicated, efficiency in the arts of conflict-resolution. To develop that efficiency the experience of conflict is, by definition, itself essential. But the process of integration is a gradual multiplication of areas of conflict, coupled with a gradual diminution of violence in those conflicts. In other words, conflict becomes more *extensive* as areas of competition become more complex, and less *intensive* as resort to violent solutions diminishes in frequency.

Finally, it should be emphasized that a process of integration is, in essence, a process of de-pluralizing society. Pluralism itself never completely disappears in any society. But a society ceases to be a 'plural society' when the stage of *coalescence* is fully reached. To put it in another way, there is pluralism in every society, even in one which is no longer a 'plural society'. For pluralism is often a competitive complex of diverse groups—and virtually every society has its rival internal groups.

When Harold Laski rebelled against the notion of 'Man *versus* the State' what he substituted in its place was a view of society which thought of political life in terms of relations between groups, rather than relations between the government and the individual. The theory that Laski was putting forward was a theory of pluralism.

A 'plural society' is not simply a society with pluralism. All societies have pluralism. What distinguishes plural societies from others is the *kind* of pluralism involved. The extreme case of a plural society is a society of total identities—of self-contained cultural systems or exclusive racial groups. This is perhaps the kind of 'plural society' which, as J. C. Mitchell suggests, comes nearest to being 'a contradiction in terms'.[1] Relationships between the groups are either at the level of bare co-existence or minimal contact. This is perhaps the 'pure type' of a plural society.

But as the integrative process gets underway, the total identities are increasingly partialized. That is, they are in contact

---

[1] 'The term "plural society" itself is a contradiction since the idea of "society" in terms of usual sociological definition implies "unity"—the antithesis of plurality. The problem of plural societies, then, lies in this contradiction—in what way can these societies be both "plural" and "societies" —indeed, if they are "plural" can they be societies?'—See J. C. Mitchell, *Tribalism and the Plural Society*, An Inaugural Lecture, University College of Rhodesia and Nyasaland (London: Oxford University Press, 1960), p. 25.

and then compromise with each other. By the time coalescence is reached, the society has been substantially de-pluralized in this special sense. As in England, the society might still have a highly structured *class*-pluralism. Yet apart from the recent immigrants England has ceased to be a plural society. England is almost a 'pure type' of an integrated nation. Complete coalescence with the Scots and the Welsh has not been fully achieved, though it is well advanced. The relationship of the English with the Northern Irish is perhaps still basically a compromise relationship, but with substantial areas of coalescence. But the preponderant English themselves have achieved cohesion. The process of national integration among the English has virtually come to an end.

Yet, for as long as certain forms of pluralism persist, there is still room for further de-pluralization. England has virtually completed national integration, but there is considerable room yet for *social* integration. There is room especially for increased erosion of class distinctions.

Yet, while national integration is *finite*, social integration is *not*. The ultimate error of Marxism is perhaps to assume that there is an end to social integration. Having made that assumption, Marxism was logical in further assuming that there was an end to the need for the state as well. Perfect social integration would indeed make the state redundant. Yet because social integration is an infinite process, the state continues to be necessary for the purpose of giving it direction.

Nevertheless, in its formulation of the role of conflict in social change, and in its conception of perfect coalescence, however unrealizable, Marxism still affords useful insights into the nature of the integrative process. As an ideology Marxism does itself often create conflict. But as a methodology it helps us to understand that conflict. After all, the integrative process is, in the ultimate analysis, the story of conflict and its role in socializing man.

6 The Tensions of Crossing the Floor in East Africa[1]

written in collaboration with

G. F. Engholm, Lakehead University, Canada

Kenya, Uganda and Tanzania emerged into independence with relatively strong legislatures. The nature of the nationalist struggle for power during the colonial period had given the old legislative council a central position in the political system, and a mystique had grown round the idea of parliament.

After independence there was a decline of the legislature in each of the three countries. And at least in Kenya and Uganda the decline was connected with the whole phenomenon of 'crossing the floor in parliament'. But it would be a mistake to assume that crossing the floor was nothing more than a symptom of the inefficiency of inherited political institutions or of the decline of parliament and party affiliations. It is a contention of this essay that the device of crossing the floor in parliament has sometimes distinct and significant functions in the political systems of East Africa.

But before we define those functions it is important to define the status of parliament itself on attainment of independence. And this can only be done by examining its relationship with the struggle for independence which had just triumphed.

THE WESTMINSTER MODEL

In a sense the story of the nationalist struggle in each of the East African countries was a story of trying to increase African

[1] This essay was originally written for the panel 'Theory and Practice of Representation' at the Seventh World Congress of the International Political Science Association, Brussels, in September 1967.

representation in the legislative council. Certainly during the concluding years of colonial rule the immediate ambitions of African leaders were oriented towards control of the legislature and its executive organ. The competitive struggles for power, later characterized by political parties operating within a framework of simple majority and single-member constituencies, were often preoccupied with whether to maintain or eliminate some fancy franchise, or other aspects of constitutional engineering, which the Colonial Office had become so dextrous at producing. Power for the nationalist movement was conceived of in representational terms. The language of liberalism was strongly evident. The road to independence was supposed to be through a process of rapid democratization and a widening franchise. As Julius Nyerere said to the Trusteeship Council of the United Nations in June 1957,

> We [contend] that the Tanganyika Government should make a statement to the effect that Tanganyika is going to be developed as a democratic state and that, since 98 per cent of the population of our country is African, this means naturally that Tanganyika is to become primarily an African state. . . . We have also asked that . . . a change should be effected within the Constitution to be symbolic of this intention to make Tanganyika democratic. . . . We suggested an increase in the number of African representatives in proportion to the number of non-African representatives. . . . We are opposed to the idea of a restricted franchise even if we had not a single European in the country or a single Asian. . . .[1]

Nyerere himself was at this time basically a 'gradualist' in his demands for greater democratization. But his conception of African political progress was typically representational. That is one reason why much of the rhetoric of African nationalism in East and Central Africa was saturated with liberal democratic dicta. Nationalist demands were for 'One Man, One Vote', 'Undiluted Democracy', 'Majority Rule' and the like.

It is this general ethos which gave the legislative council a special mystique in the colonial political system. Even when

[1] See Julius K. Nyerere, *Freedom and Unity: A Selection from Writings and Speeches* (Dar es Salaam: Oxford University Press), pp. 46–7.

Tanganyika devised a new Republican Constitution a year after independence, with new strong powers for the President, one of the four basic principles of the Constitution was declared to be the continuing 'sovereignty of Parliament'. In parts of East Africa members of the legislature possessed the privilege of displaying on their cars a large badge bearing the letters 'M.P.' Parliamentary membership also carried potentialities of influence and a gradual accumulation of affluence. The legislature, that central object of constitutional wrangles during the colonial period, had now momentarily become a symbol of power for those with a seat in it. The political élite in East Africa was, for the time being, the legislative élite.

For a while parliament continued to share the mystique which had been created by the exciting and liberating possibilities of self-government. Criticism of it was relatively slow to develop and in practice never took the form of root-and-branch condemnation of the legislature as such. But there were certain aspects of the 'Westminster Model' which were 'suicidal' for the model as soon as it was taken out of Britain. One of these seemed to be the device of crossing the floor. In Britain the right of the individual M.P. to change his Party without resigning his seat does not endanger the system. When the 'Westminster Model' was exported elsewhere, it usually included this right of crossing the floor. But outside its native environment, bereft of all the constraints and stabilizing influences, the right to cross the floor changed its character and was put to novel uses. Instead of being a rare occurrence marked by torment of conscience or by a nicely calculated opportunism, it assumed in East Africa a capacity to transform the political system as a whole.

A major aspect of the operation of any political system is the management of conflict. Crossing the floor in East African parliaments had an important role to play in conflict-management. Sometimes it served the purpose of internalizing conflict within the ruling Party. This is best illustrated by Uganda's experience. In Kenya, on the other hand, crossing the floor in 1965 resulted in externalizing what had previously been intra-party tensions. A third role of conflict-management overlaps with those other two. Crossing the floor has sometimes helped to mitigate tension and narrow the area of possible clash between groups.

A useful approach is to take those three roles of conflict-management in turn. And since the first was best exemplified in Uganda, it is to Uganda that we should look first.

THE CASE OF UGANDA

When independence was attained in Uganda in October 1962, the Government side of the National Assembly consisted of a coalition between Dr. Milton Obote's Uganda People's Congress (UPC, 44 seats), and the ethnically-oriented Buganda party, the Kabaka Yekka (KY, 24 seats). In Opposition was the Democratic Party (DP) with 24 seats.

Two forms of inter-party fluidity were soon evident in the legislature, and the term 'crossing the floor' is perhaps misleading for one of them. To switch from the Democratic Party to the UPC was indeed to 'cross the floor'. It was to move from the Opposition side to the Government side of the House. But in fact the more interesting phenomenon, and perhaps the more significant in the long run, was the record of changing allegiances within the governing coalition itself.

Dr. Obote's Uganda People's Congress (UPC) kept on growing. Initially its increasing strength owed less to its own appeal than to serious dissensions within the Kabaka Yekka movement and within the Democratic Party. Let us look at the latter first. On attainment of independence the DP Parliamentary group set out to be a serious and basically responsible official Opposition. But the leader of the Party (DP) had not succeeded in winning a seat in the National Assembly, and this rapidly led to a clear divergence between policy from the Opposition in the National Assembly and policy as unilaterally enunciated by the Party leader outside. The Party leader or president-general was Mr. Benedicto Kiwanuka.[1] The official leader of the Opposition within Parliament, on the other hand, was Mr. Basil Bataringaya. While Mr. Bataringaya was carefully trying to build the image of responsible Opposition within Parliament, Mr. Kiwanuka was indulging in a number of opportunistic tactics which cost the Party a good deal of popular respect. He even attempted (in vain)

[1] Mr. Kiwanuka held the Premiership under the phase of internal self-government on the eve of full independence.

to get the traditionalist institutions of Buganda to promote him as an indirectly-elected member from the Kingdom—although his Party had declared itself to be opposed to indirect elections and to the powers of those traditionalist institutions.

The Parliamentary leader of DP, Mr. Bataringaya, had never commanded enough support within the party to wrest the overall leadership from Mr. Kiwanuka. The former's position therefore became increasingly untenable. A number of his colleagues in Parliament crossed to Dr. Obote's Party, in part out of genuine disenchantment with DP.[1] On December 31, 1964, Mr. Bataringaya himself crossed the floor and joined the UPC, taking five other DP members with him. Although there were calls that the rest of the Parliamentary group of DP should also cross, this was resisted. And the president-general of the party, Mr. Kiwanuka, declared a resolute resistance to the apparent trend towards a one-party system in Uganda.[2]

In the meantime the UPC had also been gaining at the expense of Kabaka Yekka (KY). And, as we indicated, it was at first not so much a case of 'crossing the floor' as a change of allegiance within the governing UPC/KY Coalition itself. The twenty-four KY members of the National Assembly had all been indirectly elected—twenty-one by the Lukiiko (Buganda Regional Assembly) and three by the National Assembly sitting as an electoral college. In the earlier phases the drift from KY to UPC seemed to be a reaction against the way in which the chiefs and other traditionalists in Buganda had successfully thwarted any hope of converting the KY movement into a modern political party or of using its moral assets as a means of bringing about major reforms within the kingdom itself.

Ideologically, the KY members who joined the UPC appeared to be nearer to Obote's pragmatic brand of African socialism than to the conservative forces grouped round the Kabaka or king of Buganda. By joining the UPC the KY members were branded as traitors to the cause of upholding Buganda's traditions. But though elected by the Lukiiko, they were not removable by the Lukiiko. In any case the continuing coalition between KY and

[1] The earlier phases of these events are traced in some detail by C. Gertzel in 'How Kabaka Yekka came to be' and 'Report from Kampala' both in *Africa Report*, Vol. IX, No. 9, October 1964.

[2] See *Uganda Argus* and *Daily Nation*, January 2, 1965. See also *East African Standard*, January 11, 1965.

UPC perhaps helped to mitigate the sense of betrayal felt by those who had elected the defected KY members to the National Assembly.

UGANDA: PHASE TWO

Then, in August 1964, Dr. Obote felt strong enough in Parliament to terminate his alliance with KY. The fourteen remaining members of KY at the time crossed the floor and sat alongside the DP opposition, though they seemed to make no attempt to enter into any kind of tactical arrangement with them.

Until this break-up of the alliance, those who joined the UPC from the ranks of its opponents did not seem motivated to subvert the UPC from the inside. But following the break-up of the alliance, and especially in the course of 1965, an entirely new political manoeuvre modelled on Trojan Horse tactics made its appearance, and had repercussions which culminated in the violent upheaval of 1966. Before independence Dr. Obote had made a deal with KY whereby as a *quid pro quo* for support in the National Assembly, the UPC was to refrain from opening up branch offices and recruiting members in Buganda. The indirect election of the 21 Buganda MPs by the Buganda Regional Assembly, the Lukiiko, was part of the same deal. These MPs were originally elected as KY members.

Early in 1965 the understanding between the two parties had been partially abandoned and a few UPC branches had been opened in Buganda, principally in urban areas. Recruitment of Baganda into the UPC was slow mainly because Baganda nationalists were successful in portraying the UPC as an organization bent on undermining the Baganda way of life. The UPC attempt to render Ganda attitudes sensitive to a new set of centrally-oriented political goals was sufficiently alarming to the Buganda *establishment* to make it undertake a broad reappraisal of its strategy. What evidence there is seems to indicate that a momentous decision to try and subvert the UPC from within was taken. By February 1966 the control of the Buganda regional branch of the UPC had fallen into the hands of a faction ostensibly supporting the UPC but apparently sharing its outlook with KY supporters. The Chairman of the Buganda Regional Branch of the

UPC, Dr. Lumu, was a Minister in Dr. Obote's Cabinet. There were at least four other Ministers in the UPC Government who seemed to share political sympathies with KY.

Within Parliament the KY strategy had now apparently become one of trying to utilize the device of crossing the floor as a method of internalizing opposition to Dr. Obote, i.e. creating an opposition to him within his own coalition. In July 1965 six out of the fourteen KY Members who sat on the Opposition benches crossed the floor for the second time and joined the Government majority and the ten KY members there. But how sound was the Government majority? Most of the sixteen former KY supporters were a doubtful proposition, and a number of ex-DP and UPC members began to examine their political 'availability' as rumours of a plan to oust Dr. Obote gained ground.

The extent to which members of the Assembly had joined the anti-Obote bandwagon was dramatically revealed in February 1966. By an adroit manipulation of the parliamentary timetable, a motion was introduced in the National Assembly demanding a commission of inquiry into the disposal of certain ivory tusks and gold sent out of the Congo by the Kisangani (Stanleyville) rebels. It was alleged that Dr. Obote, the Minister of Defence and the deputy Army Commander were implicated in this Congo 'gold and ivory scandal'. The person who introduced the motion and 'led the pack' was a leading member of Kabaka Yekka, the late Daudi Ocheng. Obote was absent from the House touring in the north when the motion for a commission of inquiry was introduced. When the vote was taken those present in Parliament amounted to almost two-thirds of the total membership of the National Assembly. To the surprise of the outside world, all but one member of the National Assembly supported the motion—and this included six Cabinet Ministers. That was perhaps Daudi Ocheng's most dramatic moment of triumph. While it lasted it was also a vindication of KY's strategy of internalizing opposition to Dr. Obote by swelling the ranks of the disaffected within his own party.

The full account of Dr. Obote's recovery from this collapse of his party's unity lies outside the scope of this essay. But in brief, he came back to the capital[1] and first assured himself of the

---

[1] See M. Crawford Young, 'The Obote Revolution', *African Report*, Vol. XI, No. 6, June 1966; G. F. Engholm, 'Buganda's Power Struggle', *New Society*,

loyalty of the security forces. In a dramatic move he then got the police to arrest five ministers when they assembled for a Cabinet meeting. He suspended the Independence Constitution of 1962 and then replaced it with an interim one providing for an executive president and eliminating the quasi-federal safeguards for Buganda which had formed part of the previous Constitution. Certain counter-moves by Buganda culminated in an army attack on the Kabaka's Palace in May 1966. The Kabaka fled from the country and sought refuge in England. In the meantime the six remaining KY members in Parliament, having refused to take the oath of allegiance to the new Constitution, lost their seats. And with Buganda in a state of emergency, and its loyalty in doubt, there was no question of holding by-elections to replace them.

A striking omission in the new interim Constitution was that no attempt was made to launch a one-party system. Smaller upheavals elsewhere in Africa had quickly been used as an excuse for eliminating all formal opposition. But Uganda's experience was different. The rump of the Democratic Party in Parliament was permitted not only to continue in existence but also to act as the most important remaining source of public criticism of the Government. This was the more remarkable since Dr. Obote had taken advantage of Mr. Bataringaya's crossing of the floor the year before to declare that there would no longer be an 'official' Opposition in Uganda. This could easily have been a prelude to the abolition of 'unofficial' opposition as well, particularly considering Obote's public espousal of the one-party system as early as February 1964. Indeed, all those crossings of the floor in Parliament in the course of 1964 and early 1965 seemed to be carrying Uganda irresistably towards a one-party system. In January 1965 the national chairman of the UPC, Mr. John Babiiha, was asserting that only a one-party system could assure Uganda 'social, political and economic stability and tranquility'.[1]

Yet a year later, when the UPC was in a position to take advantage of a state of emergency to launch a one-party state, it refrained from doing so. The whole idea of winning converts from opposition parties, and thus helping to liquidate them, had

June 2, 1966; and G. F. Engholm and Ali A. Mazrui, 'Violent Constitutionalism in Uganda', *Government and Opposition*, Vol. II, No. 4, August 1967, included as a chapter in this book.

[1] *Daily Nation*, January 21 , 1965.

lost the great attraction it once had. The one-party system carried the danger of intra-party subversion—and the devices of 'crossing the floor' was the Trojan Horse which could bring this about.

In June 1967 new Constitutional proposals were made in Uganda to replace the interim Constitution which had been hastily introduced in the midst of the troubles of the previous year. The 1967 Constitutional proposals aimed to make the President stronger than ever. There were also stricter provisions curtailing civil liberties, including a new Preventive Detention Act. But again the centralization fell short of outlawing opposition and setting up a one-party system.

It is not an exaggeration to say that a major factor which has saved Uganda for the time being from a one-party system is the use to which the device of 'crossing the floor' was put. Here was a practice which could easily have led to the emergence of a one-party system, as the losers deserted their parties to join the winners. But in Uganda the practice culminated in intra-party subversion and in a resultant disenchantment for the time being with one-partyism itself, at least when this is conceived in terms of open membership.

In August 1966 the UPC frankly admitted its new suspicion of party crossings of the floor. A statement issued by the national secretariat said that in order to prevent people joining the party for 'ulterior motives', all kingdom and district assemblies would in future have to send applications for membership of UPC to the national secretariat. 'Meanwhile, the national secretariat has appealed to the National Council to examine and screen members of other political parties joining the UPC in future', the statement said.[1] The use to which 'crossing the floor' in Parliament had been put had aroused suspicions about changing allegiances in the country at large. And the trend towards one-partyism in Uganda, which had seemed so irresistable in the second half of 1964, was now being thwarted by the dominant party itself.

THE CASE OF KENYA

Kenya's experience with political parties has been, in some ways, even more complicated. But from the point of view of our analysis of conflict-management, what is of particular interest is the

[1] See *Daily Nation*, August 22, 1966.

phenomenon of externalizing, or forcing outside the party, ideological and personality clashes as illustrated by Kenya politics in recent times.

But, first, let us trace the background to this phenomenon in the story of Kenya. Between May 18 and May 26, 1963, elections were held throughout the country as a prelude to self-government. The results were as follows:

House of Representatives

Kenya African National Union (KANU)	64
Kenya African Democratic Union (KADU)	32
African People's Party (APP)	8
Independents	8

Senate

Kenya African National Union	18
Kenya African Democratic Union	16
African People's Party	2
Independents	2

On May 31, 1963, the Governor of Kenya, Mr. Malcolm Mac-Donald, formally proclaimed the country's attainment of full internal self-government. KANU was in power. A few weeks later, after discussions with the Ministers of the new Kenya Government, the Secretary of State for Commonwealth Relations and the Colonies announced in the House of Commons that Kenya would become independent on December 12, provided satisfactory progress was made at a Constitutional conference scheduled for the end of September.

The immediate points of issue between the parties continued therefore to be constitutional. KANU, the majority party, stood for a centralized, unitary state. KADU, an alliance of the smaller and less secure minority tribes of Kenya, stood for a wide area of local autonomy in each region. The small African People's Party under the leadership of Paul Ngei was essentially a Party of the sizeable and politically significant Kamba tribe. The Kamba were related to the Kikuyu, and the APP leadership had more in common with KANU leaders than they had with the dominant figures of KADU. But for a while Paul Ngei did lend some support to KADU's *Majimbo* or regionally oriented policies.

By September 1963, however, Ngei declared his disenchantment with the *Majimbo* policy and proposed to forsake the

Opposition and line up with the Government. In order to forestall any accusations of 'betraying the Kamba masses', Ngei made it a point to give advance warning of his intention of crossing the floor while addressing meetings in the heart of Kambaland—at Machakos and Kitui. On September 16 the *Kenya Gazette* announced that the African People's Party had been removed from the register of societies as it had 'ceased to exist'. All the APP members of the House of Representatives and the Senate had crossed the floor to join KANU.[1]

The result of all this was that, unlike Uganda, Kenya approached independence with only two parties after all. Their deep differences in constitutional matters were taken to London to be thrashed out at the conference. The outcome of the conference was an attempt to reaffirm both KADU's *Majimbo* principle and KANU's desire for a stronger government. But on the whole this last constitutional conference prior to independence was more a triumph for the centralists than for the regionalists. The achievement of the regionalists had come earlier—when their influence helped to give Kenya the prolix and devolved constitution which accompanied the country into internal self-government—a document which was the longest of its kind in the history of the British Empire and its dissolution. But the last constitutional conference prior to Kenya's independence tried to make amends to the centralists, though still leaving one or two matters unresolved.[2]

The possibility of KADU crossing the floor to join KANU was raised soon after the constitutional conference. The governing party extended an invitation to members of the Opposition to cross the floor en masse. But after an important meeting of the KADU Parliamentary group in October 1963, Mr. Ronald Ngala, the leader of the Opposition, explained his Party's position on this matter with firmness. Asked if his party was in favour of 'a united front' with KANU, Mr. Ngala said,

> If united front means that the Opposition should cross the floor, then that is out of the question. But if it means that

---

[1] For some of the relevant background reports see *East African Standard*, September 7, 9, 12, 13, 17, 1963.

[2] As it turned out, the most important of the unresolved issues was the North Eastern region and the future of the Somalis living there.

there should be agreement between the Opposition and the Government on delicate national issues, then that is the normal democratic way in which the party in power recognizes the Opposition.[1]

On December 12, 1963, Kenya became independent. It still had a two-party system, but pressures for the dissolution of KADU had been mounting. Some members had crossed the floor already. Towards the end of November, for example, two defections from KADU gave KANU access to what had previously been 'enemy territory'—the Kalenjin areas. 'There comes a time in the careers of politicians when they have to make an agonizing reappraisal of their position', explained a defector.[2]

But it was not until nine months after independence that KADU's power of survival faced its worst test. The Government's proposals for a Republican constitution included proposals to reduce the powers of the seven regional authorities. But the minority safeguards within the independence *Majimbo* constitution seemed to make it impossible for KANU to change the Constitution unless they got extra voting strength from at least some members of KADU, especially in the Senate. KANU asked the Opposition either to support the proposals or face a national referendum. It was expected that such a referendum would reveal much more clearly than ever how weak the Opposition was in the country and how 'inflated' its strength was in the two Houses of Parliament. KADU was therefore rightly concerned about the risks involved in forcing the Government to go to the country at that particular moment.

Nevertheless, in early November, 1964, the KADU executive decided to stand firm against the Government on the Republican constitutional proposals. But at the eleventh hour a political confrontation was avoided. Two days before the Senate was due to vote on the Republican proposals, two Masai members and one Samburu crossed the floor. This was decisive. The crossings gave the Government a certainty of the seventy-five per cent majority in the Senate to get the proposals passed. The meetings that Mr. Kenyatta had been having with the chiefs and elders of the Masai and Samburu had served their purpose. Three crossings

[1] See *East African Standard*, October 23, 1963.
[2] See *East African Standard*, November 24 and 25, 1963.

in the Senate had spared the country the expense and possible risks of what might have been an acrimonious referendum.

The KADU executive at once met to reappraise the situation. They decided that it was now 'obvious that the country has chosen to have one leadership under the new Constitution'. The vote in the Senate had not as yet been taken on the new proposals, but the Government already had the requisite voting strength. KADU decided that the time to cross the floor and join the Government was before the vote in the Senate was taken. And so, on November 10, 1964 Ronald Ngala stood in the House of Representatives and solemnly announced his Party's decision:

> I have a full mandate to declare today that the official Opposition is dissolved. KADU is joining the Government under the leadership of Mzee Jomo Kenyatta and the Opposition today will vote with the Government for the new constitution in the Senate.

Mr. Ngala's voice was almost drowned by the cheering and stamping. And then up stood a beaming Mr. Kenyatta and, to a tumultuous applause, said,

> I welcome our brothers wholeheartedly . . . I regard this day as a great day, not for KANU but for the people of Kenya.[1]

With the dissolution of KADU, Kenya became what was called 'a voluntary one-party state'. In the scramble for position as independence approached, the country had had three parties. On the eve of independence the smallest of the three crossed the floor to join the largest. Kenya therefore attained sovereign status with a two-party system. But floor-crossings again eroded the strength of the Opposition. And finally a decisive crossing of the floor by three Senators gave the Government the requisite strength for a major constitutional change. The KADU Opposition re-appraised its position—and decided to join the winners.

The one-party trend, which in Uganda was thwarted before it attained fulfilment, managed in Kenya to 'go the whole hog'. KANU became the only party—at least for a while.

[1] See *East African Standard*, November 11, 1964.

KENYA: PHASE TWO

But was not this simply another instance of internalizing by taking the Opposition into the ruling group itself? Certainly suggestions of this kind were being made not long after KADU dissolved itself to join KANU. Mr. Oginga Odinga, then Vice-President of the country, remarked some months after KADU's dissolution that former KADU leaders still had 'KADU beliefs'.

And yet Mr. Odinga's own remarks were the beginning of a new kind of split. Unlike the case of some of the KY crossings in Uganda, the KADU crossings in Kenya were certainly not an instance of infiltration. It was not a case of bringing opponents of the Government from the outside into the inner chambers of the governing party. To that extent KADU crossings were not a simple case of internalizing opposition to the Government.

And yet there is no doubt that opposition to the Government within the Party became more marked following the merger with KADU. What was the difference? The answer to the question brings in the whole relationship between the one-party state and the problem of unity. It is true that the disappearance of KADU from Kenya's political scene led to internal dissension within KANU. But KADU did not cause this dissension by joining KANU. It caused it simply by dissolving itself. In other words, even if Mr. Ngala and his colleagues of KADU had simply retired from politics after dissolving their Party, the dissension within the ruling party would still have reared its head simply because of the disappearance of a rival party.

This is one of the dilemmas facing African one-party states. A one-party system is often defended in terms of being an instrument for unity. And yet its own internal party unity sometimes depends on the stimulus of a rival party. The Tanganyika African National Union has so far averted the danger of 'withering away'. But the Kenya African National Union was faced with this risk as soon as it was deprived of the invigorating insecurity which came with a rival party. In an open letter to President Kenyatta in January 1966 the Organizing Secretary of KANU at the time, Mr. John Keen, complained bitterly of the rust, dust and cobwebs which were already covering the Party machinery. He noted 'the appalling situation of the Party'. There had not been a meeting of the Party Secretariat since February 1964 or of the party executive council since 1963. Party debts totalling nearly £20,000 had not been paid. Full-time party workers had received no salaries for months, and electricity and telephones were sometimes cut off because the requisite bills had remained unpaid. Paul Ngei, who had dissolved his own party just before independence to become a leading member of KANU, echoed John Keen's sentiments in March 1966. Ngei told the Press

> It is my opinion that the Party is not functioning. . . . I cannot see the Party dying like this when the Party is ruling the country.[1]

But it was not mere lethargy which followed upon the launching of the one-party system in Kenya. It was also mounting dissension between factions within the Party. In the course of 1965 open clashes and exchange of political abuse between leading members of KANU became increasingly uninhibited. The leader of the discontented members of the Party became Mr. Oginga Odinga, the Vice President of the country and of the Party. Clashes between him and fellow Members of the Cabinet more loyal to President Kenyatta became more publicly articulated.

Among the most loyal to President Kenyatta were, in fact, the former leaders of KADU like Ronald Ngala and Daniel Arap Moi. Indeed, when President Kenyatta decided to relieve Mr. Odinga of his portfolio as Minister for Home Affairs, he then gave it to Mr. Moi. It was about that time that Mr. Odinga made suggestions that the KADU leaders who had crossed the floor had brought their KADU beliefs with them. To these accusations Mr. Moi said

> I would like to make clear to the public that KADU joined KANU and the Government sincerely, and has consolidated those forces who were, and are, loyal to the President of Kenya. The country will no doubt know who are loyal to the President and who are not. It is easy to speak, but what

[1] For a very useful background article to Kenya at that time see John Spencer, 'Kenyatta's Kenya', *Africa Report*, Vol. XI, No. 5, May 1966. John Keen later resigned from his party office, and was briefly detained by the Government.

remains to be seen in practice is what should be taken to be the true intent.[1]

It was indeed a significant paradox. The end of KADU had both strengthened the Kenya Government and weakened the ruling party. As we have indicated, KANU was weakened when it lost the unifying effect of a rival party. The Kenya Government was strengthened when its own brand of political pragmatism found loyal support from former KADU leaders. To use the words of Mr. Moi again, 'we joined the Government and the party to consolidate forces within them loyal to the President'.[2]

In the course of 1966 events in Kenya seemed to be heading towards an ultimate confrontation between President Kenyatta's immediate supporters and the disaffected members of KANU around Mr. Oginga Odinga. Kenya's single-party system was merely an umbrella for genuine political clashes and open debate. As a newspaper of one of Kenya's neighbours noted in an editorial following a remarkable debate in the Kenya Parliament:

> It is surprising that Kenya, a one-party state, should have a Parliamentary debate on a motion seeking to express confidence in the President and his Government. And the acrimony of the debate, in which several members were ordered out and the Vice-President of Kenya walked out, comes as a surprise, despite the fact that it has been known for a long time that there were divisions in the ruling Kenya African National Union.[3]

This brief period was perhaps the golden age of liberalism in Kenya. President Nyerere of Tanzania had once said that the one-party system had the capacity to promote freer political debates than was possible in a two-party system. Party discipline, which often effectively curtailed the freedom of the individual legislator in a two-party system, could be dispensed with in a situation in which there was no rival party that might stand to gain by dissension within one's own party.

[1] See *East African Standard*, December 1, 1965.
[2] *Ibid.*
[3] 'KANU's Split is Showing', *Uganda Argus*, February 17, 1966.

To put it in another way, a single-party system has no obvious alternative government which must be denied electoral advantage. Opposing factions are looser and changeable. If there is such a thing as a 'shadow cabinet' it has not been institutionalized— and is therefore more shadowy than ever. Precisely because the fear of giving 'the enemy' an electoral advantage is less immediate and identifiable, dissension within the ruling party in a single-party system can be all the more uninhibited.[1]

But the best illustration of this vigorous debate within a single-party system has not, in fact, been Tanzania. It was Kenya in its period of vigorous liberalism within the single-party structure. Top leaders within TANU have never up to the date of writing clashed as openly and frankly as top KANU leaders were clashing in 1965–6. Kenya as an 'open society' attained the heights of candour in this short phase.

But then the device of 'crossing the floor' brought the curtain down on this period. On April 14, 1966, Oginga Odinga announced his resignation as Kenya's Vice President. The impact was far-reaching. Two assistant Ministers resigned from KANU. And then eighteen members of the House of Representatives and nine Senators crossed the floor to give Parliamentary existence to a new Opposition Party, the Kenya People's Union (KPU). Shortly afterwards the Minister of Information, Achieng Oneko, resigned and joined the rebels. It was not long before Oginga Odinga formally took over as President of KPU.

There seemed to be an immediate risk of further floor-crossings. The ruling party reacted with resourcefulness. It is reported that at a meeting of the KANU Parliamentary Group following Oneko's resignation President Kenyatta angrily demanded that all those who had crossed the floor should be expelled from Parliament. The Speaker of the House pointed out that this would be unconstitutional. Tom Mboya is credited with the alternative solution which was adopted—that those who had changed parties should be forced to go to their constituencies and stand for election again. This move was apparently rationalized on the grounds that 'having deserted KANU, the dissidents no longer represented their constituents'.[2]

---

[1] For Nyerere's stimulating discussion of this theme see his *Democracy and the Party-System* (Dar es Salaam: *Tanganyika Standard*, 1962).

[2] John Spencer, 'Kenyatta's Kenya', *op. cit.*

But this too needed a constitutional amendment. Such an amendment was rushed through. Thirteen of the defectors, faced with the loss of perquisites, applied for readmission to KANU and publicly reaffirmed their loyalty to President Kenyatta. They helped to get the constitutional amendment passed by the two Houses. But in spite of their renewed declarations of allegiance to the Party, the dissidents were told that they too would have to stand for re-election under the new law. On hearing this ten of the penitents crossed the floor once again—and rejoined the KPU.

In June 1966 the 'Little General Election' was held in Kenya in those constituencies affected by the floor-crossings. By that time twenty House of Representatives seats and ten Senate seats were involved. The campaigns were energetic and lively. And the issues which divided the two parties were indeed partly tribal. But there were also more genuine clashes of ideology and policy-alternatives than have been evident in most African elections so far. There was a neo-Marxist theme in much of KPU's rhetoric which clearly distinguished the Party from its ruling rival.

Many of KPU's members in Parliament, including Bildad Kaggia, the Kikuyu Marxist, were not returned. But the Party, however small, did survive the 'Little General Election' and continued to follow the leadership of Mr. Oginga Odinga. After a brief exercise in single-party politics, Kenya once again had a rival opposition party in Parliament.

At first sight this 'externalization' of opposition to the Government would seem to have served the cause of liberal politics in Kenya. The device of crossing the floor had given the country a two-party system once again.

And yet the total effect of the events of 1966 was in fact to reduce liberalism in Kenya. Mr. Odinga's group was larger and more powerful within KANU than it has become since then. The 'Little General Election' had itself taken its toll. Many leading figures, who would have continued to command public attention had they continued to be in Parliament, have now fallen into oblivion. Achieng Oneko and Bildad Kaggia are two such figures. Had they and their colleagues not left KANU, there would have been no 'Little General Election'. And had there been no such election, the parliamentary opposition to

Government policies would have been stronger than it is now. And Mr. Odinga's following—within the ruling party but against the Government—would have been larger and more commanding. It is also just possible that in such circumstances there would have been no Preventive Detention Act as yet in Kenya. That, however, is a less solid speculation. What the evidence does support is that crossing the floor in Kenya in 1966 resulted in giving the country an extra political party but at the cost of reduced candour in public debate and reduced effectiveness in challenging government policy. Kenya gained a two-party system and lost much of the liberalism of its politics.

LIBERALISM AND CONSENT

But liberalism is tied to the doctrine of consent in government, and this in turn is by no means unrelated to the kind of party system a country devises. It is to these aspects of the question, and their bearing on mitigation of conflict in the political system, that we must now turn.

To the question 'What is the connection between the party system and the principle of consent?' the liberal answer has tended to start from the premise that consent postulates an alternative. A people could not be said to have consented to be ruled by a given party unless there was an alternative party that they were in a position to vote for, had they been so inclined. When therefore Mr. Ngala late in 1964 decided to dissolve KADU and join the ruling party in Kenya he was in effect depriving the people of Kenya of their right to an identifiable 'shadow government'. In other words, a liberal might have argued that Kenya's two-party system had no right to commit suicide. The decision which Mr. Ngala and his colleagues had reached affected more than Ngala's own political future. It was arguable that by killing his own party Mr. Ngala had denied the country as a whole a potential alternative to KANU.

But perhaps it was not just Mr. Ngala who killed KADU. It was also those members of his Party who had crossed the floor before he decided on dissolving it. This is where we need to look at the relationship between the doctrine of consent and the phenomenon of crossing the floor.

We should perhaps begin by taking note of the concept of *composite consent*. What is consented to after a free inter-party election is not simply which party should rule. The effect of the voting is not merely in determining which party is in a majority in the legislature but also which is in a minority and by what margins of strength the different parties are separated. The balance of forces which emerges after a free election is what enjoys the *composite consent* of the electorate as a whole.

In the last general election in Kenya on the eve of independence the composite consent which resulted was to a two-party system—though with one party considerably stronger than the other.

It is possible to argue in general terms that every crossing of the floor is a distortion of the composite consent of the electorate since it modifies the balance of forces to which they had originally assented. The Uganda Parliament by the end of 1965 bore little relationship to the strength of the Uganda People's Congress at the last general election. The phenomenon of floor-crossings had inflated the strength of the UPC in Parliament and made it considerably stronger than its original electoral position would justify.

Yet in Kenya in the first **year** of independence it was possible to argue that crossing the floor was by no means always a distortion of original consent. This was because of a prior distortion arising from constituency boundaries. In July 1962 a Commission had been appointed to delimit constituencies for the Lower House of the National Assembly. In January 1963 the Report was published. It became increasingly clear that the main result of the new constituency boundaries was a heavy weighting against Mr. Kenyatta's Kenya African National Union. Clyde Sanger, writing in *The Guardian*, assessed that the sizes of the 117 constituencies varied so much that in broad terms it seemed likely that three votes for KANU would be worth only two cast for any other party—Mr. Ngala's KADU, Mr. Paul Ngei's African People's Party or the secessionist Somalis in the Northern Frontier District. Mr. Sanger continued

. . . in other words K.A.N.U. could win 60 per cent of the popular vote and yet take only a minority of seats. . . .

Electorates vary in size from Baringo East with 749 voters to Nakuru East with 47,017.[1]

When in May the elections were held, the results were not quite as bizarre as at one time had seemed possible. After all, KANU did emerge as the majority party. Nevertheless, KADU, with only one-fifth of KANU's electoral strength in the country, won the equivalent of half of KANU's seats (KADU had 32 seats in Parliament to KANU's 64). It is true that the system of single-member constituencies is not intended in any case to achieve the happy neatness of proportional representation. But in the case of Kenya's constituencies something approaching 'neo-gerrymanderism' had been at play. If therefore through a fault in the electoral arrangements KADU had got more seats in Parliament than was justified even by the canons of single-member constituencies, then crossing the floor had a restorative rather than distorting function. A few desertions from KADU made the legislature more representative rather than less so. And the composite consent of the electorate was restored.

This is certainly one area of activity in which crossing the floor could serve to mitigate some of the frustrations of being under-represented. When Clyde Sanger assessed before the Kenya elections that KANU could conceivably win sixty per cent of the popular vote and still win only a minority of seats, he appended a warning to this hypothesis. He said, 'If this happened it would not only be the perennial pessimists who would predict revolutionary violence'.[2]

THE CASE OF ZANZIBAR

Sanger was pointing precisely to the explosive risks of a certain scale of under-representation. But it was not Kenya which was soon to vindicate Sanger's theory of representational frustrations. It was Zanzibar. It is arguable that of all countries in former British Africa the one which needed floor-crossings most of all was Zanzibar between its last election in July 1963 and the actual revolution in January 1964. The results of the July elections had

[1] *The Guardian*, February 20, 1963. See also *Africa Digest*, Vol. X, No. 5, April 1963, pp. 158–9.
[2] *The Guardian*, *ibid*.

given the Zanzibar Nationalist Party twelve seats and the Zanzibar and Pemba People's party six seats. These two parties had formed the ruling alliance, holding eighteen seats in Parliament. The Opposition party was the Afro-Shirazi Party, with the remaining thirteen seats of the legislature.

And yet, in terms of support in the country, the governing coalition had won only 46 per cent of the popular vote. Through a predictable electoral fault in constituency boundaries, Zanzibar had once again a frustrated popular party in opposition, while a minority coalition held the reins of power. This was an anomaly which was predictable enough to have been rectified before the election—had the departing British authorities possessed the will to do so. But they had not. The country therefore emerged into independence with a minority government.

In different circumstances this anomaly might have mattered less. But it just so happened that in Zanzibar the ruling minority government was too closely identified with a long-established Arab élite within the Sultanate. It is true that the Zanzibar Nationalist Party had more African support than naïve external commentators sometimes assumed. The ruling coalition government would not have won forty-six per cent of the vote if it was simply an 'Arab coalition', for the Arabs were little more than a sixth of the population.

Nevertheless, although not all Africans were against the Government, virtually all Arabs were for it. That is why the ruling coalition became so closely associated in many people's minds with the long-established Arab élite.

The Arabs were economically, especially in land-ownership, still very much a privileged class. By 1963 the Arabs could no longer maintain their economic status through armed might. That is why parliamentary control assumed a crucial significance. In the words of Michael F. Lofchie,

Whereas the Arabs' position in the past rested upon their superior force as a caste of colonial invaders and upon an ability to use this force to dominate the economy, their security now depended upon the intrinsic stability of a parliamentary system.[1]

[1] Lofchie, *Zanzibar: Background to Revolution* (Princeton: Princeton University Press, 1965), pp. 270–1. See also *The Times* (London), July 17, 1963.

If the Arabs had lost control over the parliamentary system, it is conceivable that no violent revolution would have been necessary. And how could they lose control over the parliamentary system? Presumably by losing that margin of seats in Parliament without which their parties in Parliament would not have been able to form a ruling coalition.

But given that a fault in constituency arrangements had already conferred an artificial majority on the coalition of the ZNP and the ZPP, the only hope lay in a post-electoral shift in the balance of parliamentary strengths. This is what leads us to one of the great 'might-have-beens' in the political history of East Africa. It might not be too much of an exaggeration to say that if three members of the ZNP/ZPP coalition had crossed the floor to join the Afro-Shirazi Party, the Zanzibar revolution need not have taken place. Sixteen seats in Parliament would have given the Afro-Shirazi Party a majority. And if this had happened between July 1963 and early December, the departing British authorities would have had to supervise a change of government following a shift in Parliamentary support. There might indeed have been some rioting here and there, but the violent revolution which occurred within a month of British departure might well have been averted.

It is difficult to be certain when one is speculating about what might or might not have happened in this or that set of circumstances. But if Lofchie is right that the stability of the parliamentary system was the Arabs' last protection against a rapid erosion of their privileges, these hypothetical defections in Parliament from the coalition to the Afro-Shirazi Party might well have averted one of the most brutal episodes in the recent history of East Africa.

SUMMARY

We might again reiterate that increased representation in the legislative council was one of the earlier aims of nationalist movements in most British colonies in Africa. This phenomenon helped to acquire for the legislature a mystique which accompanied it into independence.

After independence the 'Westminster Model', at first popular, was then rapidly discredited. And with the apparent decline of the organized effectiveness of political parties in much of Africa, the institution of Parliament seemed to be losing its centrality in African political systems.

And yet in East Africa one form of parliamentary behaviour had sometimes far-reaching implications for political arrangements at large. And this was, as we indicated, the phenomenon of crossing the floor. In Uganda the device of crossing the floor first took the country to the brink of a one-party system. But then the dominant party took another look at what had been happening. Floor-crossing had, in part, been a form of infiltration —and while it was taking the country to the brink of a one-party system its real aim was to push the top leadership over the brink and dispose of it.

Uganda might still end up having a one-party system. But for the time being the dominant party is not overtly speeding up the process. Both in 1966 and in 1967 the Party put forward proposals for sweeping constitutional changes. But in both cases the Government did not use the opportunity to push forward proposals for a one-party system. On the contrary, in 1967 the Government specifically affirmed that it had no special proposals to set-up a one-party state.[1]

It might therefore be argued that the utilization of crossing the floor as a 'Trojan Horse' tactic had led to a situation in which the dominant party had become a little apprehensive about over-extending itself. Crossing the floor had therefore helped to create in Uganda, at least for a while, a distrust of one-partyism.

In Kenya crossing the floor had first, before independence, given the country a three-party system. Then the trend led to the liquidation of the APP—leaving the country with a two-party system. And about a year after independence the self-dissolution of KADU gave the country a voluntary one-party state.

However, the disappearance of a rival party let loose within the ruling party the ideological friction and personal rivalry which had before remained subdued. The tendency culminated in a new wave of crossings in 1966—and the formation of the

---

[1] This was affirmed by Minister Felix Onama, who had on previous occasions strongly attacked 'Western-style democracy'. See *Uganda Argus*, June 1967.

Kenya People's Party. This was a case of externalizing opposition to Government. But while the crossings of 1966 restored for Kenya a two-party system, it was at the expense of the more vigorous opposition and debate which had been possible from within the party.

Finally, we analysed the relationship between the doctrine of government by consent and the phenomenon of crossing the floor. In Kenya crossing from KADU to KANU might have helped to mitigate some of the frustrations of under-representation. In pre-revolutionary Zanzibar, however, what was significant was the final floor-crossing which never took place—the hypothetical three defections from the coalition to the Afro-Shirazi Party which alone would have given the latter the necessary majority to form a Government without a revolution.

It is these considerations which have given the phenomenon of parliamentary defections in East Africa a depth of meaning which has far transcended the apparently trivial motives which have often inspired them. At times a mere symptom, and at others a catalyst or a cause, the phenomenon of crossing the floor has often been at the very centre of problems of conflict-management in the political systems of East Africa.

7 Violent Constitutionalism in Uganda[1]

written in conjunction with

G. F. Engholm

From the country's independence until May 1966 two factors profoundly affected the nature of politics in Uganda. These were, first, *a latent violence* between groups and, secondly, *a vigorous constitutionalism* as a style of political contest. Both factors were, inevitably, connected with events and tendencies which went back well before independence.

The possibility of political violence in the country was linked to a few key issues. These included, firstly, the degree of autonomy to be enjoyed by Buganda as the largest and most developed region in the country; secondly, the unresolved problem of the Lost Counties of Bunyoro; thirdly, relations between the Baganda and other tribes, an issue which later culminated in an alleged Bantu/Nilotic cleavage; and fourthly, the tensions of party allegiances within the parliamentary system. We shall discuss these issues more fully later in this analysis.

In the meantime we should perhaps first proceed to define the second major theme of Uganda politics until the crisis of May 1966—the theme of a vigorous tradition of constitutionalism. For our purposes in this article we define 'constitutionalism' broadly to mean a procedural approach to politics; a faith in legal solutions to political tensions; a relatively open society with institutionalized competition for power in the polity. We propose to argue here that until the crisis last year, Uganda was perhaps the

[1] This paper was first published in *Government and Opposition*, Vol. II, No. 4, July–October 1967. It is reprinted here with the permission of the co-author and of the journal.

strongest example of a liberal polity surviving in Africa. The striking features of Uganda's liberal style included a spirit of open dissent to central authority; a readiness to take the government to court; a relatively non-ideological political style with a high degree of sophisticated pragmatism; and, finally, a system of institutionalized pluralism involving multi-party tendencies and permitting neo-federalism in at least some matters.

LATENT VIOLENCE

The degree of autonomy which Buganda was to enjoy in independent Uganda was perhaps at once the most directly constitutional of the major issues of national politics and one which involved the gravest risks of a violent clash. Buganda's relative autonomy and strong sense of identity constituted one of the more dramatic consequences of Britain's colonial policy of indirect rule. While permitting significant changes in the nature of native authority, that policy encouraged the survival of effective traditional kingship in Buganda. A degree of autonomy was granted to Buganda which in time both preserved Buganda's militant loyalty to itself and secured the region's favoured position in the protectorate as a whole. The Baganda themselves added to this pre-eminence by a marked response to modernity in select areas of life. Their acceptance of Western education, their sophisticated links with Christian missions, the commercialization of some of their agricultural activities, all helped to give the Baganda an extra lead in national affairs as compared with other groups. The pre-eminence which size and history had already conferred upon them was given additional protection by the Baganda themselves through their modernizing tendencies. And modernity was in turn made to serve the cause of tribal identity. To use Apter's words, the ethos of the Baganda was 'sufficiently adaptable to allow innovation to be traditionalized and thereby sanctified'.[1]

The latent violence in the situation partly arose out of Buganda's defensiveness. Her special position had deepened her self-consciousness as a region. And threats to Buganda's status tended

---

[1] David E. Apter, *The Political Kingdom in Uganda* (Princeton, N.J.: Princeton University Press, 1961), p. 27.

to provoke from the Baganda counter-threats of regional insubordination. As independence approached Buganda even staged a formal secession from the Protectorate. In September 1960 the Lukiiko or parliament of Buganda submitted a memorandum to the Queen announcing that the region intended to be a separate independent state as from the beginning of the following year. Fortunately, the colonial authorities simply ignored the verbal announcement. Yet the whole serio-comic incident was latent with possibilities of political breakdown.

What these tactics ultimately managed to extract was perhaps a greater readiness on the part of Britain and of some of the other groups in Uganda to consider the possibility of giving Buganda something approaching a federal status in the new independence constitution. The 1961 constitutional conference was itself a major exercise of political manoeuvre and bargaining. What emerged was a new affirmation of Buganda's special position, with all the potential for future conflict which this entailed. On the other hand, the fact that this neo-federal position was entrenched in the Constitution opened up the possibility of legal wrangles of interpretation in the days ahead, with all the potential for judicial constitutionalism which this in turn implied.

The Lost Counties of Bunyoro was another issue involving a prospect of violent constitutionalism. These counties had been taken away from Bunyoro and handed over to Buganda quite early in the colonial period as a reward for certain services rendered by Buganda to the imperial authority. Through the years the Banyoro had repeatedly challenged this transfer. Within the counties themselves, organized resistance to Buganda hegemony dates back to 1921 when the 'Mubende-Banyoro Committee' was formed with the object of persuading the colonial government to return the disputed areas. In 1931 the opportunity was taken to arouse British sympathies by raising the grievance before the Joint Parliamentary Committee on Closer Union, but the Secretary of State felt it was impossible to go into a matter so long settled. The Omukama, or King of Bunyoro, made formal protests in 1933. Petitions were sent to the Secretary of State by the Omukama in 1943, 1945, 1948, 1949 and 1954. The Mubende-Bunyoro Committee—which some claim to be the first political organization in Uganda—also made representations in

1951, 1953 and 1955 for the restoration of the counties to Bunyoro.

In the meantime faith in a possible legal solution to this problem was beginning to be entertained by the Banyoro. The Queen was petitioned in 1958, and there was a proposal to have the case judged by the Privy Council. But the Secretary of State maintained that no legal issues were in dispute, and the matter was purely political. This view prevailed for the time being.

In 1961 the Uganda Relationship Commission, under the Chairmanship of the Earl of Munster, recommended a referendum in the counties. But this proposal was rejected by Buganda at the Uganda Constitutional Conference in October 1961. Buganda also turned down the recommendation of the Molson Commission that the counties should be handed over *without* a referendum to avert the danger of inflaming tribal feeling. At the Constitutional Conference of 1961 the two counties of Buyaga and Bugangazi were therefore transferred to the Central Government, but the requirement that a referendum be held some time after independence was inserted into the Constitution. Here again an issue of potential violence was tied to considerations of constitutionality, with ominous risks for the future.[1]

The constitutional provision on the referendum had been that it was to be held two years or more after independence—that is, on a date sometime after October 8, 1964. In spite of the hazards, the Prime Minister, Dr. Milton Obote, decided to go ahead and hold the referendum at the earliest opportunity. As the event approached, there was a tense atmosphere in the counties themselves, in the capital, and in Buganda and Bunyoro generally. Constitutional difficulties were compounded by the fact that Sir Edward Mutesa was both Kabaka of Buganda and President of Uganda. When Dr. Obote decided that the Central Government was to take over the disputed counties more completely pending the referendum, President Mutesa refused to sign the necessary documents. In the meantime the Kabaka's Government had been settling Baganda ex-servicemen in the counties in the hope of swelling the pro-Buganda votes in the referendum. It was an elaborate instance of trying to out-manoeuvre the constitution by constitutional means, but the ruse was unsuccessful. The Government ruled that the Baganda

[1] See the Molson Report, Cmnd. 1717, May 1962.

ex-servicemen did not qualify to vote in the referendum on the grounds that they were not already on the 1962 voting register of the areas concerned. Essentially it was a disqualification on the basis of an inadequate period of residence.

The referendum was held as planned on November 4., 1964. The choice was between remaining part of Buganda, becoming part of Bunyoro, or being a separate district under the direct administration of the Central Government. An overwhelming majority voted in favour of union with Bunyoro.[1]

Once again there was an interplay of violence and constitutionalism. The security situation in the counties themselves was tense. And in Kampala two days after the referendum there were riots which resulted in three killed, twenty injured, and eighty-eight arrested. Shortly after, the strained atmosphere also led to the notorious Nakulabye incident when the Special Security Force was alarmed and seven people were killed and thirty-nine others wounded.[2]

In the meantime the Buganda Government appealed to the High Court against the referendum, arguing that it was invalid. Buganda based its case on the fact that 9,000 residents in the counties had been disqualified from voting. These were the ex-servicemen who had moved into the disputed areas since 1962. Buganda lost the case. She then appealed to the Privy Council but the appeal was dismissed in April 1965.[3]

In the meantime the principle of responsible government within Buganda claimed its victim. Michael Kintu, who had been the Kabaka's Chief Minister or Katikiro for nearly a decade, was forced to resign for 'failing to protect Buganda's sovereignty'.

VIGOROUS CONSTITUTIONALISM

It was perhaps on issues such as these that there was a causal connection between the latent violence and the vigorous

[1] 13,602 voted for union with Bunyoro, 3,542 for remaining with Buganda, and 112 for a separate district.

[2] *Uganda Argus*, November 12, 1964.

[3] The Kabaka's Government and another *v*. Attorney-General of Uganda and another. Privy Council Appeal No. 56 of 1964. See also the original Report of the Commission of Privy Councillors on the dispute between Buganda and Bunyoro, Cmnd. 1717. The final referendum resulted in the Constitution of Uganda (Third Amendment) Act No. 36 of 1964.

constitutionalism which characterized Uganda's political style. As the referendum approached leading Baganda had been making speeches which at times verged on being seditious. A former Minister of the Kabaka gave a speech at an open-air meeting saying that they would defend with their blood 'every inch of Buganda territory', including the counties in dispute. The degree to which the Central Government of Uganda permitted dissent of this kind was in part determined by the immediacy of violence as an alternative reaction to measures unpopular to the Baganda. The Baganda had almost established a 'tradition' of threatening to resort to violence, or to other acts of serious insubordination, if certain intentions of the Central Government were carried out. As we have already indicated, this tradition of defiance verging on sedition or even treason went back to the days before independence. The notice of secession which they served on the Queen in 1960–61 was only the most dramatic example of this kind of defiance. Yet, to their credit, the Baganda seldom went all out to implement their threats of violent insubordination. By *verbalizing* the country's latent violence, the Baganda might for a while have been helping to delay its actual outbreak. The safety-valve theory was operative in this case—a vigorous verbal dissent being used as a functional alternative to violent insubordination.

The immediacy of possible violence also compelled antagonists to experiment with other forms of conflict-resolution. One of these forms was, as we have indicated, the resort to the Courts. J. M. Lee, in an article published in November 1965, described Buganda as 'inveterately litigious'. He regarded this quality as tending towards 'legal quibbling' at times:

But at least it shows that the design of the Constitution cannot be ignored in studying Uganda because the law is one of Buganda's chief weapons. Uganda politics are played in an atmosphere where each side is looking for legal 'loop-holes' to be turned to its own advantage.[1]

Buganda's own faith in litigation was linked to what we might describe as *a treaty complex* which operated in her relations with

[1] 'Buganda's Position in Federal Uganda', *Journal of Commonwealth Political Studies*, Vol. III, No. 3, November 1965, pp. 175–6.

the Central Government from Colonial days. The identity of the region was supposed to have found legal expression in the 1900 Uganda Agreement concluded between Buganda and Britain guaranteeing the region certain rights in exchange for British protection. Out of this understanding gradually grew the treaty complex of the Baganda whereby major tensions with the central government were somehow referred back to a pre-existent fundamental law. In the case of Buganda's relations with the British colonial authorities, the 'fundamental law' was the 1900 Agreement. But in Buganda's relations with central government *after* independence the fundamental law became, of course, the Independence Constitution of 1962. Both these manifestations of the deep-seated treaty complex in Buganda's style of political manoeuvre helped to give rise to and reinforce the region's faith in litigation at large.

A related reinforcing agent in the earlier period was indeed the whole ethos of colonial administration and its commitment to formal procedures. There was a kind of *administrative constitutionalism* operating as the very foundation of colonial administration. The system was characterized by a strong orientation towards formal accountability in the administrators. Internally within Uganda this had a strong legal bias, tending to justify actions by reference to the appropriate document. At the national level the reference was to Ordinances; at the Provincial and District levels, to formal rules supplemented by general administrative instructions. Externally, the system validated itself with Governor's dispatches, Blue Books and Annual Reports. Such a procedural system was by no means unique to colonial administration in Uganda. In British Africa it was perhaps characteristic of most territories. But within Uganda the system interplayed with other factors and reinforced constitutionalist tendencies of later years. One peculiarity of the colonial system in Uganda was the very existence of Agreements with four Bantu kingdoms which both became a factor in administrative decisions and created a disposition in favour of limiting the central government's powers in other districts. The existence of a colonial administration acting within a system of laws of its own creation was no guarantee that after independence African leaders would also observe a similar kind of constitutional constraint. But in Uganda the idea seemed to have been, at least for a while, grafted into general African political attitudes by the very success of the 1900 Agreement.[1]

The rules of the constitutional game in Uganda required that the Baganda should be reassured periodically by a British reaffirmation of the terms of the Agreement. As the Muganda Treasurer made clear in his evidence to the Joint Select Committee on Closer Union in 1931, the Kabaka and chiefs were not satisfied by private letters of reassurance from the Colonial Office. Faced by the 'danger' of closer union in East Africa, the Baganda demanded that those assurances should be less private. They preferred to see the assurances take the form of formal statements publicly documented. This was once again a legalistic conception of political security, a recurrent frame of reference in the modern history of Uganda.

LEGALISM AND PLURALISM

What must not be forgotten is that legalism is often an important component of the liberal polity. It was certainly one of the factors which helped to give Uganda politics their strong constitutionalist tendencies. But the curious thing about Uganda liberalism is that it valued constitutional rights without necessarily valuing individual rights. Within Buganda itself the demand for conformity was great. Dissidents and political heretics were often socially ostracized and occasionally suffered an even more severe fate than that. And yet Buganda remained a central element in the country's liberalism. Much of the constitutionalist style of politics, and the tradition of challenging the government when it appeared to act *ultra vires*, owed its vigour to the militancy of Buganda as a region.

This is what brings us to the relevance of ethnic pluralism for a liberal style of politics. The British policy of indirect rule, precisely by strengthening the autonomy of Buganda and contributing to the self-consciousness of other regions, helped to

---

[1] Clauses 3, 5, 6, 11 and 12 of the 1900 Agreement gave Buganda the status of a Province; provided for the superiority of the Agreement in the event of a conflict with Protectorate law; gave legal recognition to the Kabaka, his Courts, Chiefs and Council; and restricted taxation to narrow limits. Further concessions were made in 1944 when the European provincial administration narrowed its role to advice and guidance.

prepare the way for *competitive* politics in the country. Here again a latent violence and a vigorous constitutionalism found a meeting point. Ethnic pluralism, in much of Africa, tends to be among the most politically sensitive of all social issues. The risk of violence between tribes is at the centre of Africa's twin-crises of identity and integration. Britain's indirect rule, where it was successful, tended to sharpen ethnic loyalties. To that extent it probably increased the risk of violence between tribes. But at the same time the policy created the framework for genuinely competitive politics and for a spirit of energetic dissent in at least the first few years of independence. Nigeria provided perhaps the most dramatic example of these two related consequences of indirect rule. The country started off with an almost furious liberal ethos in its national politics, with all the wrangles of strong rival political parties, all the excitement of dissent, and all the bubble of competitive political journalism. Perhaps even in its present tragedy Nigeria, outside Biafra, is more of an open society than most other West African countries. Yet that tragedy itself is the other consequence of the general ethos of indirect rule. By institutionalizing ethnic pluralism in Nigeria, the British created both the framework for latent violence and the potential for a meaningful competitive democracy in the years ahead. Institutionalized ethnic pluralism in a polity like Nigeria or Uganda was, to some extent, functionally in the same tradition as the old doctrine of 'Separation of Powers'. By creating a number of sub-centres of power within the polity, institutionalized ethnic pluralism tended to avert the danger of absolute government. Within each region of Nigeria, and perhaps pre-eminently in the North, there was indeed an intolerance of dissent. This intolerance characterized internal Buganda politics as well. Yet the strength of the regions was a form of devolution which has continued to make centralized authoritarianism in both Nigeria and Uganda less likely than it has been elsewhere in Africa.

In at least one respect Uganda until 1966 was even more of a liberal polity than old Nigeria. This can best be understood if we first remind ourselves that while the most successful application of indirect rule in Nigeria was in the isolationist North, the most successful application of the policy in Uganda was in the centrally-situated and dynamic Buganda. The Northern region of Nigeria was permitted to remain more traditionalist, more autonomous and more authoritarian internally than ever Buganda managed to be. Buganda's position at the centre of the country and of the national administrative machinery forced upon the region a degree of openness and national accountability never demanded of the Northern emirates of Nigeria. On the whole Buganda as a subpolity remained, it must be admitted, relatively *illiberal*. But her centrality saved her from being a closed society. And her energetic defensiveness prevented the country in turn from being too easily subjected to unitary control.

PRAGMATISM AND FREE SPEECH

Yet another factor which contributed to the liberalism of the Uganda polity was a kind of sophisticated pragmatism in the political culture. Ugandans have indeed been known to be intensely ideological. But here we must distinguish between visionary centralizing ideologies (like Pan-Africanism and Marxism) and immediate parochial ideologies (like a rationalized loyalty to one's own tribe). In much of Africa independence was accompanied by some degree of ideological innovation. New ideas competed for acceptance among intellectuals and political leaders. There was *Ujamaa* from Tanzania, *Consciencism* from Ghana, *Negritude* from Senegal. And even more widespread were rationalizations of one-party democracy and of unification movements.

Yet Uganda seemed to be, in relative terms, ideologically dormant. The rhetoric of its politics did not seem to share in the ferment of intellectual excitement evident elsewhere. Neither Pan-Africanism, nor Socialism, nor the vision of a one-party democracy seemed to have any great hold on the imaginations of Ugandans. In the visionary centralizing sense, the country's ethos was almost anti-ideological.

Yet, if Uganda did not lead in ideas, she certainly continued to lead in the freedom to express them. In old liberal terms again, Uganda had more freedom of expression for its indigenous citizens than almost any other African country. This did not take the form of freedom of the Press as such. On the contrary, there was hardly any freedom for the broadcasting media, and the newspapers became increasingly inhibited. What there was in Uganda was a soap-box freedom—the freedom to call a meeting at the Clock Tower in Kampala, for example, and attack Ministers of the Government by name. And for as long as that kind of freedom remained, even freedom of the Press retained some life. A newspaper might have been terrified of writing an editorial against the government, and could yet remain relatively free to report other people's attacks against the same government.

The Clock Tower was Kampala's equivalent of the Speakers' Corner in Hyde Park, London. The main difference was that the Clock Tower in Kampala had even greater democratic meaning than Hyde Park corner. Prominent critics of the government made some of their important speeches at the Tower; and Ministers of the Government sometimes turned up to defend their positions. The Clock Tower in Kampala introduced a populist theme into Uganda politics. There were times when the democratic meaning of the Clock Tower almost attained Athenian dimensions. In 1964 one prominent member of the ruling party in Uganda, Mr. John Kakonge, challenged another prominent member of the same party, Minister Adoko Nekyon, to a public debate on the meaning of 'scientific socialism' and its possible relevance for the country. Mr. Nekyon, then Minister of Planning, accepted the challenge. And these two people turned up at the Clock Tower and said their pieces—Nekyon defending the principles of private property, the family and liberal rights, and Kakonge, former Secretary General of the Uganda People's Congress, later asserting the merits of 'scientific socialism'.[1]

In the meantime party alignments had been changing. The alliance between Obote's Uganda People's Congress and Buganda's Kabaka Yekka had itself been a manifestation of Uganda's sophisticated pragmatism. The two parties seemed very different in orientation. And while one was led by a Northerner, the other was formed to defend the interests of the most privileged of the Southern regions. Yet the two parties formed an effective ruling alliance until one of them felt strong enough to dispense with the support of the other.

In the course of 1964 Uganda seemed to be drifting towards a form of one-party state as more and more members of Kabaka Yekka and the Democratic Party changed allegiances and joined

[1] *Uganda Argus*, June 1, 1964.

the UPC. In December 1964 the leader of the Opposition himself, Mr. Basil Bataringaya, crossed the floor. Yet the changing party allegiances altered the seating arrangements in Parliament without seriously reducing the vigour of debate in the polity as a whole. In the course of 1965 new issues and new forms of disagreements entered the scene. And the disagreements now were less clearly related to party labels than ever before.

EVENTS OF 1966

As the country entered 1966 the liberal openness of Uganda as a polity attained new vistas, and by so doing precipitated a series of events which culminated in the most serious explosion of violence in the country's recent history. In the Uganda Parliament in February 1966 a member of the Opposition virtually accused the Head of Government, the Minister of Defence and the deputy Army Commander of complicity in corrupt practices involving the transfer of gold from the Congo. The public accusation was itself remarkable. What was even more remarkable as a manifestation of an open society was that the accusation was formalized into a motion for the establishment of a commission of inquiry and was openly debated in Parliament. To crown the dramatic event, Parliament agreed, with only one contrary vote, that the commission of inquiry should be set up to investigate the allegations against the Head of Government and his two prominent colleagues.

Prime Minister Obote was at the time on tour in another part of the country. He took a few days to collect himself, and then left for the capital. Soon after his arrival Obote reasserted control and suspended the Constitution. Five Ministers were, in a surprise move, arrested while at a Cabinet meeting, and the Head of State, Sir Edward Mutesa (also the Kabaka), was relieved of the Presidency. And yet while the Constitution was thus suspended, constitutionalism as we have defined it, continued. For one thing, Obote did not reverse Parliament's decision to establish a commission of inquiry. He appointed three impartial commissioners— Sir Clement de Lestang of the Court of Appeal of Eastern Africa, Mr. Justice E. Miller, a judge of the High Court of Kenya, and Mr. Justice Augustine Saidi of the High Court of Tanzania. It was evident that none of the Commissioners could be suspected of being even remotely under the control of the Uganda Government. Much of the evidence on the allegations of corrupt practices was taken publicly and openly covered by the Press; Obote himself also gave evidence. What has been revealed so far would seem to clear the Government of the more serious of the charges. In any case, the mere fact that such a Commission was held at all was one of the most liberal acts of Dr. Obote's regime.

Another facet of constitutionalism which continued in spite of the suspension of the Constitution was the utilization of the Courts both by the deposed President and by the arrested Ministers.

The five Ministers were arrested in February 1966 under the terms of the (Colonial) Deportation Ordinance, pending an investigation of their activities, and taken to Northern Uganda. Their application for a writ of *habeus corpus* was dismissed by the High Court of Uganda which held that the Deportation Ordinance, despite its modification of fundamental rights, was consistent with Section 19 of the 1962 Constitution. But this was not the only legal issue at stake. The warrant for the ex-Ministers' arrest was signed on the day *following* their apprehension. This single day of 'wrongful arrest' led the arrested Ministers to threaten to take action for damages and the Uganda Government agreed, by a settlement out of Court, to pay each Minister the sum of £500.[1]

The five Ministers' next move was to appeal to the Court of Appeal for Eastern Africa in Nairobi, and it was again argued that the Deportation Ordinance was inconsistent with the human rights provisions of the 1962 Uganda Constitution. The appeal succeeded, and on receiving the judgment, Mr. Justice Fuad, of the High Court of Uganda, ordered the immediate release of the five men. On the other hand, the Deputy Director of Public Prosecutions claimed that, according to law, the five men should be produced in Court in Kampala, instead of being released at their place of detention. This apparent quibble over a point of law was of the utmost importance to the five ex-Ministers because Kampala (and indeed the nearest airport at Entebbe) was in Buganda and hence there was every likelihood of their immediate

[1] See *Uganda Argus*, March 31, 1966.

re-arrest under the emergency regulations which were in force in the Kingdom.[1]

It was, however, too late to give effect to Mr. Justice Fuad's ruling, for the Government, basing its actions on a different interpretation of *habeus corpus* procedure had already acted to bring the five men to Kampala on learning of the successful outcome of their appeal. Indeed, the Government law officers were correct, as the law relating to *habeus corpus* in Uganda was based on British practice prevailing in 1902 which required that persons illegally detained and on the point of being released should be produced before the Court. Mr. Justice Fuad's ruling was erroneously based on more recent British practice.

A further complication now arose as the aircraft bringing the five men to Entebbe airport was unexpectedly delayed in its departure, a circumstance which permitted the ex-Ministers to advance the argument that the Government had acted in bad faith in arranging for their transportation to Buganda which led, as anticipated, to their re-arrest under the emergency regulations. A further application for a writ of *habeus corpus* was therefore made by the ex-Ministers. But Mr. Justice Keatinge in the High Court held that the Government had not acted in bad faith by bringing the men into an emergency area, and the Appeal Court of Eastern Africa upheld his judgment. The Appeal Court took the view that the appellants had been fortuitously brought within an area which enabled the Minister of Internal Affairs to act under the emergency regulations. In the words of the judgment, the ex-Ministers 'were not brought within the area with the object of creating the power which was exercised by the Minister'.[2] The significant conclusion which may be drawn from these proceedings was the continuing answerability of the Government to the Courts even after the events which had shaken the country earlier in the year.

From early days of independence, the confrontation between Sir Edward Mutesa and Dr. Obote themselves had also taken the form of major constitutional clashes. It now culminated in the case brought by Sir Edward on March 11, 1966 against the Attorney General (Civil Suit No. 206 of 1966) in the High Court. Apart from a claim to costs, there were nine grounds

[1] See *Uganda Argus*, July 15 and 16, 1966.
[2] See *Uganda Argus*, December 9, 1966.

cited for the action. The three most important were perhaps that Prime Minister Obote's takeover of full power on February 24, 1966 was null and void; that the 1962 Constitution (with amendments) was still in force in its entirety and had been continually in force; and that, under the 1962 Constitution, Sir Edward Mutesa continued to be President.

No judgment was delivered from the High Court on these charges. This was because the Court procedure allowed the Government thirty days to agree to defend the suit and then another thirty days to prepare a case. But before that period was up the situation was transformed when on April 15 the Government introduced a new Constitution which effectively terminated any legal proceedings arising out of the abrogation of the 1962 Constitution. Furthermore, the new Constitution abolished Buganda's special federal status and reduced the power of her traditional institutions.

Buganda's *treaty complex* felt a new sense of outrage. The 1962 Constitution had been the legal expression of the independence agreement. It resembled a social contract creating a new society, and the parties to the contract surrendered some of their own 'natural' rights for the sake of the compact. Among the 'natural' rights of the Baganda was the right to the soil of Buganda. Yet, on the basis of the national compact of 1962, Buganda had surrendered her rights to the city of Kampala to the Central Government.

Moreover, when a social contract of this kind was broken, all rights reverted to their original holders and the logic of the situation required that Buganda should reassert her rights over the city of Kampala. The Lukiiko, or legislature of Buganda, proceeded to issue an ultimatum to the Central Government demanding that it should leave 'Buganda soil' by the end of May. Dr. Obote responded by declaring this an act of high treason. On May 24, 1966 the 'Battle of the Palace' took place. The national army attacked the Kabaka's residence, and after a sustained exchange with the Kabaka's defenders, the Palace fell. The Kabaka himself escaped, but Buganda as an autonomous entity seemed at last to have come to an end. The treaty complex of the Baganda, which had played so large a part in giving the country its constitutionalist style of politics, had culminated in a day of violent upheaval.

THE FUTURE

What of the future? As the months have gone by, it has become increasingly clear that the Buganda question in Uganda has not been settled. When the emergency in the region comes to an end, and the Baganda once again enter Uganda politics, it will no doubt be with greater circumspection than they had exercised in 1966. But the Buganda style of dissent and of legalistic response to certain challenges might yet reassert itself.

In the meantime Uganda somehow still remains more of an open society than many other African countries. Courts martial involving matters of national security are held openly and evidence for both sides frankly reported. The Government is still taken to Court on certain matters. The validity of the Constitution, though now legally confirmed on the grounds that a revolution had taken place in May 1966, had first to be publicly questioned in a Court of Law and be subjected to arguments advanced against its legitimacy. The Government's decision to extend the state of emergency in Buganda was publicly criticized and argued about. And that remarkable newspaper of the governing party, *The People*, continues to be irreverent about the Party itself, and frank even about an attempted assassination of a senior member of the Government.

The future of Uganda as a vigorous liberal polity is indeed still very much in doubt. A state of emergency in the biggest region continues, a number of people, although relatively few, are still in detention, and elections, after a recent postponement, are unlikely for another five years. But there are signs that some significant features of the old style of politics might still survive. Milton Obote remains a brilliant political tactician. In spite of the events of 1966, it is not his style to force the pace of change too precipitately. Latent violence in Uganda may, perhaps, still continue. But there is hope also for the survival of some of the old vigorous constitutionalist habits.

8 The Multiple Marginality of the Sudan[1]

The bridge concept of the Sudan is fairly common, but it is normally applied to the position of the Sudan in relation to Black Africa on one side and Arab Africa on the other. The Sudan is therefore conceived as one of the bridges between two sectors of the African Continent.

But in fact the Sudan serves comparable functions between other segments of the total African pattern. One could see the Sudan as a bridge between Arabic-speaking Africa and English-speaking Africa; between Christian Africa and Muslim Africa; between the Africa of homogenized mass nation states of the future and the Africa of deep ethnic cleavage of the present; and finally, between West Africa as a cultural unit and Eastern Africa.

And yet the use of the word 'bridge' is misleading even when applied to Afro-Arab relations. It is not really true that the Sudan plays a role of *uniting* Black Africa with Africa north of the Sahara. Arabs of the north who need to influence the Black Continent do not normally use Khartoum as the route towards that influence, nor do Black Africans who wish to put forward policies that should affect Arab orientations come to the Sudanese Government for advice and the ultilization of its good offices in that cause. The bridge concept of the Sudan claims too much. The Sudan is not bridging a chasm between Black Africa and Arab Africa, nor does it play any special linking or mediating role between these two sectors.

In this essay therefore we have preferred the term 'marginality'. Our sense of the term marginality is not quite the same as that used by Robert E. Park and subsequent sociologists. The sociological meaning of the term normally implies some kind

[1] Presented at the Conference on 'The Sudan in Africa', University of Khartoum, February 5 to 11, 1968.

of minority status, or of social deviance. The marginal man is he who hovers on the borderline between those who are in and those who are out, and his behaviour is sometimes motivated by a desire for greater absorption into the dominant community, or at least for greater grudging respect from that community.

Our sense of marginality has things in common with the sociological sense. But it is not our intention to imply any kind of deviance in the status of the Sudan, or lack of acceptance of the Sudan by this or that group. In the ultimate analysis we use the term marginality to denote specific traits in the Sudan which place it significantly in an intermediate category between two distinct sectors of Africa. Sometimes the intermediacy gives the Sudan a double identity both in her capacity as an African country in a racial sense and an Arab country in a cultural sense. But essentially the notion of marginality we intend is that which places the Sudan on a frontier between two distinct African universes—a frontier which shares some of the characteristics of both of those universes.

THE ARABS AS AFRO-ASIANS

The marginality of the Sudan as between the Arabs and the Africans has links with the marginality of the Arabs themselves, as between Africa and Asia. The Arabs as a race defy classification by continent distributed as they are on both sides of what divides Asia from Africa.

In his more parochial days (and before the breakup between Egypt and Syria) Chief Awolowo of Nigeria once asserted:

The United Arab Republic, the pet creature of Nasser, which has one foot in Africa and another in the Middle East, is the very antithesis of a workable African community.[1]

This sort of reasoning is connected with the sentiment which made Nkrumah assert that:

No accident of history . . . can ever succeed in turning an inch of African soil into an extension of any other continent.

[1] See *Awo: The Autobiography of Chief Obafemi Awolowo* (Cambridge 1960), p. 312.

Nkrumah had in mind the kind of integrationist claims made by France about Algeria, or the claims of Portugal that Angola and Mozambique were part of Portugal. But could North Africa also be regarded as a westward extension of the Arabian Peninsula?[1]

One possible answer is that it depends upon what proportion of the Arab world is now in Africa and how much of it is still outside. At the time of the Arab conquest in the seventh century, it was indeed true that the Arabian Peninsula was extending itself into the Fertile Crescent and into Africa. But had not the balance of preponderance now changed as between the different segments? In some ways is this not the equivalent of the change in relationship between England and the United States? The 'mother country' is now overshadowed by her former imperial extension—and the danger now is of Britain becoming an extension of the United States, rather than the other way round.[2]

Does the analogy hold in the relationship between Arab Africa and the rest of the Arab world? It certainly holds as between the old Arabian Peninsula proper on one side and Arab Africa and the Fertile Crescent combined on the other. Countries of the peninsula proper—Saudi Arabia especially, from which the Arab invasions of the seventh century originated—are now overshadowed in inter-Arab influence, perhaps by even Iraq and Syria on their own.

But in the context of African exclusiveness we would need to put the Arabian Peninsula and the Fertile Crescent together on one side and distinguish them from Arab Africa on the other side of the Red Sea. Yet even here the balance of preponderance is on Africa's side. As Boutros-Ghali put it in a book published in 1963, 'It must not be forgotten that 60 per cent of the Arab community and 72 per cent of the Arab land are in Africa'.[3]

---

[1] This question is also asked and discussed in similar terms in my book *Towards a Pax-Africana: A Study of Ideology and Ambition* (Weidenfeld & Nicolson and the University of Chicago Press, 1967), pp. 109–17.

[2] The best literary expression of this danger is perhaps Bernard Shaw's play *The Applecart*. The United States Ambassador applies to England's King Magnus for permission to join the Commonwealth on the argument that America is a former British possession. But King Magnus saw the danger to his Kingdom, and to the leadership of Britain in the Commonwealth, should the United States become a member of the club.

[3] Boutros-Ghali, 'The Foreign Policy of Egypt' in Joseph Black and Kenneth Thompson, *Foreign Policies in a World of Change* (New York: 1963), p. 328.

In other words, the situation was such that it had become easier to think of the rest of the Arab world as an extension of Arab Africa than the other way round. But whatever the preponderance, the main issue here is that the Arabs as a race cannot easily be classified either as Asians or as Africans in exclusive terms. In fact Pan-Africanism itself became a major paradox precisely because it involved the Arabs. Pan-Africanism was at once continentally exclusive (in that only African states were eligible) and at the same time a link between sub-Saharan Africa and the world of *Asian* nationalism. The marginality of the Arabs as a people who are neither entirely Asian nor entirely African was decisive in giving the Pan-African movement the paradoxical quality of being both Afro-centric in intention and Afro-Asian in some of its consequences. Tom Mboya of Kenya put his finger on the paradox when he observed:

> . . . From my experience at Pan-African Conferences, and observing their interest in Pan-African matters, I have come to believe that the great majority of Arabs in North Africa look on themselves as African. From our side there has been increasing recognition and acceptance of the Arabs as Africans. . . . But if there is hostility between Asia and Africa, there is bound to be a reflection of this conflict between the Arabs of North Africa and the Africans South of the Sahara.[1]

THE SUDANESE AS AFRO-ARABS

But if the Arabs constitute the most important link between Africa and Asia, the Sudanese constitute the most important point of contact between Arab Africa and Negro Africa. There is first the very phenomenon of racial mixture and inter-marriage in the Northern parts of the Sudan, coupled with the fact that a large proportion of Arab Sudanese are in fact Arabized Negroes, rather than being ethnically semitic. For many of them their Arabness is a cultural acquisition, rather than a racial heredity.

[1] See Mboya, *Freedom and After* (Boston: Little, Brown & Co., 1963), pp. 234–5. This point is discussed in a related context in my paper 'Africa and the Third World'. See Mazrui, *On Heroes and Uhuru Worship* (London: Longmans, 1967), pp. 212–13.

It is therefore the Sudanese more than any other group of Arabs that have given the Arabs a decisive Negro dimension in this racial sense. The distinction between Arabs and Negro-Africa is not dichotomous, but has the complexity of a continuum. That was one reason why the Organization of African Unity is in its composition, 'multi-pigmentational', instead of being a straight division between black Africa and the so-called 'white Africa of the North'. As we have indicated earlier that Arabs defy continentalistic generalizations, we should remember that the Arabs as a race also defy straight pigmentational classifications. They vary in colour from white Arabs of Syria and Lebanon, brown Arabs of the Hadramaut, to the black Arabs of the Sudan. Within Africa itself the range of colour among Arabs is also from white to black, though each colour cannot be as smoothly allocated to a specific area. But the stamp of blackness on Arabism comes pre-eminently from the Sudan. The Sudan has made the biggest single contribution to the fact that Arabism includes a Negro dimension. This is the sort of thing which has often impressed American Negroes on their trip through Africa. In the United States the divide between white men and Negroes is more emphatic. While it is possible to meet Negroes who are almost white, it would be impossible to think of an Anglo-Saxon American who was partly black. The dominant group was more purist in its insistence on retaining its own skin personality, but in Africa the continuum between Arab and Negro is smoother, and the Sudan especially has helped to give it this smoothness. And so W. E. B. du Bois, the great American Negro founding father of Pan-Africanism, could make the following observation:

Anyone who has travelled in the Sudan knows that most of the 'Arabs' he has met are dark skinned, sometimes practically black, often have Negroid features, and hair that may be almost Negro in quality. It is then obvious that in Africa the term 'Arab' . . . is often misleading. The Arabs were too nearly akin to Negroes to draw an absolute colour line.[1]

But it is not only the racial mixture and general acculturation in the North which makes the Sudan an important point of contact

[1] See du Bois, *The World and Africa* (First published, 1946; New York: International Publishers, 1965, enlarged edition), p. 184.

between Arabism and Negroism. There is also the division between Northern Sudan and the South, giving the country a segment which was not Arabized even culturally.

Indeed, the Sudan as a whole is not quite as Arabized as some Northern Sudanese would sometimes prefer. On the basis of the 1955–56 census it has been estimated that of the 13 million peoples of the Sudan, about 40 per cent were Arab, 30 per cent Southern, 13 per cent Western, 12 per cent Beja and Nuba, 3 per cent Nubian, and the rest were foreigners and miscellaneous. When using the language criterion, 52 per cent were Arabic-speaking and 48 per cent spoke other languages. The twelve years since that census was taken might have made some significant differences in those percentages. In any case, although the Sudan might not be quite as Arab as it is sometimes imagined, what matters sometimes is the phenomenon of self-conception among Sudanese of influence. Distinguished Arabic-speakers of the North, and distinguished Southerners, have all been known to exaggerate the ethnic chasm which separates Northerners from the peoples of the South. In the words of the then President of the Sudan African National Union (SANU), Aggrey Jadan, at the March 1965 Khartoum Conference on the Southern Sudan:

> The Sudan falls sharply into two distinct areas, both in geographical area, ethnic group, and cultural systems. The Northern Sudan is occupied by a hybrid Arab race who are united by their common language, common culture, and common religion; and they look to the Arab world for their cultural and political inspiration. The people of the Southern Sudan, on the other hand, belong to the African ethnic group of East Africa. They do not only differ from the hybrid Arab race in origin, arrangement and basic systems, but in all conceivable purposes. . . . There is nothing in common between the various sections of the community; nobody of shared beliefs, no identity of interests, no local signs of unity and above all, the Sudan has failed to compose a single community.[1]

[1] Khartoum Conference on the South, March 1965 Documents; Speech by Aggrey Jadan (Mimeo), p. 4, cited by George W. Shepherd, Jr., 'National Integration and the Southern Sudan', *The Journal of Modern African Studies*, Vol. IV, No. 2, October 1966, pp. 195, 196. I am indebted to this article for bibliographical guidance and some insights.

This is obviously a hyperbolic formulation of the differences between the Northern Sudan and the South. But when we are discussing the Sudan from the point of view of marginality, this very exaggeration has its uses. For it asserts that one and the same country is, in one area, completely Negro and, in another, completely Arab. The enclosure of these two ethnic personalities within a single territorial entity is itself an approximation to the concept of Afro-Arab marginality for the Sudan. Whether we take the Sudan as a dichotomous duality of the kind claimed by Aggrey Jadan, or we take it as an ethnic continuum, or as an inter-racial mixture, the country still emerges as a paradigm case of an Afro-Arab dual identity.

THE RELIGIOUS FRONTIER

But when we refer to a cultural difference between Northern and Southern Sudan, the difference inevitably includes a religious dimension. No other African country has been as closely identified with a schism between Islam and Christianity as the Sudan. The Nigerian Civil War has indeed been sometimes interpreted in neo-religious terms—in terms of vigorous Christian Ibos suffering the wrath of previously humiliated and profoundly conservative Muslim Northerners. But the naiveté of interpreting the Nigerian Civil War in these terms is so easy to expose that only a few popular columnists would now press it. The majority of Federal soldiers are not Muslim, nor of course is the Head of the Federal Government, Colonel Gowon. For the time being the Western Region of Nigeria is on the side of the Federal Government, and that Region is decisively Christian in power-structure.

But the naiveté of interpreting the Sudanese problem in religious terms is not quite as easy to expose. Much of the bad press that the Sudanese Government has received in many countries has rested in part on the assumption that Southern resistance was aroused as a response to religious persecution. Yet the figures of the different religious denominations in the South far from established that the South was basically Christian. In 1955 it was estimated that there were 22,500 to 23,000 Southern Muslims; 16,500 to 17,500 Northern Muslims resident in the three Southern Provinces; 25,000 to 30,000 Protestants in the South and 180,000 to 200,000 Catholics,[1] this out of a total population for the South of some 4 million.

Perhaps only the arrogance of a Christian press could describe a population which is only one-tenth Christian as being 'basically Christian'. What gave the Government's policy the appearance of religious persecution were the expulsions of missionaries and the introduction of measures to put the mission schools under the control of the Ministry of Education. Government control of mission schools is a principle which has been adopted in different forms by other governments in Africa, including the Uganda Government. On the issue of expelling Christian missionaries, again this has not been unknown in Christian countries elsewhere in Africa. A distinction needs to be drawn between religious toleration in the sense of allowing nationals to practise their own religion, and toleration in the sense of allowing missionaries from *outside* to propagate that religion on a particular scale (two-thirds of the missionaries in the Sudan used to be Italians; the rest had been a mixture of predominantly Protestant Europeans).

It is true that there are some dangers in the feelings sometimes expressed by Northerners that there is enough division between the two parts of the country without creating a sizable Christian enclave 'within' a Muslim society. But the reasoning is not devoid of sense if it is assessed from the point of view of the demands for national integration. The argument here is that if the Southerners have to have their traditional African ways changed, they had better be changed in the direction of greater homogeneity with the North. And this means Arabization and Islamization, rather than Italianization in religious terms. It makes sense therefore that Governmental policy—committed to the reduction of differences between North and South—should have prescribed the teachings of Islam to students in Southern Schools.

Western commentators sometimes assume that while it is fair game to let Christian missionaries loose among simple African villagers, it is sometimes approaching religious persecution to let Muslim missionaries loose within the same population. And so the old idea of making the Southern Provinces of the

---

[1] See *Report of the Commission of Inquiry into the Disturbances in the Southern Sudan during August 1955* (Khartoum, 1956), p. 9. See also M. O. Beshir, *The Southern Sudan: Background to Conflict* (London; Hurst and Co., 1967), pp. 6–8.

Sudan an exclusive preserve of Christian missionaries was seldom challenged. As James S. Coleman put it in referring to a dominant trend in Western attitudes at large, 'Tropical Africa held a special attraction for the [Christian] missionary. The heathen was his target, and of all human groups the Africans were believed to be the most heathen'.[1]

In the Southern Provinces of the Sudan this policy assumed monopolistic dimensions. Islam was deliberately kept out even to the extent of discouraging Muslim names or Muslim dress among the Southern population. In the rest of Africa the great instruments of national or cultural integration have often been the merchants and traders. The spread of certain important African languages or other cultural traits has often been due to the disseminating role of merchants. But in the Sudan the British took a decisive stand. As Sir Douglas Newbold, the Governor of Kordofan in the years 1932–38, put it once in blunt simplicity: 'We don't want to introduce Arab merchants from the North.'[2]

Given this desire then to bridge the gulf between the North and the South on the withdrawal of British Rule, it was almost inevitable that the North should seek to break the educational and proselytizing monopoly which Christian missions had enjoyed for so long. This determination was accentuated by the memory of the mutinies which broke out on independence as Southern dissidents sought to detach the region from the country as a whole if southern autonomy could not be assured otherwise.

It is true that the Northerners drifted into excesses in their enthusiasm for greater integration. Several missions were reported to have been told that they were not to treat patients, although no alternative medical facilities were in fact available for the populations concerned. There were also bizarre reports about Christian missionaries being expected to teach Muslim theology.[3]

And then the sheer military repression which has lasted for a

[1] See Coleman's chapter on sub-Saharan Africa in *The Politics of the Developing Areas* edited by Gabriel A. Almond and James S. Coleman (Princeton, N.J.: Princeton University Press, 1960), p. 278.

[2] See K. D. D. Henderson, *The Making of the Modern Sudan* (London: Faber, 1953). Shepherd cites Muddathir Abdel Rahim 'The Development of British Policy in the Sudan, 1899–1949' (Central Archives, 1965), pp. 10–13, on the same question.

[3] See the account in *The Economist* (London), November 19, 1960.

decade has sometimes been ruthless and devoid of adequate moral restraint. The process of integrating the South with the North may not have made much progress in the first decade after independence. It might even have been a case of two steps backwards, one step forward—by no means the most effective way of reaching one's destination if that destination is ahead rather than to the rear.

When the history of religion in the Sudan and Uganda is looked at as one entity, a different kind of continuum manifests itself. In Uganda, too, religion has for generations played a part in complicating political issues. Protestants, Catholics and Muslims have competed for each other in Uganda to secure greater influence in the nation's affairs. It has been suggested that Islam was once a unifying force in Uganda—it unified Protestants and Catholics into a single political posture. And just as an Arab government and European missionaries have been more recently vying for the control of Southern Sudan, so did Arab settlers and European immigrants struggle for supremacy in Uganda towards the end of the last century. In the words of an official of the British East Africa Company in 1888 when Arab influence was on the ascendancy in Buganda: 'These events render the question now paramount: Is Arab or European power henceforth to prevail in Central Africa?'[1]

This was perhaps the time of maximum unity between Protestants and Catholics in Uganda. When Lugard came he managed to rally the Christian armies of both denominations, and put an end to the Muslim threat and the power of the Muslim Party. But in so doing Lugard 'thus dissolved the last link binding the Catholic and the Protestants'.[2]

In different forms the division between Protestants and Catholics in Uganda persisted to Independence. Indeed, some of the political parties in Uganda were supposed to be organized on a basis of denominational loyalty. Thus the Democratic Party in Uganda came to be identified with Catholics and to attract wide support from Catholic voters. The party was initially also backed by some of the leaders of the Catholic Church. The Uganda People's Congress, on the other hand, was to some extent

---

[1] Cited by Roland Oliver, *The Missionary Factor in East Africa* (London: Longmans 1965 Edition), pp. 133-4.
[2] See Oliver, *ibid.*, p. 142.

identified with Protestants—though this identification was less easily demonstrable than the identification of the Democratic Party with Catholic aspirations. The situation was compounded by the emergence of Kabaka Yekka, a third party whose basis of affiliation was not denominational but regional. Kabaka Yekka— Kabaka Alone—was dedicated to the preservation of the proud autonomy and identity of the Buganda region. Within Buganda itself the Protestants were the élite denomination controlling the establishment. The Catholic were less privileged. But politically the Baganda were more Buganda nationalists than they were either Protestants or Catholics in their ultimate commitment.

The Muslims were much less important in the political sphere, though their influence was sometimes given a boost as a way of gaining support for one Christian sector against another, or for one political party against another.

In an exaggerated kind of way it has been suggested that Uganda was 'the Ireland of Africa', with its division between partisan Catholics and partisan Protestants. In reality the religious dimension is much less prominent, much less deeply rooted than it was in Ireland. Nevertheless, we can speak of Uganda as being, in part, a country of sectarian differences between one Christian denomination and another in the socio-political field.

If we turn our eyes now and look at Northern Sudan, we see sectarian politics at play too—only in this case it is between Muslim denominations, rather than between Christian ones. The political divisions in the first Republic of Sudan following independence had a marked sectarian theme. Even those political leaders who privately deplored the influence of religion on politics started by finding it necessary or expedient to associate themselves with the name of a respected Seyyid in order to win popular support. When the Independence Front—consisting mainly of the Umah party—emerged in 1945 with the support of Seyyid Abdel Raham el Mahdi, leader of the Ansar (Mahdist) Sect, their opponents, the national front, claimed support of Seyyid Ali el Mirghani, leader of the Khatmiyya Sect, the other major denomination in Muslim Sudan. Seyyid Ali himself, while preferring not to make public statements on political subjects, did not deny his association with the pro-Egyptian Front.

What all this means is that Sudanese politics, especially in the first few years after independence, were partly politics between Muslim denominations in competition against each other. By the same token Ugandan politics, especially in the period just before independence, but to some extent also for some time after independence, were politics between Christian denominations in competition with each other. And then between the Northern Sudan and Uganda might be placed the three provinces of Southern Sudan. The provinces constituted to some extent a line of battle between a Muslim government and Christian missions. To the north of these provinces are the politics of Muslim against Muslim. To the south of these provinces in Uganda are the politics of Christian against Christian. And the Southern provinces themselves to some extent symbolize Africa's most dramatic confrontation between local Islamic authority and expatriate Christianity.

THE LIMITS OF INTEGRATION

But these inter-denominational differences in the north should not disguise one important aspect of the character of the country. If you took the predominant northern region on its own as a measure, the Sudan is one of the most integrated countries in Africa. The greatest achievement of Islam and Arabic culture in Northern Sudan was, in the words of Yusuf Fadl Hasan, 'the creation of a feeling of cohesion among the heterogeneous inhabitants of the country'.[1]

In spite of the differences between Khatmiyya of the Eastern Sudan and the Ansar of the West, and notwithstanding significant tribal feelings among groups like the Nuba and the Beja communities, there has persisted in Northern Sudan a striking degree of national consensus.

For those who regard a capacity for some liberal competitive institutions as an index of a significant measure of national integration, the Sudan affords interesting evidence in that direction. Even the assumption of power by General Aboud in November 1958 was by no means an outcome of real parliamentary failure. Sudanese democracy at that time had neither

[1] Fadl Hasan, *The Arabs and the Sudan* (Edinburgh: Edinburgh University Press, 1967), p. 181.

stiffened into the authoritarianism of Nkrumah's regime, nor disintegrated into the corrupt anarchy of a Balewa regime of Nigeria. 'The army [in the Sudan] came to power . . . when one coalition was collapsing and another was about to be formed. The new one between Umah . . . and the National Unionist Party . . . was likely to give the stability which the old one had failed to provide. Instead, the Generals took over and the pad of parliament, which softens the blows of sudden change, was lost.'[1]

One need not go quite as far as *The Economist* in the above quotation in favourably assessing the stabilizing chances of an Umah–NUP coalition. The point to grasp, however, is that Sudanese democracy had not yet inherently failed when the army took over—except in the somewhat cynical and uncompromising sense that any democracy that is overthrown by soldiers is by definition a failure. The peaceful poll of the February 1958 elections was taken by many observers to augur well for the future.[2]

That nine months later in November 1958 soldiers decided to try their hand at politicizing was not sufficient reason to dismiss the implications of that augury.

In October 1964, General Aboud himself fell from power. Aboud's fall was itself a triumph of public opinion in the north, and an index to some degree of meaningful national consensus. A series of demonstrations in Khartoum, some of which were led by University teachers, shattered the confidence of the military regime. In some ways the fall of Aboud was the most striking manifestation yet of the democratic potential of the Sudan. It is not in every country that the military would bow to popular indignation. It is not in every country in Africa that popular indignation expresses itself in spite of possible reprisals from government forces. It is true that the military's vulnerability as a regime was partly due to its own internal division. And yet the very divisions within the military forces seemed to have been partly connected with patriotic sentiment and with a reluctance to shed too much Sudanese blood in the streets of Khartoum. One could therefore say that the fall of Aboud in October 1964,

---

[1] See *The Economist*, November 14, 1959.
[2] *The Economist*, March 15, 1958. See also, Harold F. Gosnell, 'The 1958 Elections in the Sudan', *The Middle East Journal*, Vol. XV, 1958.

was as creditable to Aboud and the military at large as it was to demonstrators in the streets demanding a return to parliamentary politics. In the conditions of Africa today, and indeed of the Middle–East, soldiers are to be given national credit when they are too inhibited to slaughter too many of their compatriots.

And yet the inhibitions of the Sudan soldiers do not extend to the south. This is what dramatizes the marginality of the Sudan in this area of national integration. On the one hand, the main part of the country has achieved a high degree of cultural cohesion. The north on its own could easily be a nation state in a classical European sense within little more than a generation. On the other hand, relations between the north and the south constitute one of the most acute crises of cleavage in the African Continent as a whole. Sudanese democracy in the north is by no means all that secure and could be overthrown again in the days ahead. But, then, so could French democracy today. But in France, as in the Sudan, there has persisted what *The Economist* once called 'a surprising instinct for democratic forms'.[1] And the instinct might be a measure of the people's capacity to identify with each other, and therefore to refrain from certain excesses of treatment. Yet the Arab-Sudanese democratic instinct has often failed to be effective as a deterrent against Arab brutalization of the south.

THE SUDAN AND WEST AFRICA

If it was Islam and its culture which partly helped to give Northern Sudan its degree of homogeneity, it was also Islam which has made the Sudan one of the few countries in *Eastern* Africa which has a strong historical connection with the flow of history in *West* Africa. In fact the country today bears the name not simply of a state, but of what has been called a 'civilization'. In the words of Roland Oliver and J. D. Fage:

> Stretching right across sub-Saharan Africa from the Red Sea to the mouth of the Senegal, and right down the central highland spine of Bantu Africa from the Nile sources to

[1] *The Economist* was referring to the Sudan. See the issue of December 7, 1957.

Southern Rhodesia, we find the axis of what we shall call the Sudanic civilization. The central feature of this civilization was the incorporation of the various African peoples concerned into states whose institutions were so similar that they must have derived from a common source.[1]

In some way Oliver and Fage defined the boundaries of the Sudanic civilization in a maximal sense. Saburi Biobaku and Muhammad Al-Hajj define a stronger link between the Niger-Chad region on one side and the Sudan on the other. But they also see the Sudanic area as being wider than even that: 'The distinction between the two regions is, of course modern, because to the early Arab geographers, '*Bilad al-Sudan*' extended from the Red Sea and the Horn of Africa in the east to the shore of the Atlantic in the west.'[2]

It would be almost true to say that the Republic of the Sudan today is, in an important sense, an extension of West Africa. In its origins the Sudanic civilization might well have spread from the north southwards, and then from the east westwards, making some of the West African kingdoms something approaching an extension of the Sudanic heart on the Nile. This interpretation is itself historically uncertain. But even if it were true that the Sudanic civilization spread, in its second stage, from the east westwards, the fact remains that in West Africa there have been a *number* of nations sharing that civilization, and there continue to be. This numerical imbalance might force us to conclude that it is the Republic on the Nile which is an extension of West Africa, rather than the other way round. But even if that is not admissible, what matters is that this east–west historical link gives the Sudan one more dimension of marginality. The rising sun on the East Coast and the setting sun on the West Coast of Africa 'both' momentarily cast rays on a slice of civilization which extends across the whole span of this part of the continent, from the Red Sea to the Atlantic Ocean.

Controversy about the direction of ideological traffic between Eastern Sudan and Western is something which has continued

[1] See Oliver and Fage, *A Short History of Africa* (Penguin Library, 1962), p. 44.

[2] See Biobaku and Al-Hajj, 'The Sudanese Mahdiyya and the Niger-Chad region' in *Islam and Tropical Africa*, edited by I. M. Lewis (published for the International African Institute by the Oxford University Press, 1966), p. 429.

to the present day. Which way did the ideas flow in the Sudanic belt? Biobaku and Al-Hajj first affirm that there has been 'constant traffic between the Niger-Chad region and the Sudan from the distant past to the present day'. The purpose of their collaborative paper is to attempt to show that the *Fulani Jihads* had given rise to the Sudanese Mahdiyya, and that the latter sought support and expansion (outside the Sudan) mainly in the Niger-Chad region. The two authors go on to argue that much of the Mahdist literature which was current in the Niger-Chad region in the 19th century found its way to the Sudan. They also claim evidence to show that the Sudanese Mahdi, Muhammad Ahmad, was influenced by ideas from the Niger-Chad region.[1]

But whatever the origins of Mahdism it was certainly Muhammad Ahmad of Eastern Sudan who led the most internationally significant Mahdist movement in Africa. In any case, after the original bubble of Mahdist ideas, it became rather difficult to be sure about the direction of the ideological traffic in this sphere of Muslim activity. Biobaku and Al-Hajj refer to the Sudan's influence on Nigeria. When the Mahdists in the Sudan were again allowed to function under the leadership of the Mahdist's son, al-Sayyid Abd al-Rahman, there was 'almost an automatic revival of Mahdism in Nigeria'. The Nigerian leader communicated with al-Sayyid Abd al-Rahman and acted as his agent in Nigeria. But the British authorities in Nigeria were more apprehensive than their counterparts in the Sudan about Mahdism at that period. Malam Said, the Nigerian leader of the movement, was therefore arrested in 1923 and deported. The British authorities in Nigeria remained sensitive to the possibilities of Mahdist uprisings, and precautions were taken insofar as this was feasible.[2]

Thomas Hodgkin has argued that Northern Nigeria for a long time remained isolated from the main stream of Islamic reform. Nevertheless, some ideological interplay between Northern Nigeria and the Eastern Sudan was fairly constant. Even when ways of reforming judicial and legal arrangements in Northern Nigeria were being explored there remained a tendency to take

---

[1] Biobaku and Al-Hajj, 'The Sudanese Mahdiyya and the Niger-Chad region', *op. cit.*, pp. 426, 431.
[2] See Alan Burns, *History of Nigeria* (4th edition, London, 1948), pp. 182ff. Also see Biobaku and Al-Hajj, pp. 436–7.

a look at the Eastern Sudan for possible guide-lines on structural changes in this sphere of Islamic life.[1]

Nigeria, of course, is not the only part of West Africa that has had this kind of ideological connection with the Eastern Sudan. The former French Soudan, now Mali, has also displayed manifestations comparable to the events which have taken place in Eastern Sudan and Northern Nigeria. 'In fact, throughout the French speaking territories of the Savannahland of West Africa, Mahdist manifestations appeared here and there, and from time to time, causing much unrest and agitation.'[2]

It is these considerations which have helped to give Eastern Sudan yet another feature of marginality—at once a piece of the Nile Valley and its heritage, and a piece of the Sudanic civilization which extends to the Western Coast of Africa.

THE BOUNDARY OF LANGUAGE

Finally a word about the Sudan as a country on a linguistic borderline. We might think of Africa as being divided into three main linguistic segments—English-speaking Africa, French-speaking Africa, and Arabic-speaking Africa. Of course, there is considerable overlapping between these countries, and especially as regards the Maghred States which are at once Arabic-speaking and French-speaking. But the fascination of the Sudan is that it signifies a borderline case between English-speaking Africa and Arabic-speaking Africa—a rarer phenomenon than the Franco-Arabic duality.

Perhaps this aspect of the marginality of the Sudan has nowhere else been better illustrated than in a simple fact concerning some courses in diplomacy at Makerere University College in Uganda. For a number of years the Department of Political Science at Makerere has organized courses in diplomacy for foreign service officials from a number of African States. In reality virtually all the states that have participated in these courses, or indeed have been invited to participate in these

[1] For the discussion on Islamic Reform by Hodgkin see, for example, his short piece 'Tradition and Reform in Muslim Africa', *West Africa*, September 22, 1956. See also Hodgkin, 'Islam, History and Politics', *The Journal of Modern African Studies*, Vol. I, No. 1, March 1963.

[2] Biobaku and Al-Hajj, *op. cit.*, p. 437.

courses, have been English-speaking states. The one exception
has been the Sudan. The Makerere Diplomatic Courses have had
Sudanese participation all along. This could not be explained
simply in terms of the Sudan's nearness to Uganda; for Uganda
has other neighbours on its borders who are not English-speakers
and who are not invited to participate in the Makerere courses.
Nor have the Sudanese appeared particularly incongruous in a
community of English-speaking Africans. They were near
enough as a category to be adequately assimilated into the body
of African diplomats attending the Makerere courses.

Perhaps the Anglo-Arabic marginality of the Sudan partly
goes back to that historical anomaly of an Anglo-Egyptian
condominium over the Sudan. The Sudan was the only country
in Africa that was at one and the same time a colony of an English-
speaking power and a colony of an Arabic-speaking country. In
reality, of course, the imperial control was effectively exerted by
Britain rather than by Egypt. But even this factor contributed
towards giving meaning to the marginality. After all the English
language was up against a pre-existent Arabic presence in the
Sudan. It needed a strong English-speaking influence in the
Sudan to give English any chance at all as a medium of intellectual discourse. It was therefore the preponderance of the British
over the Egyptians in the condominium which helped to give the
Sudan an Anglo-Arabic duality.

Today Arabic remains definitely the senior partner in this
linguistic alliance. Much of the most important Sudanese
business continues to be conducted in Arabic. In fact Arabic has
been gaining ascendancy since the departure of the British, and
has recaptured most of the educational system below University
level. From the Sudan, as from India, come reports of a declining
mastery of the English language; and debates range as to whether
the decline is something worth worrying about. Nevertheless
English does maintain an important place in the Sudan, especially
among the graduate intelligentsia.

But the place of English in the Northern Sudan is not the only
factor which has given the country as a whole this linguistic
marginality. There is also the place of English in the Southern
provinces to be taken into account. During the colonial period
the educational system set up in the South was deliberately
committed to the suppression of Arabic as far as possible. This was

part of the presumed competition between Islamic culture and British civilization in this area of Africa. In the words of one British administrator in the course of the preliminary discussions prior to the Juba Conference of 1947, 'We the British, who, whatever our failings, are better qualified than any other race, by tradition and taste and training, to lead primitives up the path of civic progress, are going to stand guard till the South can dispense with a guard, and I am not going to see the South dominated by an Arab civilization in Khartoum, which is more alien to them than our own.'[1]

Caught up in this battle of civilizations was the issue of the medium of education. And so 'the British official and missionary policy was to encourage the use of English rather than Arabic. . . .'[2]

Since Independence there has been a more concerted attempt by the Sudanese Government to give Arabic a new status in the South. Arab teachers, new Arabic curricula and increased promotion of the teaching of Arabic are all major aspects of the entire Arabization policy pursued in the South since Independence. The place of English in the next generation of Southerners may be less important than the place that English has enjoyed so far among the small group of Southern intelligentsia. But whatever the future of English in the Sudan it has so far continued to give this country a quality of linguistic twilight—an intermediate stage between the universe of Arabic in Africa and the universe of the English language.

CONCLUSION

We have tried to demonstrate in this essay that the Sudan is not simply an intermediate category between Arab Africa and Negro Africa, but is in fact marginal in a number of other ways as well. Even on the issue of Arabism in relation to Negroism there is a double level of marginality. The Arabs, as we have tried to show, are themselves a people who defy classification on the

---

[1] Letter of January 5, 1947 from B.G.A. to the Governor of Equatoria Province, Khartoum Conference on the South, March, 1965 documents. Cited by Shepherd, *op. cit.*

[2] Shepherd, *ibid.*, pp. 199–200.

basis of continents. They have nations both in Africa and in Asia. They have a quality of being Afro-Asians.

If the Arabs are Afro-Asians, the Sudanese are Afro-Arabs, both in their internal Northern mixture as Arabized Africans, and in the division between Arabic-speaking Northern Sudan and the rest of the country to the south.

As part of this cultural divide there has to be included the position of the Sudan as a focus of what is sometimes interpreted as a confrontation between Islamic Africa and Christian Africa. In reality the confrontation is between a Muslim Government and Christian Missions, or between the new policy of Arabization and the remnants of an old Christian monopoly of education in the South. This whole region of Africa downwards into Uganda has tended to include within it both inter-denominational politics within a single religion and the politics of confrontation between different creeds. The Sudan acquires a borderline quality in this religious sphere as a result.

Underlying it all is the whole issue of national integration in any case. The Sudan represents both an Africa of achieved integration and an Africa of acute structural cleavage. The achieved integration is in the North where the Sudan is well on its way towards becoming a nation state in a classical sense if it is assessed purely in terms of the cultural homogeneity observable among Northerners. But the cleavage with the south puts the Sudan also among those unhappy African countries which have acute ethnic divisions, and sometimes raging civil wars.

A fourth area of marginality of the Sudan is in relation to West Africa, whereby this country shares a civilization which stretches right across the continent, from east to west. In this fourth sense the Sudan is marginal as between the civilizations of the Nile Valley on the one hand and the Sudanic belt of cultural influence on the other. In this sense, the country is also marginal in being almost an extension of West Africa in some important respects.

Finally, we discussed the marginality of the Sudan in relation to Arabic and the English language. The country's history as an Anglo-Egyptian condominium, and its linguistic fluidity when the British took over, enabled the intellectual life of the Sudan to acquire a quality of cultural twilight.

President Nasser once placed Egypt in three concentric circles

—the Arab circle, the African circle, and the Muslim one. As an exercise in role theory, President Nasser's formulation was sociologically sound.[1] But the fascination of the Sudan is, in some ways, even more complex. This is not simply a case of a single country playing a role in different circles of allegiance. In the final analysis, the fascination of the Sudan lies in her *profound intermediacy*—as she compulsively absorbs in her being a diversity of traits. Parts of Africa which are otherwise vastly different have been known to experience a moment of self-recognition as they cast their eyes on the Sudan.

[1] I have discussed this in my article 'Africa and the Egyptian's Four Circles', *African Affairs* (London), Vol. LXIII, No. 251, April 1964, arguing that there was a fourth circle of the Non-aligned within which Egypt had sought leadership.

9 Thoughts on Assassination in Africa[1]

Perhaps no international treaty betrays a greater sensitivity to the risk of assassination than does the Charter of Organization of African Unity. The Charter consecrates its disapproval of this phenomenon under Article III—in which it expresses its 'unreserved condemnation, in all its forms, of political assassination, as well as of subversive activities on the part of neighbouring States or any other State'.[2]

Independence is a beginning. So is the month of January every year, sometimes spilling over into February. For some reason a disproportionate number of the historic acts of violence in Africa since independence have tended to happen in the opening months of January and February. It was in the month of January 1961 that Patrice Lumumba was handed over to Moise Tshombe, his enemy in Katanga. That was the prelude to one of the most significant assassinations in Africa's history. The following month the death of Lumumba was announced.

In January 1963, President Sylvanus Olympio of Togo was assassinated. And it was with Olympio's fate in the background that the Charter of the Organization of African Unity was signed a few months later.

In January 1964 the Zanzibar revolution exploded in East Africa, with vital consequences for the region as a whole. Among the immediate effects were the army mutinies of

[1] This essay was written for the panel on 'Consensus and Dissent, with Special Reference to the Developing Countries' at the Seventh World Congress of the International Political Science Association at Brussels in September 1967. It was later published in *Political Science Quarterly*, LXXXIII, No. 1, March 1968.

[2] The Charter is also available in Boutros Boutros-Ghali's 'The Addis Ababa Charter', *International Conciliation*, No. 546, January 1964. Appendix, pp. 53–62, and in Colin Legum's latest edition of *Pan-Africanism*.

Tanganyika, Uganda and Kenya which happened later the same month.

In January 1965 the Prime Minister of Burundi was assassinated. The heads of neighbouring Kenya, Uganda and Tanzania discussed the event and jointly expressed their sense of shock.[1]

Within the same period Kenya had its first assassination since independence—the killing of Mr Pinto, a prominent member of Parliament.

In January 1966 came the Nigerian *coup*—which cost the lives of the Federal Prime Minister, Balewa, and the Premiers of the Northern and Western regions. The following month Nkrumah fell. His regime was overthrown while he was on his way to Peking. From the point of view of the theme of assassination the Ghanaian *coup* had a different kind of significance—it seems to have been a studied policy of the soldiers to avoid the risk of assassinating Nkrumah. That seems to have been one reason why the *coup* was timed to take place after his departure for Peking.

Is there any special reason why the opening months of January and February from year to year should have had such a disproportionate share of Africa's great acts of turbulence? Other months have had their events too. But the deaths of Lumumba, Olympio, Balewa and the Sardauna of Sokoto; the regionally transformative Zanzibar revolution; the East African mutinies; and the fall of Nkrumah are almost in a class by themselves as events which shook Africa. Yet, while sharing January and February for their anniversaries, the events provide little evidence for a neo-Montesque hypothesis about the effect of climatic changes on major political events. Our collection of events is too widely distributed to be co-related with weather conditions in January and February. The most that one can hope for is a symbolic correlation—A new year; a new nation; a new manifestation of instability.

What is of greater interest than the month in which it occurs is, of course, the phenomenon of assassination itself. Everything

[1] This was the second Prime Minister of Burundi to be assassinated. The first was Prince Rwagasore who was shot dead with a hunting-gun as he sat in a restaurant in Usumbura, less than a month after his Lumumbist Uprona Party had swept the polls in September 1961. That, however, was before Burundi's independence. For an account of the trial and retrial of those accused of complicity see, for example, Clyde Sanger's article in *The Guardian* (Manchester), January 12, 1963.

considered, there might easily have been many more assassinations in Africa than we have had so far. The potentialities of this and other forms of political violence have been there from the start. What this essay hopes to analyse are, in part, precisely those potentialities. But it will be a postulate of this paper that the risk of assassination was not merely objectively there but was keenly felt to be there by many of the leading participants in African politics. African leadership soon developed a conscious or subconscious fear of the assassin. This fear exerted an important influence not only on their personal behaviour from day to day but also on their policies and ideologies.

In our analysis here we shall first place the issue of assassination within the context of the whole problem of legitimacy in a newly invented state. We shall then link this up with different levels of consensus, and examine these in relation to personal leadership as a functional alternative to weak legitimacy. Where authority is too personified, challenge to authority also tends to take the form of personal violence. The possibilities of assassination are maximized. However, ideology tries to mitigate these possibilities. And in any case there are assassinations which, in their impact, produce the kind of retrospective hero-worship which is itself a contribution to national identity. We shall conclude with an examination of the influence of assassination on certain aspects of Pan-African behaviour and diplomatic thought.

But, first, a definitional problem has to be tackled.

WHAT IS 'ASSASSINATION'?

An alternative rendering to the term 'assassination' is sometimes supposed to be 'political murder'. But this rendering only shifts the problem. When is a murder 'political'? If the answer is 'When it is committed for political reasons', then not every political murder is an assassination. In the course of the Zanzibar revolution thousands of people were killed. And many of these were killed for reasons which, in their racial implications, could only be described as 'political'.

Yet the killing was at the grass-root level—a petty Arab shopkeeper killed by his African neighbour; a petty landlord killed by a tenant. One of the curious things about the Zanzibar revolution—in contrast to, say, the Cuban, with which it has often been compared—was the relative toleration shown towards leading members of the previous regime under the Sultan. The Zanzibar revolutionaries showed little immediate desire to 'make a public example' of their predecessors in power. Not only were there no executions, but a special effort was apparently made by the revolutionaries to spare Sheikh Ali Muhsin, the leader of the overthrown Nationalist Party, any public indignity. Even John Okello—the temperamental Ugandan who appeared to have spearheaded the *coup*—made threats on Zanzibar Radio against anyone who had 'violent designs' against Ali Muhsin. A long detention awaited him and his kind, but there was a marked reluctance to sentence them to a physical penalty.

Yet this tolerance of the revolutionary leaders towards their predecessors was in marked contrast with the outbreak of racial vendetta at the grass-root level—neighbour against neighbour; farmer against farmer. Many of these were politically-inspired killings. But were they 'assassinations'? It is possible to argue that the Zanzibar revolution unleashed a large number of 'political murders'—but not a single 'assassination'. For the term 'assassination' does not merely mean 'killing for political reasons'. In fact, the reasons can be quite irrelevant. For example, in November 1963 headlines in different parts of the world proclaimed 'KENNEDY ASSASSINATED'—before we knew who had killed him, let alone for what reasons. Perhaps we still do not know for what reasons. Yet the death of John F. Kennedy remains a case of assassination.

What seems more plausible is that the term 'assassination' derives its meaning less from the motives of the killing than from the political importance of the victim. The victim need not be a professional politician, nor hold a formal office of state. Neither Mahatma Gandhi in 1947 nor Malcolm X in 1964 were politicians or state officials in this professional sense. Yet we think of their deaths as instances of 'assassination'.

Victor T. LeVine prefers to base the definition of 'assassination' on the role of the killer rather than the status of the victim. LeVine would also add the element of surprise into his definition. As he himself put it,

the difference between assassination and political murder is

admittedly a tenuous one; I would contend that it lies in two
areas, the role of the killer, and the element of surprise.
Assassins are usually hired or delegated, and they generally
strike without warning to the victims.[1]

That assassins usually carry out their purpose 'without
warning their victims' can surely be taken for granted. Assassins
do not normally warn the police either. As for the claim that
'assassins are usually hired or delegated', surely this—even if it
were statistically true—could have no bearing on the definition
of assassination. A king can be assassinated by his own prospective
successor.

As for the element of surprise, again this is at best an accom-
panying characteristic of assassination rather than a defining one.
What if the killer is 'theatrical' enough to telephone his victim
anonymously and tell him that he had only until Thursday the
following week to live? And what if on that Thursday the man
was indeed killed? Was the theatrical forewarning enough to
deprive the killing of the status of an assassination?

What about Lumumba when he was handed over to his
enemies in Katanga? The news of his death was announced a
month later. Many people were 'shocked' without really being
'surprised'. The phenomenon of 'surprise' implies a high degree
of unexpectedness. And yet Lumumba already bore the marks
of a violent beating-up even before he was handed over to his
worst enemies. He was being publicly manhandled as he was
being transported to Katanga. The Press informed the world
with ominous photographs of Lumumba bearing the marks of
ill-treatment as the soldiers dragged him towards the next stage.
There followed the weeks of mystery and speculation. Was
Lumumba still alive or not? When the answer came in February
1961 many people, especially in the Third World, were indeed
shocked that the worst had come to the worst. And yet somehow
it was the shock of anger, and perhaps of political anguish, rather
than the shock of surprise.

What emerges from this is that neither the speed of killing
nor the role of the killer is crucial in defining assassination. What

[1] See LeVine, 'The Course of Political Violence' in William Lewis
(ed.), *French-Speaking Africa, The Search for Identity* (New York: Walker and
Company, 1965), pp. 59–60, 68 and LeVine's footnote 15 on p. 241.

is crucial is the status of the victim. The core or essential definition is that *an assassination is the killing of someone politically
important by an agent other than the government—for reasons
which are either political or unknown.*

LEGITIMACY VS INTEGRATION

Perhaps the most fundamental problems confronting African
countries are reducible to two crises—the crisis of national
integration and the crisis of political legitimacy. For our purposes
the crisis of integration may be seen as a problem of horizontal
relationships. It arises because different clusters of citizens do not
as yet accept each other as compatriots. The sense of a shared
nationality has yet to be forged.

The crisis of legitimacy, on the other hand, is a problem of
vertical relationships. It arises not because one citizen does not
recognize another as a compatriot but because significant
numbers of citizens are not convinced that their government has
a right to rule them. Integration is a problem of neighbour
against neighbour; legitimacy is a problem of the ruled against
their rulers.

Assassinations arise both in situations of inadequate national
integration and in situations of weak legitimacy or accepted
authority. But it would be a mistake to assume that the crisis
of integration and the crisis of legitimacy need necessarily go
together. It is possible for a country to have attained a high
degree of integration or sense of nationhood while its capacity for
accepting shared authority remains underdeveloped. The reverse
phenomenon is also quite possible, and has perhaps even more
examples in history.

Assassinations are often symptomatic of both our crises. But
here again it is not necessary that both crises be present. Recurrent assassinations have been known to happen in countries with
a highly developed sense of shared nationality. Japan provides one
dramatic example of this. Robert E. Ward has argued that
Japan's history as a whole is a strange mixture of docility and
violence:

Violence and the use of armed force to accomplish political

ends have a long and honourable tradition, which is by no means limited to pre-Restoration times. The phrase 'government by assassination' gained broad currency in Japan as late as the 1930's, and with considerable justification.[1]

Ward points out that the fourteen-year period of 1932-45 marked a reversion to this form of political behaviour. The period began with the assassination of Prime Minister Inukai Tsuyoshi on May 15, 1932:

> This was merely the most conspicuous of a number of such incidents that represented protests against widespread economic—especially agrarian—distress . . . and a foreign policy held to be insufficiently nationalistic and aggressive.[2]

Here were a people with a marked degree of national consciousness. Indeed, many of the killings were widely regarded as '*patriotic* assassinations', carried out for the sake of national honour. And yet the widespread approbation of many such acts in the country was an indication that the successful creation of national identity in Japan had not been accompanied by a successful tradition of governmental legitimacy. It is true that the Emperor himself had more than political acceptance. He commanded mystical reverence as well. But in the final analysis the Emperor was perhaps more a symbol of nationhood than of secure governmental authority.

In Africa the crises of both integration and legitimacy are still acute. And political violence is often symptomatic of them both. Assassination itself as a political solution was rare during the colonial period. One could almost say that, in our definition of it as 'the killing of someone politically important, by an agent other than the government, for reasons which are either political or unknown', assassination comes near to being a post-independence phenomenon in Africa. Rival political groups in colonial Africa might have killed each other before. But the kind of political importance which a victim had to have if the killing was to be defined as an 'assassination' was, to some extent,

[1] 'Japan' in *Modern Political Systems: Asia*, (eds.) Robert E. Ward and Roy C. Macridis (Englewood Cliffs, N.J.: Prentice Hall, 1963), p. 60.
[2] *Ibid.*, p. 30.

camouflaged by the colonial situation. Thus if Patrice Lumumba had been killed mysteriously before the Congo became independent and afforded him a chance to be Prime Minister, the killing would have appeared less obviously as an assassination than it did when it took place some months after the country's independence.

But reasons of definition are not the only ones which make the killing of politically important African figures a post-independence phenomenon in the main. More weighty reasons are tied up with problems of the crises we mentioned.

British colonial governors were hardly ever killed in office—whereas within a couple of years of independence African heads of governments found themselves victims or near-victims of assassins. Why the difference? One possible answer is that the British colonial governor was well guarded. Another answer is that he mixed less with the general populace—and therefore exposed himself less to possible assassination. Both these statements might be true—and yet as *reasons* they might be of only marginal relevance.

We might get nearer the real reasons if, firstly, we reflected on this hypothesis:

That there had been few attempts on the lives of colonial governors in Africa for the same reason for which there had been few mutinies by African soldiers under the colonial regime—the range of possible retaliation measures was wider in the British Power-Spectrum than in that of the new regimes.

And yet the range of possible changes in the situation which could result from an assassination was seemingly narrower in a colonial situation than in a post-independence one. An assassin asks himself in a colonial situation 'What will happen if I killed the British Governor?' On the one hand, British power seemed great enough to be able to inflict a whole range of possible acts of revenge on the assassin alone, or on the assassin and others as collective punishment.

On the other hand, British power also seemed great enough to prevent any fundamental change in the political situation being brought about by the mere assassination of a Governor—a replacement could be sent, and the colony remain a colony under basically the same policy. British capacity for varied forms of revenge could put off an assassin by the fear of credible consequences. British capacity for maintaining the political *status quo* in spite of the loss of a Governor could put off an assassin by the fear of futility.

But in a post-independence situation getting rid of a Prime Minister could cause a more significant change in a country's orientation—just as an army mutiny after independence can effect an important change, unless it is thwarted by appeal to the former colonial power.

And even when thwarted it could—on issues like this Africanization of the officer corps in the army—prove to be a victory of the vanquished. The fluidity of the basis of legitimacy in a post-independence situation maximizes the temptation to revolt—and both military insubordination and attempted assassinations become a more common phenomenon than in pre-colonial days.

That is one reason why African independence and increased African violence are often companions—at least for a while.

CONSENSUS, PRIMARY AND SECONDARY

Linking this up with more traditional categories of political analysis, we may say that the problem of legitimacy is the old problem of 'political obligation' in political philosophy. It is the problem of why and when one obeys or ought to obey the government. Where legitimacy is fully secure, the citizens do not question the government's right to govern, though they may question the wisdom of this or that governmental action. When it is not secure, challenges to authority may allow little differentiation between dissent, insubordination, rebellion and outright treason.

In traditional political theory, the problem of political obligation involves a shifting balance between the area of consent in government and the area of compulsion. And the area of consent has itself different levels. To take Uganda as an example, one might note that there is a difference between consenting to being ruled by President Obote's Government and consenting to this or that *policy* of his government. It is possible for an opponent of Dr. Obote's regime to be in favour of this or that policy pursued by the regime. Thus there were many Ugandans outside Obote's party who supported his toughness against the kingdom of Buganda although they would not vote for Obote in a general election. In this case they accept the policy though, given a choice, they would not accept the government.

But even the idea of accepting Obote's government, or consenting to being ruled by it, has two levels. The more obvious level is in the sense of having voted for Dr Obote's party at the last election. Yet there is a sense, of course, in which even the Democratic Party, although in *opposition*, consented to being ruled by Obote's Uganda People's Congress. The whole idea of a loyal opposition implies consenting to being ruled by the constitutional government in power—although reserving the right to disagree with almost every one of its policies.

The problem in Africa in the first few years of independence was of trying to ensure that every Opposition remained a loyal opposition. It was a quest for a situation in which one could challenge decisions of the Government and not the Government's right to execute them.

In the final analysis, this was the ultimate problem of *consensus*—not a consensus on policies (i.e. secondary consensus) but a consensus on legitimate methods of policy-making and legitimate methods of implementation (primary consensus). Thus even those who did not vote for the majority party in Uganda but took advantage of the elective principle concede the right of governance to their rival party.

In this primary sense, consensus is that which makes it possible to have *compulsion by consent*. It is what makes citizens accept a certain degree of force from the Government, or even complain about that force—without feeling that the Government lacks the right to govern them at all.

But the degree of compulsion needed is sometimes in inverse proportion to the degree of secondary consensus already achieved. This secondary consensus or agreement behind certain policies is sometimes known as 'national unity' at a particular moment in time. There are occasions when we have to think of compulsion as that which we have to put into a governmental system in order to make up for deficiencies in unity. The Congo is less united than Uganda; therefore the Congo needs more coercion or compulsion in its system than does Uganda. Mainland Tanzania is more united than Uganda. Therefore mainland Tanzania or Tanganyika needs less coercion for minimal system-maintenance than does Uganda. Coercion and consensus are sometimes functional alternatives for system-maintenance.

But secondary consensus is not necessarily agreement behind policies; it can sometimes be agreement behind a leader, almost regardless of the policies he pursues.

African countries, faced with inadequate primary consensus, have sometimes invoked diverse devices in order to consolidate at least secondary consensus behind the leader. There is a tragic paradox involved in the process. On the one hand, the absence of primary consensus creates the danger of assassination because of the very inadequacy of legitimacy. On the other hand, the attempt to create secondary consensus leads to the personification of government. 'Nkrumah is the CPP; the CPP is Ghana; Nkrumah is therefore Ghana.' This is the syllogism which, in its conclusion, legitimates African equivalents of Louis XIV. But the doctrine of 'I am the State', by personifying government, can be an invitation to regicide in conditions of primary dissensus. To challenge the leader is to challenge the state. The transformation of the state therefore 'requires' the elimination of its present embodiment.

African attempts to promote 'leader-worship' are therefore caught up in this contradiction. The whole idea of promoting it is partly inspired by a desire to mitigate the potential for regicide inherent in primary dissensus. And so leader-worship sometimes verges on being almost literal. Nkrumah was the clearest example in recent African history, though by no means atypical. He permitted himself to be portrayed as a messiah. But he needed to be a political Christ without a political Crucifixion. Indeed, the whole purpose of portraying himself as a messiah was in order to avert the danger of a crucifixion. But the enshrinement of authority has entailed a personification of authority as well. And it is this which also leads to the personification of opposition.[1]

---

[1] See following chapter. See also David E. Apter, 'Political Religion in the New Nations', Old Societies and New States, (ed.) Clifford Geertz (New York: Free Press of Glencoe, 1963), pp. 82–4.

DEATH AND HERO-WORSHIP

But there are occasions when it is, in fact, the 'crucifixion' which achieves the leader-worship so vainly sought by propaganda. The clearest example is perhaps the place of Lumumba in the Congo. Before his death Lumumba was perhaps more a hero of Pan-Africanists outside the Congo than of the Congolese themselves. It is true that he was 'the nearest thing' to a national leader that the Congo had; but that was not all that 'near'. Lumumba stood for Congolese unity, but he was not himself popular enough or strong enough to ensure that unity without external help. Perhaps the forces against unity were in any case greater than any single leader could cope with. Lumumba might well have been a casualty of circumstances. Yet one thing was clear—while he lived he was essentially a factional hero rather than a national one.

But after his death the myth of Lumumba was rapidly nationalized. His death was, as we indicated, announced in February 1961. By the summer of the same year a coalition government was formed under the premiership of Cyrille Adoula, with Kasavubu still President. When the new Prime Minister Adoula ventured into Stanleyville, he made it a point to place flowers at a temporary monument of Lumumba and exclaim: 'We have achieved what Lumumba wanted: one Congo, one Congo, one Congo.'

Commenting on this phenomenon, Henry Tanner had the following to say at the time,

> The gesture . . . showed that Lumumba's place in Congolese politics has undergone a subtle but far-reaching change. Before the formation of the coalition government, the Lumumba legend had been the exclusive tool of one political faction. Now it is being invoked, with different shades of meaning and enthusiasm, by both parties in the coalition . . . even a politician who owes his power to Kasavubu, Lumumba's earliest rival, may find it wise to worship at the shrine.[1]

In July 1964, to the astonishment of the world, Moise Tshombe,

---

[1] Tanner, 'Over the Congo, Lumumba's Ghost', *New York Times Magazine*, October 29, 1961, p. 80.

the former secessionist of Katanga, was invited by President
Kasavubu to succeed Adoula as Prime Minister of the Congo.
Tshombe was widely regarded as the man behind the murder of
Lumumba. Yet he had now come back from his exile in Europe
to take over the reins of national power. On July 19, 1964, he
addressed an enthusiastic crowd of 25,000 at the Baudouin
Stadium in Leopoldville and proclaimed 'Give me three months
and I will give you a new Congo.'

On July 26 he was in Stanleyville, the Lumumbist stronghold.
He repeated his theme of 'give me three months' to a major
rally. And as one more step towards that goal of a 'new Congo',
Moise Tshombe laid a wreath at the monument of Patrice
Lumumba.[1]

Yet instability continued in the Congo. Tshombe scored a
victory over the rebels, but the whole political regime ended with
General Mobutu's *coup* in December 1965. On the first Independence Day anniversary following the *coup* a great crowd
assembled in the capital to celebrate the occasion. The day was
June 30, 1966. President Mobutu was giving the great speech
of the occasion. Suddenly he made an unexpected statement:

> Glory and honour to an illustrious citizen of the Congo, to a
> great African, and to the first martyr of our independence.
> Patrice Emery Lumumba, who was the victim of the colonialist
> plot. In the name of the Government, we proclaim his name
> on this national heroes' day . . .'.

Mobutu also declared a new policy about the Belgian mining
interests in the Congo, implying a greater assertion of Congolese
control over the country's economy. Opposition to the autonomy
of mining interests in the Congo was certainly in the tradition of
Lumumbist thought in the Congo.[2]

Not long after George Penchenier devoted one of four articles
on the Congo in *Le Monde* to Mobutu's move in proclaiming
Lumumba a hero. Penchenier pointed out that it was not merely
in the rebel-held areas that Lumumba was regarded in such
terms. 'The three short months in which he held power were

---

[1] See *Africa Report*, Vol. IX No. 9, October 1964, p. 20.
[2] See *African Digest*, Vol. XIV, No. 2, October 1966, pp. 22-3.

enough to make him a legend, and the circumstances of his death made him a martyr.' The writer went on to say:

> Six years have passed . . . The old street named Leopold III will be known in future as Patrice Emery Lumumba and a monument will be erected to his memory. The Congolese welcome these acts without stopping to think about the strange fate of a man who was followed, then betrayed, and now rehabilitated. General Mobutu has taken a political step. After having defeated the Lumumbist rebellion, he is trying to create a united Congo. Who better to help him than Patrice Lumumba?[1]

It looks as if the memory of Lumumba may contribute more to the oneness of the Congolese than anything Lumumba himself actually did while he was still alive. It all depends upon whether shared heroes constitute one of the factors which help to create national consciousness.

But why should Lumumba be a hero for reasons other than what he actually accomplished for his country while he lived? This takes us back to the place of violence in political mythology at large. Criteria for heroism in relation to violence can take one of three main forms. First, a person can be a hero because of some accomplishment in a violent activity like war. These are of course the war heroes. Secondly, a person can be a hero because of his capacity for non-violence in the face of provocation. Mahatma Gandhi and Jesus Christ fall within this second category. And thirdly, a person can be a hero simply by being a victim of someone else's violence in a particular set of circumstances. It is perhaps within this third category that Patrice Lumumba falls.

Young nations often feel a need to have an antiquity. The desire to be old becomes part of the quest for identity. And dead heroes even of the immediate past are history personified. In that lies their relevance for the development of national consciousness. Hero-worship when the heroes are alive is at best a case of secondary consensus. But hero-worship when the heroes are dead might well be a contribution to primary consensus.

[1] *Le Monde*, September 1 and 5, 1966. The English rendering of the quotation is from *Africa Digest*, *op. cit.*

But the secret both of national pride and national cohesion is to know what to forget. The desire to be old and wrinkled as a nation must be accomplished by a determination to have a failing memory. In Kenya, for example, this phenomenon is tested against what happened during the Mau Mau insurrection. On the one hand, there is a desire that yesterday's villains—the Mau Mau fighters—should perhaps become today's heroes. On the other hand, there is a determination that yesterday's heroes—the 'loyalists' who fought against the Mau Mau—should not become today's villains. A similar selectivity will be demanded of the memory of the Congolese. In the case of the legend of Lumumba, it is a selectivity which has already taken place.

As we have argued before, the very idea of a Nation can sometimes be a little too abstract, and hence a little too cold, to command ready human allegiance. To give the idea of a Nation warmth, it is often necessary either to personify it metaphorically, or, more effectively, to give it specific human form in national heroes. This is why *ancestor-worship* is important not only among tribes but also within Nations. And this is indeed why the assassination of Patrice Lumumba remains one of the most important single contributions to the development of primary consensus in the Congo.

PAN-AFRICANISM AND THE ASSASSIN

But the distinction between national consensus and regional consensus in Africa is not always easy to draw. The same factors which make nationalism and Pan-Africanism in the continent so intimately connected have also produced an overlap between problems of domestic territorial identity and problems of continental racial identity. The very fact that Lumumba was a Pan-African hero before he became a Congolese national hero emphasizes this overlap.

Problems of separatism in Africa often get into a paradoxical relationship with problems of Pan-regionalism. The old issue of Katanga's secession, the recurrent difficulty of secessionist Somalis in Kenya and Ethiopia, and even the isolation of Biafra, have in their different ways exemplified the tense connection between the politics of African separatism and problems of Pan-Africanism at large.

In what way is secessionism on the one hand and Pan-regionalism on the other related to the phenomenon of assassination in Africa? A step towards an answer can be taken by asking yet another question: what sort of issues in such areas of political experience arouse the kind of passions which produce assassins?

One major category is of issues which imply a great sense of finality once a decision is taken. And these are issues which command such a degree of emotional involvement among those affected that the apparent finality of the decision, once it is taken, seems almost unbearable to the loser. This category of issues can produce assassins even though the immediate reason for killing a public figure might be a mere side effect of the central factor which set the passions free.

Pre-eminent among the breeding grounds of assassins is a situation involving territorial partition—prospective, accomplished or thwarted partition. Partition can take different forms. The term is normally used to apply to a case like that of Ireland or India where a foreign power was involved in the partitioning. But internally generated secessionism is also a quest for partitioning a country.

Historically, Mahatma Gandhi lost his life in a situation involving separatist passions. Abraham Lincoln lost his life after frustrating a bid to partition the United States. More recently the issue of the separation of Algeria from France let loose emotions which resulted in a number of political murders, including several attempts on the life of de Gaulle.

The situation in the Algerian case was indeed complex. But to people like Jacques Soustelle, Algerian independence was at the time synonymous with the partition of France. The assassinative emotions generated were in part derived from the dread of partition and the FLN was regarded as a secessionist movement.

When one considers this relationship between separatism and assassination, the prospect in Africa can be very disquieting. It was, after all, in Africa that Europe practised the art of partition at its most elaborate. Where Europe attempted to unify those who were distinct, it left the seeds of future separatism—and Patrice Lumumba was assassinated in a secessionist province. Where Europe divided it sometimes left behind latent passions for reunification—and political killings at the grass-root level have resulted from such division. In short, balkanization is a breeding ground of political violence—including the phenomenon of assassination. And balkanization is what Africa is landed with for the time being.

Pan-Africanism is often an attempt to grapple with the consequences of balkanization. One early assassination which had Pan-African significance, as well as being somewhat connected with Africa's fragmentation, was the assassination of Sylvanus Olympio, first President of independent Togo. In this regard we might begin by noting that from the point of view of Pan-Africanism, there are three types of assassinations. There is the kind of assassination which might harm the cause of Pan-Africanism; secondly, the kind which might conceivably help the cause of Pan-Africanism; and thirdly, of course, the kind which has had little relevance for Pan-Africanism.

The assassination of Sylvanus Olympio perhaps remains the most dramatic case of a continentally divisive assassination which Africa has had so far. Olympio happened to be a pre-eminently 'bi-cultural' or 'tri-cultural' African leader in his up-bringing. He was at home among both French- and English-speaking colleagues. And his country, Togo, under his leadership, was expected to be an important inter-lingual link between the two sectors of Westernized Africa.

However, a border dispute between Togo and Ghana marred this picture of potential amity. Nkrumah had become a champion of the re-unification of the Ewe on the two sides of the border—hoping thereby to enlarge the boundaries of Ghana. Because of this border dispute, and of personality factors in the relations between Olympio and Nkrumah, Ghana became a little too hospitable in the refuge it gave to discontented Togolese 'at war' with the regime of their own country.[1]

When therefore Olympio was assassinated in January 1963, there was immediate suspicion in some circles that Ghana under Nkrumah was, either directly or indirectly, implicated. Nigeria's Foreign Minister at the time, Jaja Wachuku, articulated his suspicions perhaps a little too quickly. He regarded Olympio's

---

[1] For a comprehensive recent treatment of the border problem and its ethnic implications see Claude E. Welch, Jr., *Dream of Unity* (Ithaca, N.Y.: Cornell University Press, 1966), esp. Chapters II and III.

assassination as 'engineered, organized, and financed by some-body'. He warned that Nigeria would intervene militarily if 'the contingent of armoured Ghanaian troops lined up on the Ghana-Togo border' attempted to cross the border.[1]

Observers outside shared similar suspicions. Even the pro-Ghana American periodical at the time, *Africa Today*, saw a connection between a frontier dispute of that kind and the danger of assassination. In its own words,

> It is not the opposition which takes to the hand grenade but usually the neighbouring country whose leaders have taken up the cause of the opposition. . . . Africa balkanized will continue to be fertile ground for senseless political rivalries.[2]

But apart from the issue of frontiers, there was the issue of diplomatic recognition. With the murder of Olympio African states were faced for the first time with the whole problem of 'legitimate succession' following a case of regicide. West African governments were divided on the issue of whether or not to recognize the new Togolese Government under Mr Nicolas Grunitzky. From the east coast of Africa came the voice of Tanganyika, then almost alone as an independent state in its area. Tanganyika cabled the Secretary-General of the United Nations in the following terms:

> After the brutal murder of President Olympio, the problem of recognition of a successor government has arisen. We urge no recognition until satisfied first that the government did not take part in Olympio's murder or second that there is a popu-larly elected government.[3]

The first condition concerned the issue of whether assumption of power was by legitimate means. The second concerned a possible subsequent legitimation of what was originally an illegitimate method of assuming power. Subsequent elections

---

[1] See Helen Kitchen, 'Filling the Togo Vacuum', *Africa Report*, Vol. VIII, No. 2, February 1963, p. 9.

[2] 'Conspiracies and Balkanization', *Africa Today*, Vol. X, No. 2, February 1963, p. 3.

[3] *Tanganyika Standard* (Dar es Salaam), January 26, 1963. See also Helen Kitchen, *op. cit.*

were, in other words, capable of giving a stamp of moral dignity to a regime which originally acceded as a result of assassination or insurrection. It was like De Gaulle coming into power in 1958 as a result of military insubordination—and then organizing a referendum throughout the French Community in order to validate his standing.

The year of Olympio's murder was also the year of the formation of the Organization of African Unity. Only a few months separated the two events. The ghost of Olympio virtually dictated that dramatic part of Article III of the Charter of the new Organization—'unreserved condemnation, in all its forms, of political assassination, as well as of subversive activities on the part of neighbouring States or any other State.'

Lumumba's martyrdom had perhaps, on the whole, been a positive contribution to Pan-Africanism. It gave Africa a shared hero as the memory of nationalism indulged in unifying selectivity. Olympio's murder, on the other hand, at first deeply divided the continent, as suspicion and recrimination reigned supreme. But history is beginning to reveal Olympio as essentially the first major victim of a military *coup* in independent Africa. His death now appears to have been an omen of things to come. Whether this prophetic symbolism of his assassination would convert Olympio into a continental African hero depends very much upon whether Africa will experience a fundamental disenchantment with military regimes—and turn back with nostalgia to the first casualty of the wave of militarism.

If that were to happen, other heroes too of pre-military Africa —from Lumumba to Balewa—may contribute the vague mystique of their ancient names to the slow growth of primary consensus in the consciousness of Africa.

10 The Monarchical Tendency in African Political Culture[1]

In a sense which is not intended to disparage him, Kwame Nkrumah was both a Lenin and a Czar. His secular radicalism had an important royalist theme from the start. But our interest in this article is not merely in Nkrumah himself.[2] It is in the general phenomenon of monarchical tendencies in African politics as they have manifested themselves over the years.

We define monarchical tendencies in this article to be a combination of at least four elements of political style. There is, first, *the quest for aristocratic effect*. In Africa this takes the form of social ostentation. More specifically, it means a partiality for splendid attire, for large expensive cars, for palatial accommodation, and for other forms of conspicuous consumption.[3]

Another factor which goes towards making a monarchical style of politics is *the personalization of authority*. On its own this factor could be just another type of personality cult. But when combined with the quest for aristocratic effect, or with other elements of style, it takes a turn towards monarchism. Sometimes the personalization goes to the extent of inventing a special title for the leader—and occasionally the title is almost literally royal.

A third element in the monarchical political style is *the sacralization of authority*. This is sometimes linked to the process of

---

[1] Published in *The British Journal of Sociology*, Vol. XVIII, No. 3, September 1967.

[2] For a discussion of Nkrumah himself and his ideological mixture, see my article 'Nkrumah: the Leninist Czar', in *Transition*, Vol. VI, No. 26 (Kampala, 1966). Some of the points in this article are an elaboration of what I touched on in that article on Nkrumah.

[3] There have been in places vigorous attempts to control this quest for aristocratic effect. Tanzania has gone further in this attempt to control it than any other African country. See especially the Arusha Declaration in *The Nationalist* (Dar es Salaam), February 6, 1967. But Tanzania's ethos of frugality is an experiment which faces significant difficulties internally.

personalizing authority, but it need not be. The glorification of a leader could be on non-religious terms. On the other hand, what is being sacralized need not be a person but could be an office or institution. The institutional form of sacred authority is, however, rare in new states. Indeed, the personality of the leader might be glorified precisely because the office lacks the awe of its own legitimacy.

The fourth factor in the politics of monarchism, especially in Africa, is *the quest for a royal historical identity*. This phenomenon arises out of a vague feeling that national dignity is incomplete without a splendid past. And the glory of the past is then conceived in terms of ancient kingly achievement.

TRIBAL ORIGINS OF POLITICAL STYLES

Of the elements of monarchism we have mentioned, the one that is perhaps most clearly shared by traditional conceptions of authority is the element of sacralization. A traditional chief was not always an instance of personalized power. The situation varied from tribe to tribe and from ruler to ruler. In fact, as often as not it was the *institution* rather than the personality of the incumbent that commanded authority. But although the personalization of power in traditional Africa was thus by no means universal, the sacralization of authority virtually was. There was always a spiritual basis to legitimate rule in traditional Africa. The effect of this on modern African concepts of political legitimacy will emerge later in this analysis.

A related phenomenon is the place of eminence given to ancestors in most of African systems of thought. Partly out of this traditional glorification of one's forebears, and partly as a result of Western disparagement of Africa as 'a continent with no history', African nationalists today sometimes militantly eulogize ancient African kingdoms. This, as we shall indicate more fully later, is what the African quest for a royal historical identity is all about.

Finally, there has been in Africa since independence, and sometimes for longer than that, the tendency to contrive an aristocratic effect in one's style of life. It is to this question that we must now turn in greater detail. What has led to the building of magnificent palaces in Dahomey, Nigeria, the Ivory Coast, Liberia, Ghana and other places? Why have so many African leaders since independence betrayed a weakness for a plush effect and palatial living?

Here, too, part of the explanation might lie in the general anthropological context of African political styles. Possession as a mark of status is not an entirely new development in African life. It is true that land was very rarely owned on an individual basis. In the words of Max Gluckman:

> The earth, undivided, as the basis of society, . . . comes to symbolize not individual prosperity, fertility, and good fortune; but the general prosperity, fertility, and good fortune on which individual life depends.[1]

Nevertheless, the *exploitation* of land, as distinct from its ownership, was not without elements of individualism and competition. To quote Gluckman again:

> The secular value of the earth lies in the way it provides for the private interests of individuals and groups within the larger society. They make their living off particular gardens, pastures, and fishing pools; they build their homes, make their fires, and eat their meals on their own plots of grounds. . . . Men and groups dispute over particular pieces to serve these varied ends.[2]

Within the cooperative structure of kinship and common ownership, there was still room for individual effort and for *individual rewards of such effort*. And so, in addition to status based on age and custom, there was some social status accruing from material possessions. In certain societies, how many heads of cattle a person owned was part of his social standing. There was also bridewealth as a factor in stratification.

These early manifestations of possessive individualism in traditional Africa received a revolutionary stimulus with the advent

---

[1] Gluckman, *Custom and Conflict in Africa* (Oxford: Basil Blackwell, 1963 (reprint)), p. 16.
[2] *Ibid.*

of the money economy. As a Nigerian economist put it ten years ago,

> New statuses arise with the emergence of a new class, the rich who have made their fortune in trade either by selling the raw produce of the land or by retailing imported articles manufactured abroad. . . . The growth of this new class of rich, divorced from the land that was so important a link in the chain that bound the society to the elders, has weakened the authority of the elders. . . . The new generation that made its money in trade has challenged the traditional basis of obedience.[1]

In many cases it was this new generation which was the vanguard of the cult of ostentation. To challenge the awesome authority of a chief sometimes required a display of alternative symbols of power. The chiefs were challenged both by those who had new educational attainments, and by those who had new material possessions. And both sets of challengers were inclined to be exhibitionist. Those who had made money had a weakness for conspicuous consumption. And those who had received some education indulged in 'the misuse or overuse of long words, in the use of pompous oratory, and in the ostentatious display of educational attainments'.[2] Both forms of exhibiting the new symbols of power helped to dilute the old legitimacy of tribal elders. Western education and the money economy had produced a form of ostentation which contributed to the corrosion of some traditional ways.

In the meantime, the tendency to regard material possessions as a sign of merit and hard work received a new impetus from the phenomenon of labour migration to the towns. An increasing number of young men left the villages for the mines or for other work in the towns—and periodically came back with symbols of success. As Philip Gulliver recounts,

> In this kind of situation wage-labour becomes more than merely fulfilling youthful needs for clothes, bridewealth contributions

---

[1] Pius Okigbo, 'Social Consequences of Economic Development in West Africa', *Annals of the American Academy of Political and Social Science*, No. 305 (May 1956), pp. 127–8.

[2] James S. Coleman discusses this phenomenon in Nigeria in the colonial period. See his *Nigeria: Background to Nationalism* (Berkeley and Los Angeles, University of California, 1958), pp. 146–7.

and a little ready cash to establish a man as a husband, father and householder. Wage-labour is involved in obtaining goods and services which are not obtainable in the tribal areas and with standards which are not those of the home community— bicycles and radios, a wide variety of clothing, cash for luxuries, travel by bus and train, as well as a greater demand for the more traditional cloth, cattle, tools and utensils which are involved in tribal life.'[1]

Gulliver goes on to add that the higher and different standard of living affected not only the migrants themselves but also the people who remained at home—'for new standards became incorporated into tribal expectations and orientations'.[2]

Prestige comes to attach itself to some of these new standards. Young men then aspire to own one day at least a few of the symbols of a 'European' way of life. In the words of Mitchell and Epstein in their analysis of social status in Northern Rhodesia,

Success in achieving this 'civilized' way of life is demonstrated conspicuously by the physical appurtenances of living. The most important of these is clothes, but personal jewellery (especially wrist-watches), furniture, and European-type foodstuffs are also important.[3]

These sociological tendencies have been the very basis of a new possessive individualism in Africa. The equalitarian aspects of African traditional life, and the extensive social obligations of the extended family, exist side by side with an ethic which measures the individual's success by the yardstick of his material acquisitions. Kenya's Jomo Kenyatta tried to 'disgrace' a prominent Kenya leftist at a public meeting by pointing out that the leftist did not own a big house or a thriving business. The leftist, Mr Bildad Kaggia, was present at the meeting. President Kenyatta compared Kaggia with other old colleagues of his who had

[1] Philip H. Gulliver, 'Incentives in Labour Migration', *Human Organization*, Vol. XIX, No. 3 (Fall 1960), pp. 159–61.
[2] *Ibid.*
[3] J. Clyde Mitchell and A. L. Epstein, 'Occupational Prestige and Social Status Among Urban Africans in Northern Rhodesia', *Africa*, No. 29 (1959), pp. 34–9.

since become prosperous. Addressing Kaggia directly Kenyatta said:

> We were together with Paul Ngei in jail. If you go to Ngei's home, he has planted a lot of coffee and other crops. What have you done for yourself? If you go to Kubai's home, he has a big house and has a nice shamba. Kaggia, what have you done for yourself? We were together with Kungu Karumba in jail, now he is running his own buses. What have you done for yourself?[1]

What is significant here is the conviction that failure to prosper is an argument *against* a leader. As a socialist radical, Kaggia was urging a redistribution of land in Kenya to the poor. Kenyatta was suggesting that a person who had failed to prosper through his own exertions should not be 'advocating free things'.[2]

From this kind of reasoning is an easy transition to the feeling that enforced economic equality is an insult to the dignity of labour. The principle of 'to each according to his work' made sense—but it did not make sense to strive for a principle of 'to each according to his needs'. That is one reason why Kenya's Ronald Ngala felt that 'communism teaches people laziness'.[3]

There is a general feeling that most of those who have become wealthy in contemporary Africa have 'come up the hard way'. They have made the money themselves and have not inherited it from a long line of wealthy ancestors. It is therefore tempting to conclude that the rich in the new countries of Africa are more deserving to be rich than some of the millionaires in the Western world. Yet even those who have *inherited* their wealth from ancestors might find grace and forgiveness among a people who like to associate their own prosperity with the blessing of their ancestors. And so Dr Hastings Banda of Malawi could argue that behind every wealthy family in the Western world is a story of hard work somewhere down the family line. This is a defensible

---

[1] See *East African Standard* (Nairobi), April 12, 1965.
[2] *Ibid.*
[3] See BBC Monitoring Service Records of African Broadcasts, Nairobi in English, ME/1892/B/2, June 22, 1965. In Lenin's terms, the principle of 'from each according to his ability, to each according to his work' is a transitional principle for the 'lower phase' of communism. The ultimate aim was, of course, 'from each according to his ability, to each according to his needs'. See *State and Revolution* (1917).

assertion. But Banda has sometimes gone on to the much less defensible 'corollary' that behind every poor family in the Western world is a long tradition of a lack of initiative. In his own words,

> In Capitalist countries such as America or Britain, for example [when] some people are very rich and others are very poor, it is that the former have initiative and work very hard or that their ancestors or their grandfathers had initiative and worked hard, while the latter have no initiative and do not work hard or their forefathers did not have initiative and did not work hard.[1]

But Banda is inconsistent on this latter point. In fact he retreats into saying: 'There are others, of course, who are just unfortunate and are poor through no fault of their own.'[2] Nevertheless a general admiration of the spirit of honest acquisition is a running theme in his assessment of Westernism. Banda himself manages to combine this admiration with some degree of personal frugality. But in others the admiration of acquisitiveness could include an inner compulsion to *display* one's own successful acquisitions. Such a compulsion is, of course, what leads to general social ostentation.

But what are the implications of this phenomenon for development in Africa? How much of a social ill is a quest for aristocratic effect?

When African leaders are merely acquisitive and self-seeking, certain consequences follow. But when what they acquire is *conspicuously* consumed, a different set of consequences might emerge. The point which needs to be grasped first is that an élite can be acquisitive or even corrupt without being ostentatious. Corruption in India, for example, is at least as well developed as it is anywhere in Africa. Yet there is an asceticism in the Indian style of social behaviour which affects the Indian style of politics too. Many Indian leaders have to conform to what one observer has described as 'the Gandhian image of self-sacrifice and

[1] 'What is Communism?', speech to Zomba Debating Society, April 1964, p. 17.
[2] *Ibid.*

humility which Indians demand of their politicians'.[1] Some of
the leaders are sincerely ascetic in any case. But not all that
refrains from glittering is necessarily Gandhian.

It is arguable that a corrupt élite which is also ostentatious is
ultimately preferable to a corrupt élite which is outwardly ascetic.
The problem of measuring sincerity in India is a recurrent one.
The leader of Goa's Congress Party, Mr Purshottam Kakodkar,
disappeared from a Bombay hotel on November 28, 1965. A
nation-wide search by the police and special investigators was
carried out over a period of more than four months. In April 1966
the mystery came to an end. Mr Kakodkar wrote to the Home
Minister announcing that he had gone to a small Himalayan
town for meditation.

What were his motives? J. Anthony Lukas made the following
report to the *New York Times:*

> Some of Mr. Kakodkar's supporters say he is only a spiritual
> man who wanted a few months to commune with himself
> before plunging into politics again. Others believe his retreat
> was a stunt designed to raise his political stock in Goa, where
> elections are to take place soon.[2]

Lukas linked this event with the whole Indian phenomenon of the
sanyasi (sadu), or spiritual recluse. The cult of withdrawing from
worldly affairs can produce genuine dedication and self-sacrifice.
But it can also produce some of the worst forms of hypocrisy.
In the words of Lukas:

> A genuine sanyasi comes to the ashram [sanctuary] to find a
> guru, or teacher, who he must convince of his sincerity. He
> must take vows of obedience, celibacy and poverty before he
> puts on his robes. However, many of the 'holy men' are said
> to be thinly disguised charlatans who make good livings as
> alchemists, physicians, fortune tellers, palmists or acrobats.[3]

But why should the ostentatious acquisitiveness of the African
kind be preferable to the ascetic accumulation of Indians? From

[1] See J. Anthony Lukas, 'Political Python of India', *New York Times
Magazine*, February 20, 1966, p. 26.
[2] 'Goa Leader Discloses He Vanished for 4 Months to Meditate', *New York
Times*, April 14, 1966.
[3] *Ibid.*

an economic point of view, the Indian style of accumulation might be preferable, particularly if the asceticism is accompanied with an ethic of re-investment. The Indian would thus make money, continue to live humbly, and re-invest what he saves. On the other hand the African, in his ostentation, spends his money on luxurious consumer goods, often imported. He harms his country's foreign reserves and deprives the nation of potentially productive capital investment. From the point of view of economic development, ostentatious acquisitiveness tends to be dysfunctional.

But what are the political implications of the phenomenon? A major consideration is that if the consumption is conspicuous, it provides the populace with some index of how much money the leaders make. If the money is being made at the public's expense, the public is not being kept entirely ignorant of that fact. And sooner or later the public might demand an explanation. In short, ostentatious corruption is less stable than disguised corruption. Indeed, the ostentation might, in the long run, be the grave-digger of the corruption. It seems almost certain that in Nigeria part of the exultation which accompanied the overthrow of the regime of Sir Abubakar Balewa was due to the discredit sustained by the regime for the excessive conspicuousness of its corrupt consumption.

IMPERIAL ORIGINS OF POLITICAL STYLES

But in any case it is not merely traditional Africa that has contributed to monarchical styles of political life. The imperial experience must itself also be counted as a major causal factor. It is to this that we must now turn.

The first thing which needs to be noted is that there are certain forms of humiliation which, when ended, give rise to flamboyant self-assertion. There are certain forms of deprivation which, when relieved, give rise to excessive indulgence. After the end of the American Civil War liberated Negro slaves were, for a while, in possession of money and influence. The result was often flamboyant ostentation and a swaggering way of life. Excessive indulgence had succeeded excessive indigence. Because the Negro had been too deeply humiliated in bondage, he was now too easily inebriated with power.

Something approaching a similar psychological phenomenon has been at work in Africa. In fact Nkrumah had a certain ascetic impulse in him. It is true that he spent considerable sums on the imperial structures he inherited. But his personal mode of living was not particularly indulgent. He seems to have been more extravagant on prestigious public projects than on personal forms of indulgence. He was almost certainly less self-seeking than a large number of other leaders in Africa, Asia, and Latin America.

Nevertheless, Nkrumah did have a flamboyance which was, to a certain extent, comparable to that of many American Negroes at the time of the Reconstruction following the Civil War. A keenly felt sense of racial humiliation now exploded into a self-assertion which was partly exhibitionist. The monarchical tendency was part of this.

But the monarchical style of African politics has other subsidiary causes in the colonial experience. In British Africa one subsidiary cause was the British royal tradition itself. The myth of imperial splendour came to be so intimately connected with the myth of royalty that the link was conceptually inherited by the Africans themselves. The process of political socialization in colonial schools kept on reaffirming that allegiance to the Empire was allegiance to the British monarch at the same time. This inculcation of awe towards the British royal family left some mark on even the most radical African nationalists. When the Queen appointed Nkrumah as Privy Councillor soon after Ghana's Independence, Nkrumah had the following to say of his own people following the appointment:

> As you know, during my visit to Balmoral I had the honour of being made a member of the Queen's Privy Council. As the first African to be admitted into this great Council of State, I consider it an honour not only to myself, but also to the people of Ghana and to peoples of Africa and of African descent everywhere.[1]

The tendency of African nationalists to be flattered by the royal favours of the British monarch is perhaps what made Dr John

---

[1] *I Speak of Freedom* (New York: Praeger; 1961), p. 179.

Holmes of the Canadian Institute of International Affairs come to the conclusion that 'Africans seem to have a fondness for Queens'.[1]

But what lies behind this apparent 'fondness for Queens'? One part of the answer concerns African attitudes to the British royal traditions as such. The other part of the answer is even deeper—it concerns African attitudes to the very concept of royalty itself.

The most important element in African attitudes to British royalty is, quite simply, a lingering awe. It is that awe which made Nkrumah so sincerely appreciative of being appointed a member of the Queen's Privy Council. It is the same awe which has given the history of independent Africa four knighted Prime Ministers, one knighted regional premier, one knighted President and one knighted Vice-President—some of them are still referred to with the knightly 'Sir' by their countrymen. Many of these are now off the scene and some were regarded as conservative. But their knighthoods were seldom held against them. The Prime Ministers are Sir David Jawara of the Gambia; the late Alhaji Sir Abubakar Tafawa Balewa of Nigeria; Sir Albert Margai and the late Sir Milton Margai of Sierra Leone; the regional Premier was the late Alhaji Sir Ahmadu Bello of Northern Nigeria; the President and Vice-President were Sir Edward Mutesa and Sir Wilberforce Nadiope of Uganda. These four countries involved accounted for over sixty per cent of the population of Commonwealth Africa as a whole. At a press conference in Kampala on February 23, 1967, President Obote cracked a joke at the expense of those Ugandan regional monarchs who accepted knighthoods from the British Monarch. But on the whole accepting British knighthoods has never been a point of significant political controversy in Africa.

But is all this responsiveness to British royal traditions itself part of a deeper African attachment to the concept of royalty itself? Is there such an attachment? This is what brings us back to our thesis that republicanism is, in a sense, alien to the African style of politics. The inculcation of royal awe which the British fostered in their colonies might well have reinforced the desire for monarchical glamour in the regimes which succeeded the British Raj.

[1] See his article 'The Impact on the Commonwealth of the Emergence of Africa', *International Organization*, Vol. XVI, No. 2 (Spring 1962).

But does that mean French-speaking Africans are less monarchical in their style of politics than the English-speaking ones?
After all, the French speakers were ruled by a republican colonial
power. This is true. However, what was gained by French
republicanism was lost by the greater cultural arrogance of
French colonial policy. In a sense, the French assimilationist
policy and the British inculcation of royal awe had the same effect
on the African—they reinforced the desire for a cultural glamour
that was all African. Both the French-speakers and the English-
speakers felt a need to be proud of ancient African kingdoms. And
this need for a splendid past helped to create a desire for a splendid
present. The very choice of the name 'Ghana' for the emergent
Gold Coast was part of this phenomenon. As for the psychological
quest for parity with the British royal tradition, this comes out
in statements such as the following one approvingly quoted by
Nkrumah:

> In 1066 Duke William of Normandy invaded England. In 1067
> an Andalusian Arab, El Bekr, wrote an account of the West
> African King of Ghana. This King whenever holding audience
> 'sits in a pavilion around which stand his horses caparisoned
> in cloth of gold; behind him stand the pages holding shields
> and gold-mounted swords; and on his right hand are the sons
> of the princes of his empire, splendidly clad. . . .' Barbarous
> splendour, perhaps; but was the court of this African monarch
> so much inferior, in point of organized government, to the
> court of Saxon Harold? Wasn't the balance of achievement just
> possibly the other way round?[1]

IDENTITY AND HISTORY

This revelling in ancient glory is part of the crisis of identity in
Africa. David E. Apter has argued that African nationalism has
tended to include within it a self-image of re-birth.[2] This is true.
When I first visited the United Nations in 1960–1 it was fascin-
ating to listen to some of the new African delegates revelling in

[1] See *Political Thought of Dr. Kwame Nkrumah* (Accra: Guinea Press Ltd.),
n.d., pp. 19–20.
[2] Apter, 'Political Religion in the New Nations', in *Old Societies and New
States* edited by Clifford Geertz (New York: Free Press of Glencoe, 1963), p. 79.

the innocence of newly born nationhood. But involved in this very concept of re-birth is a paradoxical desire—the desire to be grey-haired and wrinkled as a nation; of wanting to have an antiquity. This is directly linked to the crisis of identity. In so far as nations are concerned, there is often a direct correlation between *identity* and *age*. The desire to be old becomes part of the quest for identity. A country like Iran or Egypt would not have a longing for precisely the kind that Nkrumah's country was bound to have. The paradox of Nkrumah's ambition for his country was to *modernize* and *ancientize* at the same time. And so on emerging into independence the Gold Coast, as we have indicated, first decided to wear the ancient name of Ghana—and then embarked on an attempt to modernize the country as rapidly as possible. Mali is another case of trying to create a sense of antiquity by adopting an old name. In Central Africa we now have 'Malawi'. And when the hold of the white minority government in Rhodesia is broken we will probably have 'Zimbabwe'. In Nigeria a distinguished scholar has suggested that the name be changed to 'Songhai'.[1] The desire for a splendid past is by no means uniquely African. But it is sharpened in the African precisely because of the attempt of others to deny that the African has a history worth recording.

A professor of African history in an American university has argued that:

> One of the principal functions of history is to help the 'individual define his personality'. The African, as well as Western man, must see himself within a historical context. . . . To spring from an unhistoric past it to be without character and without a place in the mainstream of universal history.[2]

This is an exaggeration, but one which has many converts among black nationalists, both in Africa and in the United States. Because of the nature of humiliation to which he was subjected,

[1] Reported in the *Mombasa Times*. This point is also discussed in my paper 'Nationalism, Research and the Frontiers of Significance', in *Discussion at Bellagio: The Political Alternatives of Development*, edited by Kal Silvert and published by the American Universities Field Staff, 1964.

[2] See William H. Lewis's review of *Africa in Time-Perspective* by Daniel F. McCall (Boston: Boston University Press, 1964). The review was in *African Forum*, Vol. I, No. 1 (Summer 1965), pp. 158–60.

the Negro has often shown a passionate desire to prove that he has a past glorious enough to form part of 'the mainstream of universal history'. Occasionally, especially in the New World, the Negro has even become what a fellow Negro has called:

. . . the rash and rabid amateur who has glibly tried to prove half of the world's geniuses to have been Negroes and to trace the pedigree of nineteenth-century Americans from the Queen of Sheba.[1]

But why the Queen of Sheba? Partly because she *was* a *Queen*. In other words, the whole concept of a 'glorious history' is too often associated with the achievements of great monarchs. Taking pride in an ancient kingdom has therefore become part of the black man's quest for a historical identity.

Sometimes, the black man's interest in some splendid phase of history in Africa is a mere cultural assertion—and does not affect policy or concrete political behaviour. An example of this is the desire of nationalists like Cheikh Anta Diop of Senegal to prove that the Pharoahs were Negroes. As he put it in a talk given at the first International Conference of Negro Writers and Artists held in Paris in 1956:

. . . the ancient Egyptian and Pharaonic civilization was a Negro civilization . . . and . . . all Africans can draw the same moral advantage from it that Westerners draw from Graeco-Latin civilization.[2]

But there have been occasions when pride in an ancient kingdom has actually resulted in a significant policy decision. Such occasions include those which resulted in renaming the Gold Coast 'Ghana' and the Sudan 'Mali'. Nkrumah has even found it possible to sympathize with the pride which the British people feel for the old Empire. As he said to a British Prime Minister once:

We know that some of the older nations were willing members of the British Empire and we appreciate the historical

[1] See Arthur A. Shomburg, 'The Negro Digs up His Past' in Sylvestre C. Watkins (ed.), *An Anthology of American Negro Literature* (New York: The Modern Library, 1944), pp. 101–2.
[2] See Diop, 'The Cultural Contributions and Prospects of Africa', the *First International Conference of Negro Writers and Artists*, (Paris: *Présence Africaine*), Vols. XVIII–XIX, 1956, pp. 349–51.

significance of that institution, just as we look back with pride on our own African history to the Empire of Ghana.[1]

The same country which was soon to declare itself an African Republic had gone out of its way to name itself after an ancient empire. The paradox has other analogies in the history of African nationalism. The late W. E. B. du Bois, a founding father of Pan-Africanism, was a Marxist; but he continued to have a proud interest in ancient African monarchs. As he once put it,

> In Africa were great and powerful kingdoms. When Greek poets enumerated the kingdoms of the earth, it was not only natural but inevitable to mention Memnon, King of Ethiopia, as leader of one of the great armies that besieged Troy. When a writer like Herodotus, father of history, wanted to visit the world, he went as naturally to Egypt as Americans go to London and Paris. Nor was he surprised to find the Egyptians, as he described them, 'black and curly haired'.[2]

IDENTITY AND HEROIC LEADERSHIP

But when the tasks of creating a national future and creating a national past are undertaken at the same time, there is always the danger that the present might be caught in between. The adoration of ancient monarchs might overspill and help to create modern equivalents. Ancient kingdoms and modern presidents are then forced to share royal characteristics.

Du Bois's own first visit to Africa was after the Pan-African conference in Lisbon in 1923. By the accident of a pun, the paradox of monarchical republicanism was implicit in his very mission to Africa. Du Bois tells us:

> I held from President Coolidge of the United States status as Special Minister Plenipotentiary and Envoy Extraordinary to represent him at the second inaugural of the President King of Liberia.[3]

[1] Speech in honour of Harold Macmillan on his visit to Ghana in January 1960. See 'Hands off Africa!!!', *op. cit.*, pp. 56–7.

[2] W. E. Burghardt du Bois, *The World and Africa* (first published in 1946), New York: International Publishers, 1965 (enlarged edition), p. 121.

[3] See George Padmore (ed.), *History of the Pan-African Congress* (first published in 1947), London: William Morris House, 1963.

Another ideological influence on Pan-Africanism was Marcus Garvey, the West Indian who launched a militant Negro movement in the United States after World War I. In his own autobiography, Nkrumah came to admit that he was greatly impressed by the ideas of Marcus Garvey. It is not clear which Garveyite ideas left a durable mark on Nkrumah. What needs to be pointed out is that the paradox of monarchical republicanism was present in Garvey too. The International Convention of the Negro People of the World which he called in August 1920 was characterized by a kind of royal pomp and fanfare.

Garvey was elected provincial president of Africa. . . . As head of the African republic he envisaged, his official title was 'His Highness, the Potentate. . . .'[1]

Forty years later Kwame Nkrumah was President of a more modest African republic. His equivalent of a quasi-monarchical title was the *Osagyefo*, or the redeemer.

Yet this again is by no means a uniquely African phenomenon. Perhaps the need for heroic leadership of kingly dimensions is felt by most new nations. It was certainly felt by that 'first new nation', the United States of America. In the words of Seymour Martin Lipset, 'We tend to forget today that, in his time, George Washington was idolized as much as many of the contemporary leaders of new states.'[2] George Washington was the 'Osagyefo' of his America—adored with the same extravagance as that which came to be extended to his Ghanaian counterpart two hundred years later. The curious thing is that Washington was supposed to symbolize the triumph of republicanism over monarchism in his time. In the words of a former professor of Princeton University:

At that moment of history Tory ideas of royal prerogative controlled Europe; and the two Americas, with a large part of Asia, were dependent on Europe. Washington was to defend

[1] See E. U. Essien-Udom, *Black Nationalism, A Search for an Identity in America* (Chicago: Chicago University Press, 1962), pp. 38–9.

[2] See Lipset, *The First New Nation: The United States in Historical and Comparative Perspective* (New York: Basic Books, 1963), pp. 20–1.

against the partisans of royal or aristocratic absolutism the cause of Republicanism merging into Democracy.[1]

Yet before long the Senate and the House of Representatives of the new United States were discussing what title their first President should bear. A majority of the Senate favoured 'His Highness, the President of the United States, Protector of their Liberties'.[2] There was strong opposition from the House of Representatives. And the Senate later agreed to the simpler title of calling him 'The President of the United States'. But the Senate gave in not because it thought 'His Highness' would be wrong, but because it did not want to set a precedent of bitterness in its relations with the House of Representatives.

As for the attitude of Washington himself, he wanted the subject dropped, not because he himself was strongly opposed to 'exalted titles', but because he felt that his political opponents in the country might portray the title as a betrayal of the principles of their revolution.[3]

Yet although an actual exalted title for Washington was formally avoided, the idolization of Washington as a national hero went virtually unchecked.

When the [Revolutionary] war was won, Congress voted him an equestrian statue in bronze. 'He was to be represented in Roman dress holding a truncheon in his right hand and his head encircled with a laurel wreath.' There was a Roman amplitude about his life work, and in magnanimity of character he was as great as 'the noblest Roman of them all'. . . .[4]

The Washington cult gathered momentum. Marcus Cunliffe, the English author of what Lipset calls 'a brilliant biography of the first President', brings this out very well. He says:

In the well-worn phrase of Henry Lee, he was *first in war, first in peace and first in the hearts of his countrymen* . . . He was

---

[1] Paul Van Dyke, *George Washington, The Son of His Country, 1732–1775* (New York: Charles Scribner, 1931), pp. 3–5.

[2] See Douglas Southall Freeman, *George Washington, A Biography*, Vol. XI (*Patriot and President*), New York: Charles Scribner's Sons, 1954, p. 186.

[3] *Ibid.*

[4] Van Dyke, *op. cit.*, p. 5.

the prime native hero, a necessary creation for a new country.
. . . Hence . . . the comment made by the European traveller
Paul Svinin, as early as 1815: 'Every American considers it his
sacred duty to have a likeness of Washington in his home, just
as we have the images of God's saints.' For America, he was
originator and vindicator, both patron *and* defender of the
faith, in a curiously timeless fashion, as if he were Charle-
magne, Saint Joan and Napoleon Bonaparte telescoped into one
person . . .[1]

The idea that Washington was one of the few men ever to
succeed in changing the course of world history has substantially
persisted to the present day. Van Dyke has argued that Washington affected the future of mankind more deeply than did Napoleon. To use his words,

> If young Washington had been among the hundreds scalped
> at Braddox's defeat, it would have had on the political develop-
> ment of the world a deeper and more durable effect than if the
> young Napoleon had been killed at the bridge of Lodi.[2]

IDENTITY AND SACRED RULERS

But admiration of secular heroes can too easily assume a sacred
dimension. This tendency is again particularly marked in the
political situation of a new state. In his discussion of 'political
religion' in the new states, David Apter has argued that:

> The 'birth' of the nation is thus a religious event, forming a
> fund of political grace that can be dispensed over the years.
> The agent of rebirth is normally an individual—an Nkrumah,
> a Touré who, as leader of the political movement, is midwife
> to the birth of the nation.[3]

[1] Cunliffe, *George Washington, Man and Monument* (New York: Mentor
Books, 1960), pp. 20–1.
[2] Van Dyke, *op. cit.*, pp. 4–5.
[3] See Apter, 'Political Religion in the New Nations' in Clifford Geertz
(ed.), *Old Societies and New States* (New York: Free Press of Glencoe, 1963),
pp. 82–4.

Apter then cites the adulation accorded to Nkrumah, illustrating
with the eulogy by Tawia Adamafio, the former Chairman of the
Convention People's Party:

> To us, his people, Kwame Nkrumah is our father, teacher, our
> brother, our friend, indeed our lives, for without him we
> would no doubt have existed, but we would not have lived;
> there would have been no hope of a cure for our sick souls, no
> taste of glorious victory after a lifetime of suffering. What we
> owe him is greater even than the air we breathe, for he made
> us as surely as he made Ghana.[1]

Here again the analogy with George Washington is compelling.
In his biography of Washington, Cunliffe refers to the dying
Roman emperor Vespasian who is supposed to have murmured:
'Alas, I think I am about to become a god.' Cunliffe goes on to
add:

> George Washington . . . might with justice have thought the
> same thing as he lay on his deathbed at Mount Vernon in
> 1799. Babies were being christened after him as early as 1775,
> and while he was still President, his countrymen paid to see
> him in waxwork effigy. To his admirers he was 'godlike
> Washington', and his detractors complained to one another
> that he was looked upon as a 'demi-god' whom it was treason-
> able to criticize. 'O Washington!' declared Ezra Stiles of Yale
> (in a sermon of 1783). 'How I do love thy name! How have I
> often adored and blessed thy God, for creating and forming
> thee the great ornament of human kind!'[2]

Editors of newspapers, speech-makers, and poets in early America
often indulged in eulogizing Washington in godly dimensions.
The editor of the *Gazette of the United States*, an extravagant
admirer of Washington, used at times the kind of epithets which
were later to be echoed by the Young Pioneers of Nkrumah's
Ghana. A factor which contributed to the expulsion of an arch-
bishop from Ghana in 1962 was the spread of slogans claiming

---

[1] Adamafio, *A Portrait of the Osagyefo Dr. Kwame Nkrumah* (Accra: Government Printer, 1960), p. 95. See Apter, *op. cit.*
[2] Cunliffe, *op. cit.*, pp. 15–16.

that Nkrumah would never die. Some members of the clergy in Ghana expressed reservations about the ethics of teaching such slogans—and a crisis ensued for a while for churchmen in the country.[1] Yet claims of immortality for heroes also go back at least to that 'first new nation', the United States. As that Editor of the *Gazette* put it in his euology of Washington:

> Fill the bowl, fill it high,
> First born son of the sky,
> May he never, never die,
> Heaven shout, Amen.[2]

A letter from Boston published in the same newspaper expressed similar sentiments about the first President:

> So near perfection, that he stood
> Upon the boundary line,
> Of finite, from the infinite good,
> Of human from divine.[3]

The *Gazette* was perhaps the most pro-Washington newspaper at the time. But eulogies to Washington were to be found in other newspapers as well. It was the *Daily Advertiser*, for example, which published a poem by a New York woman which said of the national leader:

> The man's divine—let angels write his name
> In the bright records of eternal fame.[4]

It is this extravagance of early adoration of George Washington which made him the Osagyefo of young America.

In Africa in more recent times this *degree* of adulation was by no means typical. Only Nkrumah was adored in terms which were anywhere near those used in the admiration of George Washington. Nevertheless, almost everywhere in Africa there

[1] For a brief discussion of some of the implications, please see Ali A. Mazrui, 'Africa and the Egyptian's Four Circles', *African Affairs*, London (April 1964).

[2] Cited by Freeman, *op. cit.*, p. 212.

[3] Letter to the Editor, *Gazette of the United States*, April 25, 1789. Cited by Freeman, *op. cit.*, p. 184.

[4] The *Daily Advertiser*, June 26, 1789. Cited by Freeman, *op. cit.*, p. 212.

has been a tendency to spiritualize the head of state or government in these initial years following independence.

It is this tendency towards sacred leadership which, perhaps more than any other factor, makes republicanism somewhat unsuited to the style of politics of new states. This is to assume that republicanism is usually a governmental system of secular orientation, but the assumption is more than merely defensible historically. What monarchical republics of Africa have now been out to assert is the new doctrine of the divine right of founder-Presidents. Nor is the doctrine entirely without justification in countries which have yet to establish legitimacy and consolidate the authority of the government. As Apter has put it, 'the sacred characteristic becomes essential to maintain solidarity in the community'.[1] The British Queen may be no more than a *symbol* of national unity; but the head of a new state may be an essential *basis* of such unity. He, too, might need to be accepted as 'God's anointed'—and feel 'this hot libation poured by some aged priest!'

This is where Africa's own traditional royal ways become pertinent in at least those communities which have a monarchical background. Some modern equivalent is sometimes needed for the old Stool of the Chief. As K. Macnell Steward, the West Indian poet living in Ghana, once put it,

> Here, faith, religion, centres in one thing—
> The Stool: take this away—the nation dies
> And even colour fades out of the skies
>   of Africa. . . .
> In you mute things repose a nation's soul.[2]

Hence titles like 'osagyefo' for Presidents of Republics. Such titles help to lend traditional sacredness to modernizing leadership. The words themselves have connotations that might sometimes defy the visiting student of African politics. As Ruth Schachter Morgenthau has put it,

> We are accustomed to discuss the pattern of authority within parties as collective, or personal, charismatic, institutionalized

---

[1] *Op. cit.*, p. 83.
[2] See his 'Ode to Stools and Stool Worship', *African Affairs* (Journal of the Royal African Society), Vol. LII, No. 208 (July 1953), pp. 185–97.

but each word has a history and a set of associations, mostly Western. How are we to understand references to *Fama*, roughly 'king' in Malinke, used in referring to Sékou Touré of Guinea?[1]

There have indeed been occasions when attempts to 'royalize' an African republic have been resisted by the leader himself. The most striking example of this so far has been Julius Nyerere. He has tried to discourage even such minimal ways of adulation as having streets named after him or having too many photographs of himself distributed to the public. And when, on the eve of the presidential election in Tanzania in 1965, Zanzibari newspapers were saying 'Let us elect President Nyerere as our President for life', Nyerere warned the people of Zanzibar about the dangers of excessive surrender to a leader. He said:

> I might stay on until I am too old to do my job properly and then tell my son to act for me. When I died he might claim a right to the Presidency—and call himself Sultan Nyerere I; and there might be a second and a third.[2]

But in many ways Nyerere is an exception. And, in any case, the mere fact that there were public demands for his installation as President for life is an indication of the responsiveness of ordinary Africans to certain monarchical ways.

CONCLUSION

It was perhaps fitting in the history of African nationalism that the three most moving cases of exile in the colonial days should have concerned African monarchs. There was the flight and exile of Emperor Haile Selassie of Ethiopia following Mussolini's invasion of his country. This was an event which gave early African nationalists and Negro radicals in the New World a deep sense of personal humiliation.[3]

[1] Morgenthau, *Political Parties in French-Speaking West Africa* (Oxford: Clarendon Press, 1964), p. xviii.
[2] See *East Africa and Rhodesia* (London), Vol. XLII, No. 2138, September 30, 1965, p. 72.
[3] Nkrumah tells us his reaction when, on arrival in London in 1935, he saw the placard of a newspaper stand 'Mussolini invades Ethiopia'. 'At that

Then there was the exile of the Kabaka of Buganda in 1953—a case of an African king defying a British governor, and then being sent away from his people as punishment.

A few years earlier there had been the exile of Seretse Khama, King of the Bamangwato—kept away from his people by the British because he had married a white girl.

All three exiles during the colonial period were pregnant with powerful symbolism for African nationalists everywhere. The sense of racial humiliation was sharpened by the very fact that these were African *kings* who were suffering the indignity of expulsion from their own kingdoms.

Today exile of African rulers by colonial powers is, by and large, a thing of the past. But the royal theme in African nationalism has only found new expressions. The capital of Pan-Africanism is Addis Ababa, which of course, is also the capital of an old dynastic African empire. The President of the Ivory Coast has built himself a Palace which is almost an African equivalent of Versailles. The President of Malawi invokes witchcraft to spiritualize his absolutism. The President of Kenya has at times come near to borrowing the symbols of 'the King of Kings' himself. The highlight of the Kenyatta Day celebrations on October 20, 1965, for example, nearly became a 'Last Supper'—commemorating the last supper that President Kenyatta had before being arrested in connection with the Mau Mau uprising.[1]

Both the palaces and the political prayers are sometimes intended to create the necessary awe towards authority and make national integration possible. In a sense, the phenomenon bears comparison with the dual position of Elizabeth II—Queen of England and Head of the Anglican Church. This tie between Church and State in England is now little more than a formal legacy of British history. But in Africa the spiritualization of the head of state is part of the struggle for national cohesion. And for as long as that spiritualization continues to be deemed

---

moment it was almost as if the whole of London had declared war on me personally.' He glared at the faces that passed him, wondering whether they appreciated the essential wickedness of colonialism. 'My nationalism surged to the fore.' See his *Autobiography* (Edinburgh: Thomas Nelson, 1957), p. 27.

[1] See *The Times* (London), October 7, 1965. For protest against the supper, couched in racialistic anti-African terms, see *East Africa and Rhodesia*, October 14, 1965, p. 108.

necessary, the secular rationalism which we normally associate with republicanism will have a touch of incongruity in an African political universe.

Yet the sacralization of authority, as well as its personalization, is a phenomenon mainly of the peak of political power in an African country. It is the head of government or the head of state who comes to symbolize 'the soul of the nation'. What is a more widespread phenomenon is the general quest for aristocratic effect. This manifests itself not merely in the paramount leader, but also further down in the pyramid of élite status. And the tendency is persisting even after the *coups* in those countries which have ousted their old political regimes. Not long after the Nigerian *coup*, one of the leading columnists in the country lamented in the following terms:

> What a nice gesture it would have been if the military leaders had reciprocated [the people's call for self-imposed austerity] by leaving the official residences built by the ostentatious politicians strictly alone . . . If, as it is widely believed, they were advised that their personal prestige would be enhanced by moving into these mansions, I say it is nonsense. . . . It was a mistake for them to move into the palatial edifices which had become objects of much resentment among the people.[1]

The writer allowed that Major-General Aguiyi-Ironsi might indeed have had to move into the State House 'for the sake of protocol'. After all, he was not only Supreme Commander but also head of state. 'He needs the royal environment of State House, Marina.' But what about the provincial governors? What about senior military men generally?

> Nigerians would have loved to see them riding around in their official military vehicles, escorted by their troops. But not in the Rolls-Royces bought by flamboyant politicians. Not escorted by police out-riders, sirens wailing and traffic brought to a standstill. This nation needs a sense of urgency, a toning down of high living . . . a manifestation of that exemplary

[1] Peter Pan, 'The First 100 Days: Spirit of the Revolution', *Daily Times* (Lagos), April 28, 1966.

self-denial which was so lacking among the politicians . . .
And the leadership must come from the Army.[1]

This was a voice of an African intellectual rebelling against the
recurrent quest for aristocratic effect within the leadership of his
country even after a major national shock like a violent military
coup. But the aristocratic and kingly aspects of African styles of
politics have deep roots, both in African traditions and in the total
impact of the colonial experience. African conceptions of earned
rewards, the spiritualization of ancestors, the quest for a historical
identity, the assertion of cultural equality, the general desire for
political glamour, have all contributed their share to the
monarchical tendencies in African politics. Behind it all is the
newness of African politics, and the need to strengthen the
legitimacy of the regimes with sacred symbols and romantic awe.

[1] *Ibid.* Some of these factors are also discussed in my book *The Anglo-
African Commonwealth: Political Friction and Cultural Fusion* (Oxford: Pergamon
Press, 1967).

11 Moise Tshombe and the Arabs: 1960—1968[1]

In the first seven years of its independence (June 1960 to July 1967) a number of factors went towards making the Congo an embodiment of an African tragedy. But few of those were perhaps more poignant than the fact that one of the ablest of all Congolese politicians was also among the least patriotic in the terms understood by contemporary Africa. There was little doubt that Tshombe was, in personality, political adroitness and intellectual calculation, a bigger man than ever Lumumba was. In nationalistic terms, Lumumba had the right political convictions but he had the wrong qualities for leadership. He seemed confused in tactical judgment and unpredictable in his political moods. He was less than mature in his governmental behaviour.

Tshombe, on the other hand, demonstrated a polished style of political manoeuvre and an air of sophisticated calculation. What was wrong with Tshombe were his political ethics. Conor Cruise O'Brien, who was a United Nations' officer at the time of Katanga's secession and conducted negotiations with Tshombe, described Tshombe in a lecture given at Makerere University College in 1964 as 'the best politician that money can buy'. If Lumumba lacked competence but possessed a Pan-African conscience, Tshombe had the competence but entirely lacked the conscience. Tshombe had the right skills but the wrong views, Lumumba the right views but the wrong skills. The ultimate pathos of the history of the Congo in its first seven years was that it did not produce a leader who could combine the best of Tshombe with the best of Lumumba—the adroitness of Tshombe with the

[1] An earlier version of this essay was presented at the Seventh World Congress of the International Political Science Association in Brussels in September 1967, and published in a revised form in *Race*, January, 1969. It is reprinted here with the permission of the editors.

ambitions of Lumumba. In short, the tragedy of the Congo was that the Lumumbist ethos did not find a Tshombe to bring it to fruition and fulfilment.

Be that as it may, Moise Tshombe had earned a distinct place in Africa's history. Few leaders have aroused as deep feelings or been more central to major debates. The first few years of Africa's independence have also been the years of Tshombe as a dominant theme in the headlines of the continent.

This story of Tshombe has points of contact with the story of Arab participation in African affairs since 1960. Wittingly or unwittingly, it has perhaps been pre-eminently Tshombe who was often instrumental in giving the Arabs some of their most active roles in the major issues of independent Africa. It is with this theme that this essay is primarily concerned—against the background of the fact that it was an Arab country, Algeria, which in June 1967 acquired the power to send Tshombe home to face a death penalty passed upon him.

ALGERIA'S INDEPENDENCE AND KATANGA'S SECESSION

But let us first go back to that dawn June 1960, the month of the Congo's independence. 1960 was also the year of the independence of sixteen other African countries.

A number of questions arose as the brush of sovereignty re-decorated the map of Africa. At first it looked as if a pervasive sense of fellowship was going to characterize relations between the new African states. The bonds of a shared continent, of a shared colour, and of a shared colonial experience held the promise of inter-African cordiality, if not inter-African intimacy.

And yet two diplomatic issues were soon to tear the continent apart. The first was the tempestuous beginning of the Congo's independence; the other was the tempestuous ending of French rule in Algeria. African states took sides on these matters—and there was more than one side to take. These were the issues which led to the division of African states into the Casablanca group and the Monrovia group, at loggerheads with each other. And within the Monrovia group was the Brazzaville cluster of French-speaking states.

The problems of Algeria and the Congo in those first few

months of Africa's independence in 1960–61 were then the two issues which, quite early, shattered all hopes of a homogeneous diplomatic climate in the new Africa.

Curiously enough, the principle of secession was involved in both issues. It is true that the immediate spark which started the Congo's conflagration was the mutiny of the Congolese army. The mutiny was certainly the factor which suddenly created a situation of potential external intervention. The anarchy which ensued on the breakdown of military discipline led first to the coming of Belgian troops in the Congo, and then—at the invitation of Lumumba—to the coming of the United Nations with the task of restoring law and order. But order might have been restored more smoothly if all that was at stake were the mutinous troops. After all, order was restored in East Africa quite speedily in 1964 after the mutineers had been subdued by British troops.

What delayed the solution of the Congolese crisis in 1960 was the fact that, soon after the army had mutinied, the first major political upheaval took place. The richest province of the country, Katanga, declared its independence. The leader of Katanga in her bid to secede from the Congo was, of course, Moise Tshombe.

In strict legality, the problem of Algeria too in 1960 was a problem of secession. The French position on Algeria had for a long time rested on the claim that Algeria was a province of France—very much as Katanga was a province of the Congo. If then the National Liberation Movement in Algeria was demanding independence from France it was, by at least a legal fiction, demanding the right to secede. Ferhat Abbass, the diplomatic head of the Algerian National Liberation Movement, was legally the Moise Tshombe of Algeria, making a bid to tear a province of France from the metropole.

For African radicals like Nkrumah, the analogy was false to its very bowels. In the words of Nkrumah,

That Algeria, a country in Africa, is French is a ridiculous concept. France belongs to the continent of Europe; Algeria belongs to the continent of Africa. . . . Africa is not an extension of Europe or of any other continent.[1]

[1] See Nkumrah, 'Positive Action in Africa', in *Africa Speaks* (eds.) James Duffy and Robert A. Manners (Princeton, N.J: D. Van Nostrand, 1961), pp. 49, 53.

But there were a number of countries in the French-speaking sector of black Africa which virtually accepted the old French claims to Algeria, at least for a while. Some of them were perhaps slower in changing their views about Algeria than General de Gaulle himself. Apart from Guinea and Mali, hardly any of the French-speaking countries were *ahead* of the General in their thinking about the future of Algeria. In gradual and sometimes painful stages, the delusion that Algeria was part of France was abandoned. But most of the French-speaking African states south of the Sahara were reluctant to force the pace of Algerian liberation.

In October 1960 independent Africa's first diplomatic faction came into being in Abidjan in the Ivory Coast. It was a meeting summoned by the Ivory Coast to discuss the possibility of the Francophone African states mediating between France and Algeria. But the motivation was apparently not so much to speed up Algeria's independence as to try and avert the risk of more active UN support for the FLN. Friends of the FLN had been asking for a referendum in Algeria, supervised by the United Nations, to ascertain the people's will on the issue of Algeria's separation from France. The French-speaking African countries meeting in Abidjan were against this proposal. It was this group which, two months later, became the Brazzaville group—the 'Union of African States and Madagascar'. In their communique they described the proposed United Nations' solution to Algeria as 'a negative solution, consisting in an illusory resort to UNO, for the organization and control of a referendum in a country which does not come under the guardianship of UNO'.[1]

This was the beginning of institutionalized factionalism in African diplomacy. The same states which were against directing United Nations efforts towards solving the Algerian problem were also against directing those efforts to solve the problem of Katanga's secession from the Congo. According to these states, the United Nations was by all means to provide technical assistance to the Congo—but, to use the words of the Brazzaville Declaration, 'UNO is not required to substitute for the Congolese authorities'. In other words, the world body was not to give

[1] See the Brazzaville Declaration, Appendix 13, in Colin Legum's *Pan-Africanism: A Short Political Guide* (London: Pall Mall Press, 1965 edition), p. 198.

support to the central Government in its attempt to put an end
to Mr Tshombe's Unilateral Declaration of Independence.

TOWARDS THE BIRTH OF O.A.U.

Once this Francophone diplomatic faction was institutionalized,
another followed suit. The radical faction of African diplomacy
came to bear the name of an Arab metropolis. The African states
which had supported Lumumba's position on the Congo had been
feeling the need for greater coordination. In January 1961 they
met in Casablanca. The heads of Ghana, Guinea, Mali, the United
Arab Republic, Morocco and the Algerian Government in Exile
met in that old North African city—and the radical Casablanca
faction of African states came into being.[1] It was on the side of
Lumumba in the Congo and on the side of the FLN in Algeria.

But January 1961 was the ominous month when Lumumba
was handed over by Kasavubu to Moise Tshombe ostensibly for
safe-keeping. A month later the disturbing news was announced.
Lumumba had been assassinated in Katanga, apparently with the
connivance if not instigation of Moise Tshombe. There was a wave
of indignation throughout the Third World. Within Africa itself
perhaps none were more angry about Lumumba's assassination
than the Casablanca countries.

The diplomatic battles for the cause which Lumumba had
stood for continued. But there was also a human side to the
vacuum caused by Lumumba's death—especially in relation to
his own family. And so Egypt became the new home of Lumumba's widow and Lumumba's children. Partly for cheap diplomatic reasons, partly for high nationalistic ideals, and partly
for simple humanitarian considerations, Egypt became the refuge
and educational haven of the offspring of Africa's most celebrated
martyr.

In May 1961 the Monrovia faction of African diplomacy came
into being, consisting of the old Brazzaville states, plus a number of
the other 'moderate' African states. The Casablanca states were
not there. The African division was becoming deep.

---

[1] Also represented were Libya and Ceylon. But Ceylon was more of an
observer. And Libya was not represented by the head of government nor did
it later sign the Casablanca protocol.

Nigeria's Prime Minister at the time, the late Alhaji Sir Abubakar Tafawa Balewa, took the initiative in calling another conference a few months later to try and bridge the gulf. The conference was to take place in Lagos in January 1962. Algeria was still not independent, but it did have a provisional government in exile. Sir Abubakar invited the Algerians. The first objections came from some of the French-speaking members of the Monrovia group. Before long Africa was divided afresh on whether the Algerians should be given full diplomatic status at such a conference or not. The Casablanca states made Algeria's attendance as an equal a condition of their own attendance. They could hardly do less for one of their own members of the Casablanca group. On the eve of the conference they declared their boycott of it.

There were some Arab states which were not members of the Casablanca group. These were Tunisia, Libya and the Sudan. But even these could no longer participate in the conference if the issue was whether Algeria was to be accepted or not. So they too withdrew from the Lagos gathering.

Nigerians were deeply hurt by the so-called 'Arab boycott'. The *West African Pilot*, Nnamdi Azikiwe's newspaper, carried an editorial entitled 'Arab First, Arab Last'. But much of the Nigerian indignation might, in reality, have arisen from their suspicion that Kwame Nkrumah was the man who had instigated the Arabs against the Lagos conference. There was certainly evidence that Nkrumah was opposed to the idea of such a conference even before the Algerian issue became live. There was therefore a marked suspicion in some quarters that the question of Algeria's representation at the conference had simply been a pretext, rather than a genuine explanation of the Casablanca boycott of the Lagos meeting. But the truth of the matter is that both Nkrumah's personal opposition to Balewa's initiative and the desire of the Casablanca states to stand by Algeria when her status was at stake played their part in determining the course of events.

It was not until the middle of the following year that Africa's institutionalized factionalism was ended—at least for a while. At a historic meeting in Addis Ababa in May 1963 the Organization of African Unity was born, pledged to put an end to the diplomatic groupings which had until then put a strain on interstate relations within the continent. Both the Casablanca and the Monrovia blocs were liquidated; and early the following year even the Francophone U.A.M. as a political organization was, at least for a while, dissolved. So too was PAFMECSA in Eastern Africa.

But even if we accept the proposition that the Organization of African Unity was successful in ending institutionalized factionalism, the O.A.U. most certainly did not end factionalism itself. By that time Algeria had become independent. But the Congo retained its vitality as a perenially divisive factor in African diplomacy at large.

TSHOMBE AND AFRO-ARAB NONALIGNMENT

At first all seemed well because Katanga's secession had been forcefully ended by the United Nations, and Moise Tshombe had gone into semi-voluntary exile in Europe for the time being. The United Nations moved out of the Congo, and the country was at last ostensibly permitted to handle its own affairs.

But in July 1964 yet another strange phenomenon emerged from the womb of the Congo. To the astonishment of the rest of the world, Congolese President Joseph Kasavubu announced that Tshombe would succeed Prime Minister Cyrille Adoula who had come to the end of his tenure of office. Tshombe, who had become a symbol of latent Congolese disintegration, was now being called upon to return to his country and take over the reins of power and the direction of national unity. From a symbol of secessionism he was being asked now to become an instrument of consolidation. Africans themselves in other parts of the continent were at first uncertain how to react to the appointment of Tshombe as Prime Minister of the Congo. But before long a conviction re-asserted itself that to recognize Tshombe was to forgive him for those moments of betrayal in the first few months of his country's independence. And so many African countries refused to have any dealings with Moise Tshombe. Among those who were the most forthright in refusing this recognition were, in fact, the Arab states.

Later in 1964 an Arab country seemed to have within its power the chance of giving Moise Tshombe some legitimacy in the diplomatic circles of the Third World. Cairo was the host city to a conference of nonaligned countries. Tshombe immediately grasped the potentialities of the situation. If only he could attend the meeting at the head of the Congolese delegation, he would *ipso facto* have made some progress in his quest for diplomatic recognition.

Would Cairo refuse the Congo the right to representation at the conference?

The question hinged on whether the Congo's representation at the meeting would be headed by Tshombe. Egypt seemed to be in a predicament. On the one hand, she probably felt that outright alienation of a major African country like the Congo might be diplomatically expensive. On the other hand, there was no doubt that many of those who were participating at the meeting of nonaligned states in Cairo would have found it unacceptable to share a conference chamber with Moise Tshombe.

Indeed, on October 4, the Foreign Ministers who had been preparing the agenda for the summit conference of nonaligned states in Cairo had approved a resolution in favour of excluding Prime Minister Tshombe from the conference. President Nasser thereupon sent a cable to President Kasavubu personally inviting Kasavubu to come but leave Mr Tshombe behind. Mr Tshombe had already announced his intention to attend the conference. The sponsors of the conference said in their cable to Kasavubu that Tshombe's attendance would not be desirable in view of the feelings expressed by some of the other delegations. Kasavubu was assured that this was not an attempt to interfere in the internal affairs of the Congo but was 'above all a sincere desire to avoid unnecessary difficulties liable to impede the work of the Conference'.[1]

Undeterred by all this, Moise Tshombe left for Cairo. The Cairo airport authorities refused his plane landing rights, although Tshombe had apparently been issued with the UAR visa in Leopoldville. His plane was diverted to Athens. From Athens the determined Mr Tshombe boarded a commercial Ethiopian airliner bound for Cairo. He arrived there on October 6.

The authorities in Cairo held him in comfortable isolation while further consultations were held. It was reported that a few states at the conference, including Nigeria, Liberia and Senegal,

[1] *The Times* (London), October 6, 1964.

defended Tshombe's right to attend the conference. But most of the other delegations expressed reservations. A leading voice against Tshombe's attendance was the President of Algeria at the time, President Ben Bella. He had declared in advance that he would not attend the conference if Tshombe was present. And he described Tshombe himself as 'a travelling museum of imperialism'.[1]

In the face of Tshombe's 'gate-crashing' tactics President Nasser called the heads of other states in Cairo to a special session. And the heads approved the Foreign Minister's earlier decision that Tshombe's participation at the conference would be 'inopportune'.

Leopoldville seemed to have interpreted the decision as an Arab insult against the Congo. Congolese security forces sealed off the embassies of the United Arab Republic and Algeria. President Nasser told Mr Tshombe that he would not be permitted to leave Cairo until the Congolese Government withdrew its police cordons around the UAR and Algeria embassies in Leopoldville.

On the next day the Congolese Government lifted the guard, and the embassy staffs of the UAR and Algeria left for Brazzaville, escorted to the ferry by a detachment of troops. President Nasser then permitted Mr Tshombe to leave the United Arab Republic.[2] Mr Tshombe thus returned to Leopoldville after his abortive trip to Cairo. He was given a tremendous welcome by thousands of Congolese, who chanted, 'Long live Tshombe, Arabs go home'. How different was this from the cry in 1967 when Tshombe was in the hands of the Algerians and the Congolese Government wanted him back to come and face his death sentence. In this case instead of 'Long live Tshombe, Arabs go home', the cry from the Congo, from the middle of Africa, was 'Down with Tshombe, Arabs send him home'! Be that as it may, on October 17, 1964, at a mass rally in Leopoldville, Prime Minister Tshombe accused Egyptian and Algerian leaders of plotting to kill him and of defying the national sovereignty of the Congo by taking it upon themselves to decide on the composition of the Congolese delegation at the Cairo conference of

[1] See Peter Mansfield's report in the *Sunday Times* (London), October 11, 1964.
[2] See *West Africa*, October 10, 1964 and *Africa Report*, Vol. IX, No. 10, November 1964, p. 19.

non-aligned nations. Recalling that Arabs had long been involved
in the Congolese slave-trade, Mr Tshombe declared that all Arab
citizens from the United Arab Republic and Algeria would be
requested to leave the Congo. Seldom had the animosity between
the Arabs and Moise Tshombe been as intense as it was following
that meeting of non-aligned powers in October 1964.

THE ARABS AND INTRA-AFRICAN INTERVENTION

In the meantime African states at large had begun to feel less and
less inhibited in actively supporting Tshombe's opponents within
the Congo. Among those who took a leading part in siding with
the rebels against Tshombe were, in fact, Arab states. In a letter
dated December 24, 1964, addressed to the UN Security Council,
Tshombe charged that Algerian and Egyptian officers were
actually serving with rebel forces on the Northeast frontier of his
country.

But by what canons of diplomatic behaviour could Arab intervention in the Congo at that time be defended?

This brings us to two related concepts in African diplomatic
thought—the principle of Continental Jurisdiction and the idea
of Racial Sovereignty. The principle of Continental Jurisdiction
is the one which asserts that there are certain African problems
which should only be solved by Africans themselves. This sounds
like an African Monroe Doctrine, but there is an important
difference. The trouble with the Monroe Doctrine is that it is not
continental but hemispheric. It has given the Colossus of North
America jurisdiction over the affairs of South America and related
islands. In African diplomatic thought, there is something
unnatural in hemispheric jurisdiction—it would have made
better sense if the unit of exclusiveness was the continent rather
than the hemisphere. Americans and Canadians could then form
one continental system; South and Central America and the
Latin Islands another system.

This principle of continental exclusiveness as enunciated in
Africa is not intended to *replace* the principle of state sovereignty.
Like the Monroe Doctrine itself, it just introduces an additional
dimension to the doctrine of non-intervention, but with a
different unit of exclusiveness. Thus a Cuban 'intervention' in

the Dominican Republic would be a 'domestic' affair of Latin America according to the principle of Continental Jurisdiction, but an *external* violation of the rights of the Dominicans according to state sovereignty. A new level of *externality* could be said to have been introduced by the *North* American intervention in the Dominican Republic in 1965. In other words, just as a Ghanaian interference in Nigerian affairs is less 'external' than, say, Chinese interference in Nigerian affairs would be, so Cuban interference in the Dominican Republic would be less 'external' than American intervention could be deemed to be.

The principle of Continental Jurisdiction is related to another principle implicit in African diplomatic thought—the principle of Racial Sovereignty. Sometimes the unit of exclusiveness is not strictly a continent but a 'race' in a loose sense. The concept of 'Latin America' is itself partly continental and partly 'racial' in a loose linguistic sense. But an even better example is that of the Arabs. Egyptian and Saudi 'intervention' in the Yemen is a 'domestic' affair of the Arabs according to Racial Sovereignty, even though it is an external violation of self-determination for the Yeminis according to state sovereignty.

North Africans are, in fact, well placed to benefit by both the principle of Continental Jurisdiction and of Racial Sovereignty. That of Continental Jurisdiction gives Algeria and the United Arab Republic some kind of 'family' right to interfere in the affairs of the Congo; while the principle of Racial Sovereignty gives them a family right to take sides in Yemeni quarrels. By the same token the idea of Continental Jurisdiction gave black Africans the right to mediate in the border dispute between Algeria and Morocco. What has yet to be brought to the test is the right of black Africans to interfere in North Africa in the way that North Africans have sometimes interfered in the affairs of the Congo. This is not to suggest that, given similar situations, Arab Africans will react in a less Pan-African spirit than black Africans have done. If a civil war like that of the Congo were to break out in a North African country, and one side started recruiting mercenaries from Gibraltar, Portugal and South Africa, black Africans might feel as free to help the other side as Arab Africans have felt in helping Tshombe's opponents. And the broader unity between the two sides of the Sahara could still survive this Trans-Saharan intervention. All we know at the moment is that there has not as yet been a North African Congo.[1]

An additional touch of vindicating irony for Arab intervention was provided by the kind of white mercenaries that Tshombe employed in his fight against internal challenges to his power. Algeria, which had got mixed up with the politics of Katanga's secessionism in 1960, was to touch the history of the Congo in other ways too. Many of the die-hard white settlers of Algeria, bitterly disillusioned after Algeria's independence, ended up in Tshombe's pay roll. A major recruiting market for Tshombe seemed to be among the angry malcontents from French Algeria. Some were former members of the French Army. There were occasions when France itself seemed to be a major centre of military purchases by Moise Tshombe. Section 85 of the French Penal Code had sometimes to be invoked against offenders—a section which apparently provided up to five years' imprisonment for recruiting troops on French soil 'on behalf of a foreign power'. Tshombe's recruiting agencies disguised their activities well whenever they thought the French authorities were extra alert. But the point which is being made here is simply the fact that out of the bitter loss of Algeria came an extra source of mercenaries for Tshombe. From the ranks of former Algerian malcontents, Tshombe recruited some of his henchmen. And from the resources of the old National Liberation Front of Algeria, Tshombe's opponents in the Congo sought in turn military sustenance.[2]

ABDUCTION IN AFRICAN POLITICS

Tshombe's side in the Congo in 1964–5 ultimately won. It won in spite of the help that the Arab states, Uganda and other African countries gave to the rebels against Tshombe's Government. Yet Tshombe's military victories against his Congolese opponents did not assure him power for long. Differences between

[1] See the paper 'African Doctrines of Non-Intervention' in my collection *On Heroes and Uhuru-Worship: Essays on Independent Africa* (London: Longmans, 1967).

[2] Journalists' reports in August 1967 indicated that former white Algerian adventurers continued to 'grace' the ranks of white mercenaries involved in the Congo.

him and Kasavubu were aggravated, and it soon appeared as if the two were going to wrestle for the highest office in the land—the Presidency. But in December 1965 General Mobutu put an end to the contest between politicians, and took over power himself. Moise Tshombe once again left for exile in Europe.

His next dramatic re-appearance in world news was in July 1967 when the plane on which he was travelling was high-jacked over the Mediterranean and brought to Algiers. Ben Bella had, as we indicated, once described Tshombe as a 'travelling museum of imperialism'. But now Tshombe's travels had brought him to the reluctant destination of Algiers—and into the embarrassed custody of Ben Bella's successor, Colonel Boumedienne.

Kidnapping as a form of political vengeance or prelude to civic justice falls within a variety of traditions in political behaviour at large. In Africa—north and south of the Sahara—abduction has tended to be pre-eminently a Francophone style of gamesmanship and intrigue. This is not to suggest that there has been no abduction in the politics of English-speaking Africa. It is merely to point out that, whether by accident or not, Francophone Africa has had a more consistent 'tradition' of kidnapping than other parts of the continent.

Sometimes France herself has been implicated in this phenomenon. In the course of the Algerian war, for example, there were cases of dramatic abduction conducted with the full contrivance of French authorities. Then there was the kidnapping of Ben Berka, the Moroccan radical, from a street in Paris in 1965—a kidnapping and suspected killing which compromised again the French police itself. And in French-speaking black Africa there was in 1967 the forceful restriction of Guinea's Foreign Minister by the Ivory Coast—a whole Guinean delegation from the United Nations having been virtually hi-jacked from a plane. The only difference in the case was that the plane carrying the Minister and the delegation was not 'hi-jacked' in the sky but when it had momentarily landed at an airport in the Ivory Coast on the way home to Guinea.

The Congo itself has been a long story of hostages and counter-hostages. Tshombe's own men have been known to kidnap United Nations' personnel. Curiously even these included Arabs. Late in 1962, in his last-ditch effort to keep Katanga out of the Congo, Tshombe's men abducted five Tunisian soldiers. It took a tense period of negotiations and United Nations' toughness to get them released.

And now the most dramatic abduction in the history of modern Africa has involved Moise Tshombe himself. In July 1967 the plane on which he was travelling was hi-jacked, and brought to the capital of Algeria. The Congolese Government requested his extradition to the Congo so that he could face the death sentence which had been passed on him for treason. The Algerian Supreme Court sat to decide whether the offences with which Tshombe had been charged were political or not. They decided that some of the offences were plain criminal—and Tshombe was therefore extraditable. It was now up to the Algerian Government itself to decide whether or not Tshombe was to be extradited.

It has been suggested that the abduction of Moise Tshombe afforded an opportunity for an African Nuremberg. Nuremberg was of course the great international trial[1] of Hitler's collaborators which established in current international law that there were such things as legal crimes against humanity for which it was no defence to say that one was obeying the orders of one's government.

If Hitler's henchmen were charged with crimes against the human race, Tshombe and his henchmen were now presumably to be charged with crimes against the African race. And yet an African Nuremberg would only have made sense if it was held under the auspices of the Organization of African Unity or comparable Pan-African umbrella. Only if Tshombe had been handed over to the OAU or to a comparable Pan-African body would his trial have become sufficiently internationalized to bear an adequate comparison with the phenomenon of Nuremberg.

Perhaps the real analogy of Tshombe's 'judicial abduction' was not Nuremberg but the Eichmann trial. Eichmann, who had helped Hitler exterminate hundreds of thousands of Jews, was himself kidnapped while in exile—and made to face trial in Israel more than fifteen years after the death of Hitler.

TSHOMBE, AFRICA AND ARAB–ISRAELI TENSIONS

This is where our analysis touches the issue of Israel at large. Perhaps one cannot complete a discussion about Tshombe and

[1] See *East African Standard* (Nairobi), July 24, 1967.

the Arabs without finally touching on the question of the Arabs and the Israelis—least of all in view of the coincidence that the abduction of Tshombe in July 1967 followed so closely upon the defeat of the Arabs by Israel in June.

What needs to be noted first is that there is probably a significant correlation between denunciation of Tshombe and support for the Arabs among politically-conscious Africans. At least at first glance there are indications that the strongest critics of Tshombe and the strongest supporters of the Arabs against Israel overlap quite noticeably. In order to understand this apparent overlap, an important theme in African ideologies needs to be examined.

At the beginning of the Middle East crisis President Nyerere sent a cable to President Nasser assuring the UAR of the support of Tanzania 'in the defence of your rights against imperialism'.[1] There was speculation elsewhere in the world as to why Tanzania was being so categorical in its support of the Arabs against Israel in the 1967 conflict.

The explanation had two inter-related facets. One was the attitude of African radicals towards North Africa; the other was their attitude towards Israel. For several years now black African radicals have been sympathetic towards North Africa. What should be remembered is that they would probably have been so even if Israel had not been created. In addition, black African radicals have also tended to be somewhat uneasy about Israel and its links with the West. It needs also to be remembered that the radicals would probably have been uneasy about Israel even if there had been no Arab–Israeli animosity on the world scene.

To some extent it is curious that the radical nationalists south of the Sahara should more readily accept Arabs as fellow-Africans than other black Africans have sometimes managed to do. It is curious because, in its essence, African nationalism is a race-conscious nationalism—and one might therefore have expected it to be more *purist* in its radical definition of 'African'. Yet the same black radicals who felt most strongly about Tshombe's use of white mercenaries also felt least strongly about Gbenye's use of Arab military help in the Congo.

The truth of the matter is that within the African continent

[1] See *The Nationalist* (Dar es Salaam), June 1, 1967.

itself African nationalism does become less racially exclusive as it assumes greater militancy. On the whole, it is perhaps the mystique of the African *continent* rather than that of the Negro *race* which has tended to inspire Pan-African radicalism. White settlers have not been part of the continent long enough to be integrated into the mystique of the continent in spite of differences of race. But the Arabs of North Africa have indeed now been integrated into the fabric of Africa. They are a more permanent feature of the African continent than any white community can as yet confidently claim to be.[1]

It is partly this consideration which enabled African radicals to accept Arab intervention in the Congo more readily than they could approve of the intervention of white mercenaries. In general, hostility to North Africans has been more evident among conservative black Africans—especially the old Brazzaville group —than among radicals like Sékou Touré, Modibo Keita, Kwame Nkrumah when he was in power, and Julius Nyerere today. Pan-Africanism at its most ambitious has always been trans-Saharan. A refusal to recognize the Sahara as a dividing line between black and Arab Africa has therefore been characteristic more of radical African nationalists than of conservative ones. And so has the refusal to accept the utility of white mercenaries in a situation like that of the Congo.

In short, we can say that *Africanism of leftist persuasion* is a school of thought which is at once markedly sympathetic towards Arab North Africa and particularly antagonistic towards white-ruled Southern Africa. Tshombe became a symbol of those who collaborated with Southern Africa; and Israel a symbol of those who conspired against Egypt and North Africa. By extension Israel became suspect to African radicalism on almost the same grounds as Tshombe was suspect. The African National Congress of South Africa cabled President Nasser from Dar es Salaam at the beginning of the Middle Eastern crisis in 1967 expressing its support for Nasser in his conflict with Israel and describing the war threat in the Middle East as 'being directly engineered as an act of provocation and aggression by Anglo-American powers'.[2]

---

[1] See Mazrui, *Towards a Pax Africana: A Study of Ideology and Ambition* (Weidenfeld and Nicolson and Chicago University Press, 1967), p. 212. See also pp. 109–25.

[2] See *The Nationalist* (Dar es Salaam), June 1, 1967.

This tendency to suspect Israel on almost the same grounds as those on which Tshombe has been suspected has also a 'tradition' behind it. That significant meeting in Casablanca in 1961 which brought into being the so-called 'Casablanca bloc' devoted its time to discussing not only the Congo and Algeria but also the problem of Palestine. The African Charter which emerged expressed deep concern 'about the situation created in Palestine by depriving the Arabs of Palestine of their legitimate rights'. The communique on the Charter went on to denounce Israel as 'an instrument in the service of imperialism and neo-colonialism not only in the Middle East but also in Africa and Asia'.[1]

The signatories to this denunciation included Sekou Toure of Guinea, Modibo Keita of Mali and Kwame Nkrumah of Ghana—the radical triumvirate of black Africa at that time.

Were these three sub-Saharan Africans denouncing Israel because of positive feelings for North Africans as comrades? Or was it for genuine negative feelings against Israel as enemy? On balance Nkrumah's reasons were Pan-African rather than anti-Israel. It was a question of denouncing Israel to please North African friends, rather than out of a genuine antagonism against Israel.

And yet there were elements in Israel's policies at the time which made it easier for African radicals to suspect her. Israel's special relationship with France at the time had compromised her on issues like Algeria in her struggle for independence and in regard to the French Sahara tests. The voting pattern of Israeli behaviour in the United Nations could be construed as being basically pro-French even on such highly sensitive nationalistic issues in Africa. And on the Congo the Israelis sometimes appeared distinctly anti-Lumumbist in the causes they seemed to support. It made it easier for Arab publications to argue in the following terms:

If the Israeli Chiefs really supported the Africans, why did they not announce their support for the legal power [Lumumbist] in the Congo, the body on whom depends the victory of the Congo over her imperialist enemies? Instead the Israel Chiefs supported Moise Tshombe, Prime Minister of Katanga.[2]

[1] Appendix 15, Legum op. cit., p. 206.
[2] See comments in The Arab Observer, Vol. I, No. 21, November 13, 1961, p. 18.

In other words, there was enough ambiguity in Israeli policy towards African nationalism to give Israel's opponents ammunition against her. It was also enough to make African radicals suspicious of Israel even if these black radicals had no special Pan-African links with North Africans.

One can of course be anti-Israel without being anti-Jewish in general. But the distinction between the two feelings can sometimes be blurred. Both the Arabs and the Israelis have sometimes been known deliberately to blur it for propaganda reasons. There is little doubt that Israelis have been known to play on the general horror of anti-semitism which many liberals have. Indeed, much of the sympathy which Israel enjoys among liberal intellectuals is due to the fear that liberals have of appearing to be anti-Jewish. Hitler was at once the greatest enemy of Jews in history and the greatest benefactor of Israel. As it has often been noted, the brutalities of Hitler's anti-semitism and his gas chambers gave Zionism a great boost. Hitler destroyed Jews—and in the very macabre and cruel process, Hitler also helped to create the state of Israel. At any rate this seemed to be the position that the Tanzanian Government took in 1967 when in a parliamentary session its ministerial spokesman attributed the birth of Israel to the guilty conscience of the Western World. And commenting on apparent Israeli attempts to equate anti-Zionism with anti-semitism Minister Hasnu Makame said to the National Assembly of Tanzania:

> It is a terrible irony of history for Israel to cooperate with the former prosecutors of the Jews in hoisting the crime of anti-semitism on the shoulders of Moslems and Arabs. Moslems do not accuse Jews of killing Mohamed [like Christians have accused them of killing Jesus]. Nor is Nasser a Hitler—however much Westerners may hate him.[1]

But in fact it has not been only Israelis and Western liberals who have failed to distinguish between anti-Zionism and anti-Semitism. The Arabs also have sometimes deliberately tried to blur the distinction. The significant Jewish finance and investment in Southern Africa has sometimes been referred to by the Arabs, complete with suggestions that major contributions to

[1] See *The Nationalist* (Dar es Salaam), July 4, 1967.

Israel's economic viability came from Southern Africa. As for the alliance between these Jewish financial interests and Moise Tshombe, this too could be adroitly alluded to. So could the racial origin of Tshombe's most prominent, influential and unequivocal supporter in Africa on the issue of Katanga's secession from 1960 to 1963—Sir Roy Welensky, then Prime Minister of the Federation of Rhodesia and Nyasaland. The Jewish origins of Tshombe's comrade-in-arms at that time afforded the Arabs an extra area of political innuendo in their less public propaganda activities. Tshombe had a number of strategic and tactical discussions with Sir Roy, and was even known to meet the Press at Sir Roy's residence.[1]

These are some of the factors which, in a series of historical accidents, have sometimes compromised the image of African Jewry and of Israeli policies on some issues affecting Africa. And when in July 1967 Tshombe appeared to be the Eichmann of Africa, awaiting judgment for his 'crimes against the African race', history did indeed seem to have indulged her twisted sense of humour once again.

In the meantime, the Arabs had in June 1967 sustained a humiliating defeat at the hands of Israel. Again there was a link between this and Sir Roy Welensky's old country, Rhodesia, which was now in more extreme hands. The response of white Rhodesians to Israeli successes in June 1967 was apparently enthusiastic. There was clear evidence of empathetic identification in the white Rhodesian response. Israel was small; the Arab countries and their populations were large. And yet the Arabs had proved to be militarily impotent in the face of Israel. By the same token, Rhodesia was small; the African continent was large and its population impressive. And yet Africans were militarily impotent in the face of Ian Smith's government. Indeed, Rhodesia should be internally even weaker than the rulers of Israel—for Smith represented a minority government imposed on a potentially 'treacherous' black population whereas the Israeli Government had majority support in its own country in its anti-Arab policies. And yet both Israel and Rhodesia had

---

[1] I knew a Jewish colleague at Columbia University who expressed embarrassment over the fact that Sir Roy Welensky was Jewish. We both agreed that this fact was irrelevant, but the colleague angrily felt that a 'Jew should know better'—than be on the side of 'racists'.

reduced to impotent anger populations vastly bigger than their own.[1]

By July 1967 Tshombe was perhaps in part a scapegoat for African frustrations in the face of Rhodesia and her allies. In addition there was also talk in that month about making Tshombe the scapegoat of Arab frustrations over Israel as well. This followed from the widespread speculation at the time on whether the Algerians, then holding Tshombe in their power, would attempt to extract extra support against Israel from the Congolese Government in exchange for Tshombe's extradition to the Congo. But these were on the whole journalistic rumours yet to be vindicated.[2]

BIAFRA, KATANGA AND THE OAU:

Meanwhile, events in another major African country had culminated in a tragic civil war. Nigeria and the Congo were in fact Africa's largest states south of the Sahara. The Congo had suffered from convulsive instability from the very beginning of her independence, but Nigeria was for a while a model of serene liberal democracy.

But the difference between the two countries was soon drastically narrowed. In January 1966 independent Nigeria experienced its first military *coup*. Two regional premiers and the federal Prime Minister were killed. The *coup* was interpreted as an 'Ibo *coup*' because of its Ibo leadership. In July 1966 came the 'counter-*coup*', replacing the Ibo leadership. Events from then on seemed to be leading irresistibly towards a military confrontation between the

---

[1] A Scandinavian colleague who did some research in Rhodesia soon after the Arab–Israel conflict of 1967 confirmed the tendency of many white Rhodesians to identify themselves as 'the Israelis of Africa', surrounded by hostile but less distinguished neighbours.

[2] See, for example, *Uganda Argus* (Kampala), July 1967. For an account of the kidnapping as given by one of the British pilots who travelled with Tshombe on the plane see Captain David Taylor, 'Kidnap in the Sky', *The Sunday Express* (London), October 1, 1967. See also 'Crisis over Algiers', *The Sunday Express*, October 8, 1967. For a legal discussion of the implications of abductions see Daniel Marchand, 'Abductions effected outside National Territory', *Journal of the International Commission of Jurists*, Vol. VII, No. 2, Winter 1966, pp. 243–68.

Federal Government and the old Eastern Region of Nigeria. On May 30, 1967, Biafra declared herself an independent state. The Federal Government responded with military force—and the civil war was on.

The rest of Africa was for quite a while reluctant to interfere in the war. And behind that reluctance was, *inter alia*, the memory of events in the Congo some years back. But by the middle of 1968 four African states—Tanzania, Zambia, Gabon and the Ivory Coast—had recognised Biafra. The Nigerian civil war was becoming international.

In September 1968 Algiers became once again the focus of an important Afro-Arab event. The Organization of African Unity held its summit meeting there. By far the most important subject discussed at the Conference was the Nigerian Civil War. At first sight this had no direct bearing on Moise Tshombe. But it did touch the issue of Afro-Arab relations, not least because of the active military involvement of the United Arab Republic in the war on the side of the Federal Government.

There appears to be little doubt that the site of the summit conference was an asset to the Federal side of Nigeria. There was first this simple fact that the Arab states, including the host country, were in their sympathies inclined towards Federal Nigeria. President Houari Boumedienne of Algeria took the line in his opening speech that secessionism was an invitation to imperialist interference in Africa.

Another asset to the Federal side at the conference was the role of President Mobutu of the Congo (Kinshasa). In fact Mobutu attempted to get the full discussion of the Nigerian problem ruled out of order, but the Chairman, Sir Dawda Jawara of the Gambia, after sounding delegations, permitted discussion to take place. President Mobutu then warned the conference about what would happen if Biafra succeeded in breaking away: latent secessionism was present all over Africa. President Mobutu was speaking from experience—he cited his own country's difficulties with Katanga's bid to secede under Moise Tshombe.

This point attained extra effect in Algiers from the simple fact that Tshombe was in detention somewhere in the neighbourhood of the very conference. His future apparently came up in informal discussions in the course of the summit meeting. There was a time when a formal decision by the OAU on Tshombe's future was expected, but this issue was shelved for the time being. Tshombe's role at the summit meeting in Algiers was therefore reduced to that of being a background ghost of an arch-secessionist. He symbolized the link between separatism and imperialist interference in Africa. And so, when the resolution on Nigeria came up at the meeting, it was formulated in terms of supporting the Nigerian Government's efforts to re-unify the country. The resolution called on the Biafrans 'to co-operate with the Federal Authorities with a view to restoring the peace and unity of Nigeria.' When the vote was taken, 36 were for the resolution, 4 were against it, and 2 abstained (Rwanda and Botswana). The 4 who voted against were the four states who had already recognized Biafra.

On the issue of the Middle East itself, the resolution which emerged from the summit conference of the OAU was considerably milder in tone than the one which was passed by the Organization's Council of Ministers in Addis Ababa in February 1968. The earlier resolution had spoken about 'Zionist aggression'. This was objected to by a number of African states. The summit resolution hardly mentioned Israel by name, but it did demand the withdrawal of all foreign troops from Arab soil, and urged the strict application of the United Nations' Security Council's resolution of November 1967. Voting on the Middle-East resolution was 36 for, none against, and 3 abstentions (Lesotho, Swaziland, and Botswana). A country which would probably have voted against the resolution was not represented at the summit meeting. This was Malawi. Dr. Banda had recently become increasingly anti-Arab since he was at the same time becoming more friendly with South-Africa. He had made a number of public references to the memory of the Arab slave trade in Eastern Africa and to the racial implications of the civil war in the Sudan. Dr. Banda had then decided to boycott the summit meeting of the OAU in Algiers, partly because of his hostility to Arab states, but also because of his growing disenchantment with the usefulness of the OAU. In the eyes of some of those present at Algiers, Dr. Banda had become a symbol of 'counter-revolutionary forces in Africa'. And his attitude to the Arabs once again illustrated that anti-Arabism was more evident among black African conservatives than among black African radicals.[1]

Not long after the summit meeting in Algiers, events in Kinshasa seemed to be partially deciding the fate of Moise Tshombe. The Foreign Minister of the Congo was sent out to Congo (Brazzaville) to try and persuade Pierre Mulele, a former rebel leader and revolutionary from the Congo, to return home. Mulele was given to understand that he would benefit by the amnesty offered by Mobutu's Government to rebels and exiles from the Congo. But on arrival back home, Mulele was detained and President Mobutu announced that he would be tried by a military tribunal as a 'war criminal'. Much of Africa was indignant at the way in which this man was lured officially by the Foreign Minister to return home on a false understanding, and then be tried on a capital charge. He was sentenced to death, appealed to Mobutu for clemency, but President Mobutu instead sanctioned his execution.

Among the countries which reacted strongly against this seemed to be Algeria. The press there denounced it as a cheap form of brutality. It seemed quite clear, that for the time being, the Algerian Government would not be able to hand over Tshombe to the Congolese Government in Kinshasa with a clean conscience. The ultimate fate of the prisoner in Algeria was as undecided as ever, but repatriation was for the time being ruled out.

CONCLUSION

There are occasions when a single personality assumes so much importance to a country or region that almost all major events are touched by his political significance. Nor need such a personality be a hero in order to radiate such relevance. He can indeed be a political figure more widely cursed than acclaimed.

[1] See West Africa, September issue, 1968. Consult also Africa Confidential, No. 19, September 20, 1968. Also relevant are the following dispatches: 'Congo willing for Tshombe Release: Banishment Plan', and 'Congo Rules out O.A.U. Discussion on Mr. Tshombe', East African Standard, September 11 and 12, 1968. On Dr. Banda's anti-Arab stand see, for example, 'Dr. Banda would fight Arabs if he had army', East African Standard, September 18, 1968. On Algeria's 'pledge' not to extradite Tshombe following Mulele's execution see East African Standard, October 17, 1968.

Such a person in Africa since 1960 has been Moise Tshombe. Major factors in the evolution of African diplomacy have converged on him as a point of dispute. The whole issue of separatism and its legitimacy in contemporary Africa was tested in a most dramatic form as a result of Tshombe's secessionist initiative in Katanga. The problem of what criteria should be regarded as relevant in determining the legitimacy of a political regime assumed new complexities for Africa when African states had to decide whether or not to recognize Moise Tshombe as Prime Minister of a newly reunified Congo barely four years after he had taken the leadership in attempting to break the country up. The issue of foreign mercenaries and their role in African disputes was again first raised and tested as a result of Tshombe's initiatives. The idea of strategic utilization of white soldiers of fortune, which later bedevilled the Nigerian Civil War, was almost a brainchild of Moise Tshombe. And non-alignment as a diplomatic creed found its most militant manifestations at the time of the confrontation of the big powers in the Congo in the second half of 1960 in the wake of Katanga's attempted secession. As Prime Minister of the Congo barely four years later Tshombe attempted to rejoin the ranks of the non-aligned as a way of improving his Pan-African credentials—but he had his ambitions frustrated.

All these are areas of political experience that this paper has touched upon. But the ultimate focus of the paper has been that other major factor of diplomatic life in contemporary Africa,— the delicate balance of Afro-Arab relations and the whole phenomenon of the quest for continental Pan-Africanism. For this issue too Tshombe has recurrently assumed a critical pertinence. The story includes Arab intervention in the early Congo rebellions, Arab participation in preventing Tshombe's admission to the conference of the non-aligned in Cairo in 1964, Arab attempts to demonstrate that the friends of Tshombe in Southern Africa were also the friends of Israel. Even the simple fact that when Tshombe was abducted he was taken to the Arab capital of Algiers, and the subsequent role of Algiers as the site of an African re-evaluation of secessionism in Nigeria against the memory of attempted secessionism in Katanga—all these were occasions which helped to demonstrate that persistent and sometimes crucial connection between the story of Moise Tshombe and the politics of Afro-Arab relations at large.

12 Tanzaphilia[1]

What is *Tanzaphilia*? It is neither a disease nor an exotic flower. It is a political phenomenon. I would define 'Tanzaphilia' as the romantic spell which Tanzania casts on so many of those who have been closely associated with her. Perhaps no African country has commanded greater affection outside its borders than has Tanzania. Many of the most prosaic Western pragmatists have been known to acquire that dreamy look under the spell of Tanzania. Perhaps many Easterners too have known moments of weakness.

What explanation can one advance for this striking phenomenon?

OPIUM OF AFROPHILES

The first thing which needs to be noted is that Tanzaphilia has been particularly marked among Western intellectuals. If we are seeking to know its causes we should perhaps first seek to understand what in an African country is likely to appeal to Western intellectuals.

Intellectuals everywhere in the world have a weakness for fellow intellectuals. A major element in the mystique of Tanzania is, of course, Julius K. Nyerere himself. He is the most intellectual of all English-speaking Heads of African States. He has commanded the same admiration among Anglo-American intellectuals that Leopold Senghor used to command among French ones. Westerners sometimes saw in these two men an incarnation of their own cultural achievement.

As I have argued elsewhere, Julius Nyerere is perhaps the most

[1] Reprinted with permission from *Transition*, Vol. VI, No. 31, June–July, 1967.

Anglicized of all Heads of State in East and Central Africa. Again I emphasize that by 'Anglicized' I do not mean 'Anglophile'. I do not mean that Nyerere is more pro-British than this or that other leader. But I do mean that Julius Nyerere has an intellectual turn of mind which is unmistakably a product of the Western system of education, both in Tanganyika where he had his early education and at Edinburgh University from which he graduated. I remain convinced that Nyerere would have been a different kind of person if he had been educated in, say, Saudi Arabia, Afghanistan or Communist China. Nyerere is what he is partly because of himself and partly because of the impact of his intellectual preparation in the Western tradition. And yet he is still among the most radical leaders today.

What needs to be remembered is that intellectual acculturation is not to be confused with ideological conversion. If Nyerere had been 'pro-Western' instead of 'Westernized', this would have been something which could change overnight under the impact of powerful disenchantment. A pro-Western African could cease to be pro-Western tomorrow if he suddenly discovered something shockingly evil about a particular Western policy. The discovery of C.I.A. activities in Africa could profoundly disillusion an African who might, only the day before, have been more naively trusting in American candour and good will. Similarly, many Western Marxists became deeply disenchanted with the Soviet Union, and sometimes even with Communism, under the shock of the brutal Soviet suppression of the Hungarian revolution. Many Indian communists were thrust into an agonizing reappraisal under the shock of China's invasion of India in 1962. And who knows how many Africans began to hate the United Nations as soon as the murder of Patrice Lumumba was revealed?

All these are indications that ideological conversion is a more superficial state of mind than intellectual acculturation. To be in favour of this country or that, to be attracted by this system of values rather than that, are all forms of ideological conversion. And under a strong stimulus one can change one's creed. But it is much more difficult to change the process of reasoning which a person acquires from his total educational background. No amount of radicalism in a Western-trained person can eliminate the Western-style of analysis which he acquires. After all,

1 See the interview I gave to *The People* (Kampala), April 8, 1967.

French Marxists are still French in their intellectual style. Ideologically they may have a lot in common with Communist China or communist North Koreans. But in style of reasoning and in the idiom of his thought, a French Marxist has more in common with a French liberal than with fellow communists in China and Korea. And that is why a French intellectual who is a Marxist can more easily cease to be a Marxist than he can cease to be a French intellectual.

Applying this to Julius Nyerere, we find that someone like him can more easily cease to be 'pro-Western' than he can cease to be 'Westernized' in his basic intellectual style and mental processes. And it is the latter quality which has often captivated Afrophile Western intellectuals.

Many Western intellectuals are, in their own countries, starved of intellectual leadership in politics. They would like to see a man of ideas at the helm in their own countries. And yet their own electorates have repeatedly let them down. For a brief period John F. Kennedy satisfied this craving for intellectual leadership that many Western intellectuals have had. And yet even Kennedy achieved intellectual greatness almost by accident. When he was first elected, many intellectual sceptics in his own country regarded him merely as a clever young manipulator, with a lot of wealth on his side. But he turned out to be more inspiring than expected.

Nevertheless, the real measure of the place of intellectualism in Western politics was not John F. Kennedy but Adlai Stevenson. Here was a great American intellectual who had failed twice to snatch the presidency from a gallant but mediocre rival. Stevenson was the great symbol of the impotence of intellectualism in Western politics, especially in the Anglo-Saxon world.

And then some of these frustrated intellectuals turned their eyes towards Africa—and saw Julius Nyerere in remote Tanganyika. Here was an intellectual in full command of his country. Here was an Adlai Stevenson in Africa—but victorious against the forces of mediocrity. What the American electorate had denied itself, the Tanganyikan peasants had bestowed upon themselves.

Even the very fact that Nyerere could be affectionately referred to as *Mwalimu* was a major difference in the status of intellectualism between the political ethos of Tanganyika and that of the

Anglo-Saxon world. What aspiring President or Prime Minister in America or Britain would let himself be known as 'the Teacher'? Such an epithet would be enough to compromise his image. Only his enemies or critics could come up with such a name for him. Harold Wilson, like Julius Nyerere, was a teacher once. Wilson tutored at Oxford for a while. But Wilson would definitely regard it as a liability in public relations if he were known by the British equivalent of 'mwalimu'. The British political ethos is too anti-intellectual to let the national leader be its mentor.

And so Wilson himself is hardly recognizable any longer as an intellectual. He has become too much of a straight politician—too cynical and calculating. And so British intellectuals too are without an Adlai Stevenson in power. Very few regard Wilson as one of their own kind.

What should be remembered is that just as there is a deep anti-intellectual tradition in Western politics, there is also a deep anti-political tradition in Western intellectualism. The old saying that 'politics is a dirty game' helped to deprive politics of aesthetic stature. The deceptiveness, the quest for popularity, the intrigues, the broken promises, all combined to give political activity a quality which offended some of the aesthetic ideals of intellectualism. And so many intellectuals have tended to despise the game of politics itself.

It is a contention of this essay that part of the mystique that Nyerere has had for Western intellectuals is that he has not really been a politician. Relatively speaking, he has not as yet been forced to be one.

POLITICAL HYGIENE

A major reason why Nyerere has not been forced to be a full politician so far is, of course, the sheer support he has enjoyed in the country. In relative terms, he has not been forced to plot and intrigue in order to remain in power. He has an easier country to handle than Nkrumah had, or Obote has had. The cleavages between tribes and other kinds of groups in Tanganyika have not been as deep as they have been elsewhere. There has also been a tradition of acceptance of authority in Tanganyika greater than has been evident elsewhere. Even during the colonial period Tanganyika did not have a militant form of nationalism. There was a certain *gentleness* in Tanganyika's 'struggle' for independence which made it hardly a struggle at all. And it was fitting that Tanganyikans should have accepted the leadership of a gentle personality like Nyerere.

But there were perhaps other reasons why Nyerere has not emerged as a stereotype politician of the kind distrusted by Western intellectuals. And one reason is precisely the fact that Nyerere himself is too much of an intellectual. He too has believed that politics has a great potential for being a dirty game. But to him what can so easily make politics dirty is precisely what Western intellectuals themselves have often jealously valued the multi-party structure of competition for power. In his stimulating analysis of 'Democracy and the Party System', Nyerere said:

> Why, then, have so many come to associate 'politics' with trickery and dishonesty? It is not, I am sure, that politicians are a naturally dishonest set of individuals. But if you are going to start from the premise that there *must* be more than one party, you may find before long that complete honesty becomes almost impossible to maintain.[1]

He goes on to argue that political honesty and party politics of the Western style are often in a state of tense incompatibility. At election time 'each party is led into conducting its election campaign by the "political" tactics of evasion, distortion and even downright lies about the other party's motives and intentions. Not does it stop there. Once in Parliament, as we have seen, members of the opposing parties must still observe the rules of party unity which, in themselves, must inevitably stifle not merely freedom of expression but, indeed, honesty of expression.'[2]

When in 1965 Tanzania therefore experimented with competitive elections within a single-party structure, the motivation was, to some extent, political hygiene. If dirt in politics was to be avoided, it was essential to avoid the conditions which give rise to it. Pre-eminent among those conditions is inter-party political

[1] See his pamphlet *Democracy and the Party System* (Dar es Salaam: *Tanganyika Standard*, 1962), p. 13.
[2] *Ibid.*, p. 14.

contest. It was far healthier to devise elections in which members of the same party competed for office. In such elections the Party itself would be in a better position to control the degree of mutual mud-slinging which its members were to be permitted to indulge in. And in any case a shared loyalty to the same party principles in a single-party system could go some way towards reducing the kind of virulent and cheap antagonism which members of opposing parties in Western systems sometimes felt against each other.

In the elections of 1965 TANU did control the language and style of campaign between candidates. It also narrowed the kind of issues which could be raised. There was a determined attempt to prevent the election degenerating into a breeding ground of deadly social bacteria that might harm the body politic. That is why the 1965 Tanzanian election was an exercise in political hygiene.

This again was a matter which had a direct appeal for certain intellectual tastes. 'Clean elections' constituted an aesthetically satisfying ideal. Clean elections in new countries can sometimes be particularly difficult to achieve. And yet here was Tanzania making a brave attempt.

Western liberals were also pleased for other reasons by the 1965 electoral experiment. In the first flush of Afrophilia as independence was achieved some Western liberals had believed too readily in the democratic intentions of some African leaders. A number of Western scholars burst into print in defence of the African one-party state, convinced that Africa was about to display to the world a new form of democratic genius.[1]

But then disenchantment set in. One after another of African leaders in both Francophone and Anglophone countries capitulated to the temptations of power—and betrayed the democratic optimism of that first Independence Day. Ordinary African citizens, who felt the brunt of political mismanagement, felt also the disenchantment most directly. But in addition many Afrophile Western liberals experienced a sense almost of personal

[1] For a critical survey of some of these theories see the recent book by Aristide R. Zolberg, *Creating Political Order* (Chicago: Rand McNally, 1966). See also Ruth Schachter (Morgenthau), 'Single-Party Systems in West Africa', *American Political Science Review*, Vol. LV No. 2, June 1961; and Morgenthau, 'African Elections: Tanzania's Contribution', *Africa Report*, Vol. X, No. 11, December 1965.

betrayal as their old eulogies of African democratic instincts were reduced to mockery.

And yet the record in Africa was far from being uniformly depressing. The tendency towards cheap authoritarianism had its exceptions. And among the most promising of those exceptions was the case of Tanzania under the leadership of Julius Nyerere. To some Western liberals, Nyerere was almost the last hope. Could he save a little of their old pride? Could he vindicate at least a little of their old faith in the feasibility of new democratic forms in Africa?

In 1965 Nyerere's country rose to the occasion. Genuinely competitive elections within a one-party structure were held. That they constituted a real choice for the electorate was demonstrated by the fact that several Ministers lost their seats. It was a great experiment—promising as well as precarious. In this case Tanzaphilia was a form of escape for disenchanted Western Afrophiles.

THE COURAGE OF BETRAYAL

These great experiments and inspirational ideas are an indication that the mystique of Nyerere is not simply in his being an intellectual. It is also in his being a gifted and imaginative one. Of all the top political figures in English-speaking Africa as a whole, Nyerere is perhaps the most original thinker. But here it is perhaps worth distinguishing between an original thinker and an independent thinker. In some ways Kamuzu Banda of Malawi has been a more consistently independent thinker than Nyerere has been, though less of an original thinker than Nyerere.

At least until the bold Arusha Declaration, Nyerere's ideas were, on the whole, *safe* ideas. The policies they advocated were widely advocated in many other parts of the continent. The originality of Nyerere consisted not in the policies advocated but in the arguments advanced in their defence.

On the other hand, there has not been much of an abstract thinker in Hastings Banda. Originality of thought at this level does require some capacity for abstract analysis—and Kamuzu Banda has not gone out of his way to display such an ability. What there has been in Banda is a marked capacity to arrive at decidedly independent decisions—even if they are at variance with the climate of opinion in the African continent as a whole. It is this quality which makes Banda more of an independent thinker than Nyerere—if less of an original one.

At least until recently, there was in Nyerere a marked concern with Pan-African respectability. He was all too conscious of African public opinion at large. This was never more dramatically illustrated than after Tanzania's use of British troops to subdue her own mutinous soldiers. All three East African countries had had to resort to the use of British troops, but only Tanzania felt it necessary to call a special meeting of the Organization of African Unity to clear her name. She called this meeting in spite of the slight tension the move created with her two East African neighbours. Uganda's Head of Government, Dr Milton Obote, was driven into expressing public scepticism about the meaningfulness of the O A U cleansing ceremony in Dar es Salaam.[1]

There have been other cases since then of Tanzania's preoccupation with Pan-African respectability. Even the militancy of Tanzania on the issue of Rhodesia had a little of this preoccupation.

Not until the Arusha Declaration and its aftermath can Tanzania claim to have demonstrated a political boldness at all comparable to that exhibited by Banda in his very heresies. Banda has been the Bourguiba of sub-Saharan Africa—heretical and irritating, but also refreshingly blunt. There are times when it takes revolutionary courage to be a pragmatist. Habib Bourguiba had the boldness to mention to his fellow Arabs the possible need of a rapprochement with Israel. Hastings Banda is demonstrating to his fellow Africans the feasibility of a rapprochement with South Africa. Both leaders have deviated from the militant norms of their fellow kind. To be so defiantly pragmatic in the company of militant revolutionaries is perhaps itself a form of revolutionary heresy.

But with the Arusha Declaration and its aftermath Nyerere has given Africa an alternative form of political boldness. Nyerere has had the courage to try and reduce his dependence on Western aid and assistance. Banda has had the courage to try and increase his economic dealings with South Africa and

[1] See also Mazrui, *On Heroes and Uhuru-Worship: Essays on Independent Africa* (London: Longmans, 1967), pp. 92-4.

Portugal. He has negotiated new trade agreements with both. Nyerere is out to demonstrate the lesson that what Africa needs is self-reliance in each individual country. Banda is out to prove that what Africa needs is inter-dependence even between a poor black country and the wealthy South Africa. Both Nyerere's experiment and Banda's overtures are, in effect, policies which demand significant political courage. I do not myself regard the two approaches as equally honourable. I find Tanzania's policies more defensible than Malawi's. But there is no doubt that each is an exercise in sheer boldness.

THE WHITE MARXIST'S BURDEN

But it has not been merely the reduction of Western aid that the new Tanzanian militancy is supposed to accomplish. It is also designed to increase exertions by Tanzanians themselves.

The ethos of anti-parasitism and hard work in Tanzania is older than the Arusha Declaration. It goes back to the slogan of *Uhuru na Kazi*, or Freedom and Work, which accompanied the country into independence. It got translated into the self-help schemes of 1963–4, and into the regulations about maximum utilization of land in the country as a criterion for possession of that land on lease from the state. And finally in October 1966 the ethos of hard work in Tanzania culminated in the National Service, compulsory for sixth form and university graduates and for products of comparable educational institutions. The National Service was to consist, in part, in nation-building forms of toil like digging and construction. A person was to spend two years in the service before starting a regular career.

By the time that the National Service was launched Tanzania's ethos of anti-parasitism was assuming certain features of anti-intellectualism. There seemed to be a growing feeling among policy-makers that African intellectuals could very easily become parasites. And the way to prevent this was to initiate those intellectuals into the rigours of manual labour.

But even this incipient anti-intellectualism in Tanzania some-how captivated a significant number of intellectuals outside Tanzania. In the final analysis, there is a deep-seated masochism in many intellectuals. They sometimes enjoy seeing fellow intellectuals elsewhere 'humbled'. Western intellectuals sometimes enjoy manual labour in the same way in which Marie Antoinette enjoyed playing the peasant girl and shepherdess in the grounds of her palace. An exhibitionist posture with a shovel or a wheelbarrow taken by a well-educated intellectual, is definitely in the tradition of 'Back to Nature' romantic movements. Scratch a certain kind of Western intellectual in Africa and you will see the spirit of Marie Antoinette in her artificial village in the grounds of the Palace of Versailles.

The curious thing has been that the ultimate leader of anti-intellectual tendencies in Tanzania is himself an intellectual. In this respect Nyerere is reminiscent of Franklin D. Roosevelt. Roosevelt was a millionaire. Yet his New Deal policies were the nearest point to socialism that the United States had ever got at that time. In a sense, he was starting a new movement to squeeze the rich in the interest of the poor. And since he himself was from a rich family, Roosevelt was regarded as a 'traitor to his class'.

The Report of the Tanzanian Presidential Commission on the Establishment of a Democratic One-Party State does refer to Roosevelt's difficulties with the Supreme Court on the constitutionality of his radical measures to deal with the Depression.[1] But from the point of this article, the real point of similarity between Roosevelt and Nyerere hinges on their attitude to their own respective sectors of society. Just as Roosevelt had attempted to squeeze the rich for the sake of the poor, Nyerere has been trying to squeeze the intellectuals for the sake of the masses. To that extent Julius Nyerere, like Franklin D. Roosevelt, might indeed be described as 'a traitor to his class'.

But these might well be forms of 'treason' which are creditable to the 'traitors'. They represent a wider loyalty of heroic dimensions. And perhaps Nyerere's 'treason' to his own class might, in historical retrospect, be as vindicated as that of Roosevelt was.

This brings us to yet another species of Tanzaphilia—the kind experienced by Western Marxists. In the old days of Tanzania's 'multi-racialism' and humanitarian rhetoric, Tanzania was the darling of Western liberals. She was commended for being 'moderate', and for being sensitive to the value of the individual

---

[1] *Report*, Presidential Commission on the Establishment of a Democratic One Party State (Dar es Salaam: Government Printer, 1965), p. 31.

and the virtues of an open society. Those were the days when a Western radical, then working at Kivukoni College, lamented that Tanganyika was suffering from *four* social ills—'poverty, ignorance, disease and empiricism'.

Tanzania today is significantly less empirical and more ideologically committed than it was at that time. It has now more clearly captured the dedicated allegiance of a number of Western Marxists. There are advantages in this. Western liberals can be as evangelical as Western Marxists, but Western Marxists might sometimes have the added advantage of helping the country to recover an ideological balance which the colonial experience might have distorted.

The danger arises when the evangelism is carried too far. This is as true with liberal as with Marxist evangelism, but it so happens that at the present moment it is the Western Marxists who have abandoned themselves to inadequately restrained proselytism in Tanzania.

A major target has been the University College, Dar es Salaam. A number of Western Marxists, in alliance with other Marxists, have apparently been contriving to 'socialize' the University College.

As I have affirmed elsewhere, I accept the proposition that it is the duty of any University in the modern world to allow for the study of socialism. This is because socialistic ideas have an important bearing on twentieth-century realities—and the University that leaves no room for their analysis is betraying its function and its duty to remain in touch with reality.

But it cannot be repeated too often that this is a different matter from converting a whole University into an institution for the promotion of socialism. There does remain a distinct difference between a University and an ideological institute.

It is true that there is no university in the world which is totally free of ideology. And if there were it is unlikely to be a good university. But a genuine university should not be intellectually monopolistic. It should be multi-ideological rather than uni-ideological. It should permit maximum interplay between different interpretations of reality.[1]

If Tanzania feels a need for an ideological institute, that might well be a good reason for establishing one. But such an institution

[1] See *The People* (Kampala), April 8, 1967 and May 19, 1967.

should surely remain a distinct enterprise from the University College.

Yet the pressure to convert the University College into an ideological institute has tended to come more from inside the University College than it has done from the outside. And when it has come from the outside, it has often been at the instigation of forces within the University College itself.

As I have asserted before, there has indeed been a group of radical academics who have had less faith in the concept of a University than President Nyerere himself. Yet I am not convinced that these radicals—themselves products of distinguished Western universities—would themselves dream of sending their children to be educated in something like the old Kwame Nkrumah Ideological Institute in Ghana or the Lumumba Ideological Institute in Kenya. I doubt if any of them would send their children to the Patrice Lumumba University in Moscow. They are all for transforming the University of East Africa into an ideological institute. But if the experience of British socialists is anything to go by, the ultimate academic ambition they have for their children is often admission into Oxford or Cambridge. Indeed, many British radicals send their own children to public schools.

This is not to deny that there is often a wealth of sincerity and genuine social conscience among Western radicals who come to Africa to be of service. And some of their ideas for reform might well constitute a genuine contribution to a healthier future for African countries. But a balance needs to be kept. Western radical zeal in Africa—as indeed Eastern proselytism—can all too easily deteriorate into a new form of cultural arrogance. There is some risk of a 'White Marxist's Burden', disguised as a socialist crusade. As long as there is some restraint all round, this risk need not be fatal. There is room for debate between the different schools of reform movements in East Africa. What there is no room for is a weird, hybrid creature from the womb of the nineteenth century—a poet-ideologue called 'Karl Kipling'.

CONCLUSION

It is to the credit of Tanzania that she had managed to command the varied loyalties and affection of a wide range of external admirers. From Gandhians to Maoists, humanitarians to ruthless revolutionaries—all these have been known to fall under the soothing spell of Tanzaphilia.

The range is partly chronological. Tanganyika was the favourite of liberals before it became the favourite of radicals. It was a moderate country before it became a militant one. And its union with Zanzibar gave it an added dimension of revolutionary fervour.

But a chronological interpretation of the range of admirers that Tanzania has known is inadequate. The range of the country's admirers has been impressive at every point of the country's evolution, however many may get disillusioned on the way.

No short article can ever be adequate as an explanation of the phenomenon of Tanzaphilia. Here is a country which has at times appealed to people's diverse sensibilities. The ambition of purified politics, the ethos of symmetrical austerity, the romance of 'Back to Nature' and to the discipline of the countryside, the opposition to ostentation and opulence—these are all factors which touch deep into the *aesthetic* sensibilities of intellectuals.

But Tanzaphilia has also been an *ideological* commitment to the goals of self-reliance and egalitarianism. As an ideological commitment, it delves deep into *moral* responses.

It is these considerations which make the phenomenon of Tanzaphilia at once an aesthetic experience and a profound ethical longing. Tanzania's durability as a fact of political life depends upon a number of factors. But ultimately it depends upon a continuing compatibility between an intellectual leadership and a popular sense of mission in that remarkable African country.

13 Political Censorship and Intellectual Creativity[1]

The basic dilemma facing the printed word in Africa is whether it should be used to create a nation or used to create an intellectual heritage. In the short term, the two uses are not necessarily compatible. The immediate problem of creating a nation might demand self-censorship, and involve a policy of trying to avoid dissension between groups and protect the legitimacy of government from the dangers of reckless public criticism. But the task of creating an intellectual heritage might demand exactly opposite requirements. It might demand precisely an atmosphere of dissension and public debate—a capacity for frank self-censure rather than self-censorship. We might therefore admit that in the short term the climate in which an intellectual heritage grows is, alas, the sort of climate which could at times be fatal for political stability.

THE AFRICAN PRESS

In the middle of this dilemma between constructing a nation and constructing a heritage is, of course, the African Press. We might therefore usefully start with an appraisal of the Press situation in Africa today. In general, we might first observe that English-speaking countries in sub-Saharan Africa are greater newspaper readers than their Francophone counterparts. Nigeria, partly because of its size, and partly because of the vigorous temperament of some of its peoples, has been a particularly rich area in journalism. Daily newspapers alone have been estimated

[1] This essay was first presented at a Seminar on 'The Press in Africa—is it Dying?' organized by the Makerere Extra-Mural Department. The essay was then published in *East Africa Journal*, December 1966.

to vary between 15 and 20. We shall later touch upon the role of some of these newspapers in the early days of Nigerian nationalism.

In continental black Africa the next country after Nigeria in number of newspapers is, according to some estimates, Kenya. The number has fluctuated, but somewhere in the region of half a dozen daily newspapers has been more the rule than the exception for several years. In fact, per head of population, Kenya is a more 'newspaper-reading' country than Nigeria.

Kenya has had more newspapers than Ghana. Yet Ghana has had in turn—in proportion to her population—more newspaper readers than virtually any other African country.

There is one French-speaking country which is in a class by itself in terms of the number of newspapers it has had. This is the Malagasy Republic, which has been credited with up to eighteen newspapers—though having only 45,000 readers.[1]

Certain questions arise as to the implications of having many newspapers but fewer readers (as in Malagasy) or more readers and fewer newspapers (as in Ghana). And these questions have direct bearing on the dilemma we have mentioned between building a nation and building an intellectual heritage.

There is a school of thought which regards the Press as something which ought to be a free market place of ideas and information. According to this school, the more newspapers there are in the country the greater is the diversity of ideas competing for acceptance in the market place.

This notion might be resting on a fallacy. Liberalism itself does not seem to realize that what it needs is not the phenomenon of different ideas expressed in different newspapers as such. It is different ideas expressed in the *same* newspaper which would really constitute a competitive intellectual market—a place where opinions do genuinely contest for more general acceptance.

After all, a large number of newspapers catering for different tastes would merely result in self-contained compartments of mutually-exclusive readerships. To use British examples, the reader of *The Daily Worker*, to use its older name, might never

[1] For brief accounts of some of the situations see 'Press and Radio in Africa', *Africa Report*, Vol. IX, No. 2, February 1964; 'A Symposium on Africa', *Africa Report*, Vol. XI, No. 1, January 1966; Joseph S. Nye, Jr., *Pan-Africanism and East African Integration* (Cambridge: Harvard University Press, 1965), pp. 68-9, 78-80.

know what is discussed in *The Times*—nor of *The Times* what the pages of *The Daily Worker* are agitated about. In order to have a real market place of competing ideas, the ideal would be a situation in which 'Daily Workerish' opinions and 'Timesian' pronouncements appear in the same newspaper—accessible to the same readership. Different opinions expressed within different compartments of society do not really compete with each other for general acceptance.

From the short-term point of view of national integration, what a new country might need is not, in any case, necessarily the highest possible diversity of thought. The price of diversity of thought could in the extreme be loss of communication itself. A population split up into little clusters of readers of multiple little newspapers is perhaps a population which is not using the medium of the Press for maximum communication at the national level. Given the same number of readers, the fewer newspapers a country has the greater should be the communicative utility of those newspapers. In this case one is not splitting up the readership too much. And so Ghana achieves greater communication among its people with its three newspapers than the Malagasy Republic does with its eighteen newspapers.

Social communication is, of course, a major requirement in the process of welding different groups into a nation. If among the factors which are needed for national integration is that of exposing the different groups to the same media of information and ideas, one's advice can only be 'Keep the number of newspapers down. Do not split the readership too much'.

Yet the trend in much of Africa is not towards having too many newspapers expressing different views. It is more towards having a few newspapers all expressing the same official viewpoint. Faced with the dilemma of having to choose between intellectual creativity and political stability, many Africans have opted for the latter. The Press has been either directly circumscribed or urged to impose a censorship on itself of its own accord. As Tom Mboya frankly put it once,

> Because the leaders are trying hard to create unity, they become sensitive to anyone who appears to act as though he constituted an opposition and did nothing but criticize the government's efforts. Freedom of the press in a new country

has, therefore, got to be limited: not so much restricted by legislation, but rather deliberately guided; for its main functions include not only giving news but also taking part in the national effort and contributing towards the building of a nation.[1]

That a free press could undermine the legitimacy of a regime is a view which is, alas, vindicated by the triumph of African nationalism itself. When all is said and done, British colonial rule permitted a high degree of freedom of expression. One could almost say that there is not a single former British colony today which, after independence, enjoys as much freedom of expression as it enjoyed under colonial rule. The British did indeed send some nationalists to jail for various offences, but in general there was still significantly more freedom of dissent, of organized opposition and public criticism of the government before independence than after. And yet what did that freedom lead to? The colonial regimes fell from power. The freedom which the British permitted their subjects undermined their own legitimacy as a ruling power. How then can the new African regimes, which have succeeded the British, be expected to take the same risk?

INTELLECTUALISM

And yet it was not freedom of agitation alone which brought down the British. It was also the relative spread of education and the emergence of a class of modern intellectuals in the colonies. If freedom of dissent is today viewed with suspicion by African governments because it had helped to bring down their British predecessors, should education also be suspect because it too had contributed to the same end result?

In fact, the birth of modern politics in Africa had three parents instead of the usual biological two. Nationalism, journalism *and intellectualism* shared a moment of intimacy—and the urge for liberation was consummated.

It is indeed true that the whole idea of 'an intellectual' is a relative one. To the question 'What is an intellectual?' the answer must be that it depends substantially upon the society that one is

1 *Freedom and After* (London: André Deutsch, 1963), p. 101.

looking at. And one could classify societies according to the degree
to which their cultures are influenced by the printed word. In a
society with a high degree of literacy, the criteria of what constitutes an intellectual are more complex than they are in a poorly
literate society.

When standards of education in Africa were low, it did not
take much to be classified as an African intellectual or African
'scholar'. In his book on the political history of Ghana, David
Kimble—formerly a Professor at the University College, Dar es
Salaam—tells us that 'the term "scholar" . . . aroused much
awe among illiterates'. As for the definition of the term, we can
discern it from Kimble's account of the strong reaction the term
came to arouse in colonial administrators. The reaction against
African 'scholars' extended 'to cover all who were articulate in
English, from the barely literate to the well-informed critic'.[1]

Nevertheless, this was the beginning of the equation between
African 'intellectuals' and African 'politicians'. To the question
of 'Who are the African politicians?' the answer used to be 'It is
the African intellectuals'. There developed a so-called 'Colonial
Office Attitude' to educated Africans—perhaps typified by an
assessment registered in Colonial Office records in 1875 that 'the
"educated natives" or "scholars" . . . have always been a thorn
in the side of the Government of the G. Coast. They have been
at the bottom of most of the troubles on the coast for some years
past.'[2]

It is such conclusions which illustrate how closely intertwined
were the roots of modern African nationalism with the roots of
modern African intellectualism.

JOURNALISM

The third factor, as we have indicated, which helped to bring
into being modern African politics was the phenomenon of African
journalism.

Yet, curiously enough, the genesis of African journalism lay

[1] *A Political History of Ghana: The Rise of Gold Coast Nationalism 1850–1928*
(Oxford: The Clarendon Press, 1963), pp. 87–93.

[2] Minute of February 6, 1875, by A. W. L. Hemming (later Head of the
African Department of the Colonial Office); CO/96/115. See Kimble, *ibid.*,
p. 91.

in dry official publications of colonial governments. As one student of history of the Press in Africa put it,

> The Press in Africa began with publications owned and/or operated by officials of the British Government. It began in Sierra Leone in 1801 with the publication of *The Royal Gazette*. Twenty-one years later Ghana (then the Gold Coast) followed Sierra Leone's example with the publication of *The Royal Gold Coast Gazette*.[1]

Something similar seems to have happened in East Africa. It is not for nothing that the word for newspaper in Swahili is 'gazeti'.

All these then go to illustrate that the Adam and Eve of newspapers in Africa were government gazettes. But then history once again indulged her ironic sense of humour. The medium which had been used by colonial governments was adopted and adapted by African nationalistic forces and directed against those governments themselves. In West Africa Azikiwe rapidly became a giant of journalism. As Ronald Segal observes in his profile of Zik,

> It was by his journalism . . . that Azikiwe gave a new impetus to Nigerian nationalism. He started a chain of newspapers, the most important of which was the *West African Pilot*, and revolutionized West African journalism by the daring and directness of his editorials and news coverage. Concentrating upon racial injustices and the need for positive action to emancipate Africa, he energetically spread his message throughout the territory, nursing circulation by provincial news coverage and by efficient distribution, and establishing four dailies, in Ibadan, Onitsha, Port Harcourt and Kano.[2]

Kwame Nkrumah was also convinced quite early of the need for an alliance between nationalism, intellectualism and journalism. Nkrumah's tendency to philosophize and write books was part of his intellectualism. As for his belief in journalism, it found its

1 John Nelson Williams, 'The Press and the Printed Word in Africa', *Oversea Quarterly*, Vol. III, No. 8, December 1963, p. 243.
2 *African Profiles*, Penguin African Library, 1962, p. 199.

most militant expression when he brought into being the *Accra Evening News* in 1948. Explaining why he launched the newspaper, Nkrumah tells us in his *Autobiography:*

> I failed to see how any liberation movement could possibly succeed without an effective means of broadcasting its policy to the rank and file of the people.[1]

Chief Obafemi Awolowo of Nigeria was another African nationalist who was moulded by journalistic and intellectual influences. In September 1934 he entered the employment of the *Nigerian Daily Times* as a reporter-in-training. That was only the beginning of a long association with journalism. Even when he later became a law student in the United Kingdom he kept up his journalistic activities free lance. In the course of his journalistic career, Awolowo wrote on varied subjects. They included an article on Shakespeare's *Julius Caesar.* Indeed, Awolowo's intellectualism is so frank that he acknowledges Shakespeare as one of the influences which moulded him. To use Awolowo's own words:

> Shakespeare is my favourite. I have read all his plays, and have re-read some of them—like *Julius Caesar, Hamlet, The Tempest, Antony and Cleopatra* and *Henry V*—more than three times. Some of the mighty lines of Shakespeare must have influenced my outlook on life.[2]

Jomo Kenyatta's journalistic experience goes even further back than Awolowo's. As General Secretary of the old Kikuyu Central Association he started and edited the first Kikuyu journal—the *Muigwithania*—from 1928 to 1930.[3]

As a generalization we might therefore say that in many countries of Africa the role of the Press changed from being essentially governmental to being essentially opposed to the Establishment as then evolved. Even the settler Press in Kenya was often a

---

[1] Nkrumah, Ghana: *The Autobiography of Kwame Nkrumah* (Edinburgh: Thomas Nelson and Sons Ltd., 1960 reprint), p. 76.

[2] *Awo: The Autobiography of Chief Obafemi Awolowo* (Cambridge University Press, 1960), pp. 70, 85-6, 90-1.

[3] See Preface to Kenyatta's *Facing Mount Kenya* (1938) (London: Secker and Warburg, 1959 reprint), p. xix.

Press of dissent, tending recurrently to be critical of the colonial government's position on this or that issue. The settler Press was on the whole critical from the *Right* of the political spectrum. But at least it had the vigour and sense of independence which comes with being sceptical of officialdom.

CONSTRUCTING AN INTELLECTUAL HERITAGE

The question which now arises is whether newspapers in independent Africa are about to resume their earliest role in the history of colonialism—and become government gazettes, or *magazeti ya serikali*, all over again. In at least some African countries what were once vigorous newspapers have indeed been reduced to official gazettes or government bulletins. In other African countries there is clearly a similar possibility. It is felt by many African leaders that the journalistic freedom which had helped to create African nationalism could not be trusted to create African *nationhood*. Relative freedom of the Press helped to achieve independence; but it could not be relied upon to achieve national integration after independence. Or so the argument goes.

And yet there are two fundamental fallacies in this whole line of reasoning. One is the assumption that avoiding conflict is the same thing as achieving integration. And so African governments often go to great lengths to avert the appearance of dissension in the country and try and eliminate every risk of serious conflict either between groups or between the state and some groups. What is not realized is that such an 'absence of conflict' is artificial. National integration does not consist merely in forcing people to smile sweetly at each other. It consists in accumulating the experience of peaceful resolution of conflict. And one cannot acquire such experience unless peaceful conflict is permitted to take place. One form of such conflict is verbal debate between speech-makers or open controversy between writers. It is indeed true that such debate could lead to less peaceful outbreaks between the debating antagonists. But similar outbreaks could also occur as a result of trying to enforce an artificial 'stability'. In any case the different groups in a society will never learn the techniques of non-violent quarrelling unless governments are prepared to risk a violent accident now and then. One does not learn to swim unless one risks a violent gulp or two.

This then is the first fallacy of those who argue that open clashes of opinion are harmful to nation-building. They are wrong in assuming that to avert conflict between groups is the same thing as to integrate those groups. They forget that the groups could never be integrated unless risks of conflict are taken.

The second fallacy of this kind of reasoning is that its view of integration overlooks the fact that the process of building takes a matter of several generations. It is not enough to maximize communication between the different groups who live in Uganda or Kenya *today*. It is also necessary to maximize communication between the nationals of today and those who will be living here thirty or fifty years from now. Once you think of nation-building in terms of several generations, constructing a nation and constructing an intellectual heritage cease to constitute a dilemma. They become an inter-related process. And you cannot build a significant intellectual heritage worth being remembered by the next generation unless you refrain from stifling the creative instincts of the present generation.

And what is an intellectual heritage? It could indeed be oral, passed from mouth to mouth down the ages. But a heritage is at its richest when the thoughts of one generation are captured in print and handed down verbatim. For too long much of Africa has had to rely on oral tradition, on word of mouth from father to son. But neither a literary tradition nor a philosophical one can achieve its maximum richness without the written word. Without the written record too many of yesterday's insights are lost—too much is expected of memory. A thousand years ago what were the inhabitants of this part of the African continent like? We might discover through archaeology what kind of pottery they used or what kind of tools they employed. But this is because pottery and tools are durable remains that can physically survive to be discovered. It is much harder ever to find out what kind of political ideas ancient East Africans had, or what kind of philosophical stories they told each other, or what kind of poetry they recited to each other. Because our ancestors lacked the printed word, we have been denied an intellectual heritage which goes far back in time.

But are we going to sentence future generations of East Africans to the same intellectual deficiencies? We are today equipped with that great preservative of culture—a widespread capacity to commit our thoughts to writing. This capacity would be useless if the only thoughts we were allowed to commit to writing were those of harmless mediocrity, too light to stand the slightest chance of rocking the national boat.

CONCLUSION

Equipped with the printed word, the present generation of East Africans stands at the beginning of an entirely new intellectual tradition in the history of the region. We could bequeath to future East Africans a wealth of poetry and novels, of drama, of philosophical and speculative writings. They in turn could add to it, and pass it on to their descendants. As the literature builds up, it would one day be divided into periods according to dominant trends at a particular age. Historians of literature might one day speak of a romantic period of African literature, or of the neo-classical period of African philosophy—distinguishable from other great periods in the same cumulative African intellectual tradition. And this tradition would be diffused to the different levels of the populace through the popularizing tendencies of a vigorous press, relatively free.

It follows then that at this particular moment of its history Africa should perhaps momentarily turn away from 'ancestor-worship' to 'posterity-worship'. She should look to the future and decide what she would like to bequeath to her revered descendants. From this dawn of independence a whole new epic of African creativity could unfold. And our gift of the intellect to the next generation might at the same time become a bond of nationhood.

SECTION D

PERSONAL INTIMACY AND
SOCIAL TENSIONS

14 On Revolution and Nakedness[1]

Far away, many dust-laden miles away in Arusha some little
man in the administration, such as are to be found in all the
governments the world over, in his little white shirt and collar
and his little Western tie, or in his national dress that gives him
prickly heat around his neck whenever the weather gets
excessively hot and humid, has decided that the Masai must
wear clothes.[2]

This bitter lament against a new policy statement from Tanzania
early in 1968 formed part of the debate which was unleashed by
the declaration of that policy. The authorities in Tanzania had
decided that the Masai had been permitted naked indulgence for
far too long; that their withdrawal from normal attire constituted
a withdrawal from the main stream of progress in their country.
It had therefore been decreed that no Masai men or women were
to be allowed into the Arusha metropolis wearing limited skin
clothing or a loose blanket. The Masailand Area Commissioner,
Mr Iddi Sungura, kept on issuing a number of warnings to the
Masai threatening retribution if they clung to awkward clothing
and soiled pigtailed hair.[3]

From prominent Masai across the border in Kenya came protests. A Kenya Masai Member of Parliament holding a ministerial position, Mr. Stanley Oloitipitip, asserted that Tanzania
was denying the Masai the right to be themselves. Another
Kenyan Mr John Keen threatened to turn up at Arusha, the new
capital of the East African Community, dressed in his Masai
attire and see what the authorities there would do to him. Tanzanian authorities in turn replied in this debate across the border

[1] This is reprinted with permission from *Transition*, No. 39, 1968.
[2] See Richard Brooke-Edwards, 'A Fourth Freedom', *Transition*, No. 34,
December–January 1968, p. 39.
[3] See, for example, *The Daily Nation* (Nairobi: February 6, 1968).

that such interference in the policies of Tanzania towards modernization and national integration was totally unacceptable. The Masai of Kenya could remain in their pristine traditionality but the Masai of Tanzania were to be converted to the trappings of modernity.[1]

This whole controversy on the future apparel of the Masai has links with an important theme in the history of nationalism and of revolutionary fervour. Our concern in this paper is not with the Masai controversy as such. It is with this wider theme of the place of dress and nakedness in the history of thought. In its ramifications, this is a human phenomenon which has contacts with such important issues as firstly, *authenticity*; secondly, *identity*; and thirdly, *rebellion*, both religious and political. One might discuss each of these in turn.

NATURE UNCOVERED

In order to understand some of the implications of the concept of authenticity we have to relate it to other intellectual ideas. What is authentic is often deemed to be that which is not artificial. That which is not artificial is often deemed to be that which is natural. Major intellectual movements in world history have romanticized nearness to nature and lamented the growth of civilization and industrialization because of the presumed concomitant growth of artificiality in man's life. The idea that expanding complexities of social organization maximize man's distance from the essence of things has been discerned in the works of political philosophers like Rousseau, and of poets like William Wordsworth. The romanticization of the Noble Savage was at the heart of these critiques of developed life. Rousseau sometimes argues that civilized life enfeebles man and makes him too dependent on gadgets and artificial comforts. Equipped with all his artificial aids civilized man is indeed at a great advantage, but if you stripped him of these, and confronted him with bare nature, the effeminate ways of civilization will expose his lack of vigour. In Rousseau's own words,

> Give civilized man time to gather all his machines about him, and he will no doubt easily beat the savage; but if you were to

[1] See *Daily Nation* (Nairobi: February 8 and 16, 1968).

see a still more unequal contest, set them together naked and unarmed, and you will soon see the advantage of having all our forces constantly at our disposal, of being always prepared for every event, and of carrying oneself as it were, perpetually whole and entire about one.[1]

Sometimes the Noble Savage was placed by philosophers and literary figures in the Americas. The Noble Savage was the Indian, in Alexander Pope's words,

> . . . whose untutor'd mind
> Sees God in clouds, or hears him in the wind;
> His soul proud Science never taught to stray
> Far as the solar walk, or milky-way;
> Yet simple Nature to his hope has giv'n,
> Behind the cloud-topt hill an humbler heav'n . . .[2]

But with the greater interest in Africa which came with the great debates about the slave trade, the Noble Savage in European imagination came to be located also in the African continent. The African came to be regarded as natural man par excellence. He might lack the capacity to blush, but commanded full ability to be bold. In the words of the poets Day and Bicknell,

> What tho' no rosy tints adorn their face,
> No silken ringlets shine with flowing grace?
> Yet of etherial temper are their souls,
> And in their veins the tide of honour rolls;
> And valorous kindles there the hero's flame,
> Contempt of death, and thirst for martial fame.[3]

In our own time the image of the African as a child of nature has been inherited by the movement of negritude, of which the most distinguished spokesman on the African continent is Leopold Senghor, the poet-President of Senegal. Senghor defines

[1] See Rousseau, *A Dissertation on the Origin and Foundation of the Inequality of Mankind*, Everyman's Edition of *The Social Contract and Discourses* (London: J. M. Dent and Sons, 1955), p. 164.

[2] Pope, *Essay on Man* (1732).

[3] Thomas Day and John Bicknell, *The Dying Negro* (London 1775), pp. 7-8. First published 1773.

negritude as 'the sum total of the values of the civilization of the African world. . . . More precisely, it was the communal warmth, the image-symbol and the cosmic rhythm which instead of dividing and sterilizing, unified and made fertile.'[1]

And Jean-Paul Sartre, the French philosopher, also draws attention to the 'proud claim of non-technicalness' which is at the heart of negritude. The nearness to nature is persistent. In the words of Sartre 'in concerning himself first with himself, the Negro proposes to gain nature in gaining himself'. Sartre then proceeds to cite the poet who said,

> they abandon themselves, possessed to the essence of
>   all things ignoring surfaces but possessed by the
>   movement of all things,
> needless, taking no account, but playing the game
>   of the world,
> truly the elder sons of the world
> porous to every breath of the world
> flesh of the flesh of the world throbbing with the
>   very movement of the world.[2]

The nearness to nature which is attributed to the Negro becomes associated with spontaneity; spontaneity finds expression sometimes in responsive sexuality; and sexuality connotes the nakedness of things. The entire life style of the Negro is romanticized into one constant work of natural creation. To quote Sartre again,

> Techniques have contaminated the white worker, but the black remains the great male of the earth, the sperm of the world. His existence—it is the great vegetal patience; his work —it is the repetition from year to year of the sacred coitus. He creates and is fertile because he creates. The sexual pantheism of these poets is without doubt that which first strike the reader. To labour, to plant, to eat, is to make love with nature. . . .
>
> > Behold yourself
> > Erect and naked
> > Shaft you are and you remember

---

[1] See Senghor, *Prose and Poetry*, translated by John Reed and Clive Wake (London: Oxford University Press, 1965), p. 99.

[2] See Sartre, *Black Orpheus* (Paris: *Présence Africaine*), pp. 43–4.

> But you are in reality the child of this fecund shadow
> Which feeds of the milk of the moon
> Then you slowly shape yourself into a rod
> On this low wall entwined by the dreams of flowers
> And the perfume of the idle summer.[1]

If the Negro is sometimes conceived as a symbol of masculinity, Africa is sometimes conceived in decidedly feminine terms. But in both conceptions the theme of nakedness is again recurrent. Leopold Senghor thinks of his part of Africa in such feminine terms. In the words of his famous poem,

> Naked woman, black woman
> Clothed with your colour which is life, with your form
>   which is beauty!   .
> In your shadow I have grown up; the gentleness of your
>   hands was laid over my eyes. . . .
> Naked woman, black woman
> I sing your beauty that passes, the form that I fix in
>   the Eternal,
> Before jealous Fate turn you to ashes to feed the roots of
>   life.[2]

THE DRESS OF IDENTITY

But it is not simply the issue of authenticity which is at stake in this area of political argumentation; it is also the issue of identity. Identity is sometimes in regard to a particular individual and the kind of quality and personality he has; and sometimes it is in regard to a member of a particular community, nationality or religious affiliation and the cultural traits exhibited by such a community. The identity of the individual on his own may indeed include these traits inherited from his cultural group, but insofar as they define his own distinctive personality, these traits are combined with other qualities. Whether a man is temperamentally cheerful or moody, whether he is warm-hearted or reserved, whether he is meticulous and formal in his behaviour, or easy-going and jovial—all these are intensely personal characteristics which may not necessarily be derived from the social

---

[1] *Black Orpheus, op. cit.*, pp. 45–7.
[2] Senghor, *Prose and Poetry, op. cit.*, pp. 105–6.

group to which a person belongs. The characteristics may sometimes be accentuated or mitigated by cultural factors, but in
general there are personality factors in each individual which are
distinctive to the person and not typical of the community from
which he springs.

Dress is related to this issue of the distinctive person. There
has been a school of thought which has assumed that you can
indeed judge a man by the way he dresses. It was Shakespeare's
character Polonius who, in his fatherly advice, made the famous
statement, 'For the apparel oft proclaims the man'. A man of
good taste might therefore be judged by the way he dresses. The
class to which he belongs might be discernible by his general
attire. In general etiquette, dress is sometimes in relation to the
particular occasion to which a man is called upon to respond. A
man turning up at a formal dinner in a bush shirt is dismissed in
Western terms as Bohemian. Some restaurants in the more
Westernized parts of Africa would insist on a tie and perhaps a
jacket for dinner, but not necessarily for lunch. The two meals
have been ritualized and permitted to demand distinctive attire
for those who participate in the ritual. In some British universities
the academic gown becomes important for some ceremonial
occasions and a less flamboyant gown becomes indispensable for
some of the dinners at college at high table. The person who
ignores these conventions is again judged to be inadequately
attuned to the civilized values of the society. And old Polonius
might once again nod his head saying 'For the apparel oft
proclaims the man'.

But these very examples themselves illustrate how closely
related are the *personal* aspects of dress to the *cultural*. The identity which is established by personal attire sometimes presupposes
the tastes and norms of the society as a whole. The Bohemian
who turns up for dinner without a jacket or a tie is a Bohemian
by the canons of the society *within* which he is operating. But as
between one society and another there may also be a place for
dress as a distinctive differentiating characteristic. It was Franz
Fanon, the late revolutionary thinker from Martinique and
participant in the Algerian Insurrection, who once said:

> The way people clothe themselves, together with the traditions
> of dress and finery that custom implies, constitutes the most

distinctive form of a society's uniqueness, that is to say the one that is the most immediately perceptible. Within the general pattern of a given custom, there are of course always modifications of detail, innovations which in highly developed societies are the mark of fashion. But the effect as a whole remains homogeneous, and the great areas of civilization, immense cultural regions, can be grouped together on the basis of original, specific techniques of man's and women's dress.[1]

In the streets of Marrakesh and Algiers one therefore often knows that one is in a Muslim country. If one opened one's eyes in Bombay or New Delhi, the dress of many of the passers-by would be part of the revelation that one was in the midst of an Indian civilization. An exposure to Disneyland or other pleasure centres of California would soon familiarize the stranger to some of the dress manifestations of the American sub-culture.

In reality the idea of differentiating civilizations by the way its members dress is rapidly being antiquated by events. Perhaps the most successful cultural bequest from the West to the rest of the world has in fact been precisely Western dress. Mankind is getting rapidly homogenized by the sheer acquisition of the Western shirt and trousers. The Japanese businessman, the Arab Minister, the Indian lawyer, the African civil servant have all found a common denominator in the Western suit.

To some extent this is what made the case of the Masai an elegant exercise in sheer cultural obstinacy. Here were a people who refused to climb on the bandwagon of Westernized apparel. The Area Commissioner of Masailand in Tanzania was particularly frustrated to note that even those Masai that had been exposed to modern education continued their attachment to Masai modes of personal adornment. Area Commissioner Sungura admitted to being surprised to find amongst a group of 'bright-looking English-speaking secondary school-taught Masai youth' a young man called George Koyo who was complete with ochre-soiled clothing and hair, 'showing no sign whatsoever of his education which is better than mine'.[2]

---

[1] Fanon, *Studies in a Dying Colonialism*, translated from the French by Haakon Chevalier (New York: Monthly Review Press, 1965), p. 35.

[2] See *The Daily Nation* (Nairobi), February 6, 1968.

The whole Tanzanian policy of seeking to 'modernize the Masai' by getting them to wear trousers seemed to be a direct attack on the most distinguishing aspect of the cultural identity of the Masai. Surprise was widely expressed that Tanzania, which in many ways had stood for the African right to be distinctive, should at the same time have embarked on one of the most blatant acts of enforced de-culturation since the great debate on female circumcision among the Kikuyu in Kenya half a century earlier. In fact one participant in the debate on the Masai, O. N. Njau, argued on the futility of enforced de-culturation by citing the example of the circumcision debate. In the words of Njau,

Far back in the early 1930's the missionaries saw the need of advising Kikuyu of the obvious fact that circumcision of girls was unnecessary. Despite the much publicized campaign against this practice, even today more than 70 per cent of all Kikuyu girls are circumcised. The then Colonial Government attempted to carry out this advice and I remember that, as late as 1957, circumcized girls were not admitted in the then inter-mediate schools. However, as we all know, there must have existed many loopholes as Kikuyu women are among the best educated in this part of Africa.

Njau also discussed the impact of Westernism on Indians and Pakistanis. To some extent he echoes the view of John Plamenatz, the Oxford philosopher, that the Indians are perhaps the most deeply Westernized of all non-Western peoples.[1]

But Njau notes,

Indians and Pakistanis have been acquainted with the Western civilization for centuries, yet they proudly use their traditional dress.[2]

A governmental policy that the Masai become more Westernized in their dress, when pursued in a nationalistic country like Tan-zania, had historical as well as cultural anomalies. Nyerere himself had once complained how in a certain period of colonial rule

[1] Plamenatz, *On Alien Rule and Self-Government* (London: Longmans, 1960).
[2] 'Masai and Their Fashions', Letter in *East African Standard* (Nairobi), February 17, 1968.

Africans themselves regarded it as a compliment rather than an insult to be called 'Black Europeans'.[1]

African poets have on occasion satirized the so-called black *evolué* or *assimilé* who had absorbed too readily the trappings of the conquering nation. To use the lines of David Diop of Senegal,

> My brother you flash your teeth in response to every
> hypocrisy
> My brother with gold-rimmed glasses
> You give your master a blue-eyed faithful look
> My poor brother in immaculate evening dress
> Screaming and whispering and pleading in the parlours
> of condescension.[2]

But what ought to be borne in mind is that nakedness, while revealing the body of a man, may at the same time be disguising

[1] President Nyerere's *Address to the Tanganyika National Assembly*, December 10, 1962, special publication, p. 21. In this regard it is instructive to compare the Masai controversy with the agitation about mini-skirts in Tanzania. In October 1968 some girls wearing mini-skirts were man-handled by members of the TANU Youth League in Dar es Salaam. Riot police had to be called in to handle the youth. A resolution ('Operation Vijana') was proposed to ban mini-skirts, wigs, and tight trousers from Tanzania with effect from January 1969, but younger members of the ruling party thought January was too far away and embarked on measures to speed up the change. The Afro-Shirazi Youth League in Zanzibar soon endorsed the move by their sister organization on the mainland. In a resolution marking the close of a three day seminar the Afro-Shirazi Youth League pledged they would work resolutely to eliminate such remnants of foreign culture in the country. In the background of these resolutions was the memory of Kariakoo Market Place, Dar es Salaam, a few days earlier when these youthful gangs stopped girls wearing mini-skirts and tight dresses and assaulted them, and riot police carrying guns and tear gas helped to disperse huge crowds at the market place.

It was clear that Tanzanian disapproval of the semi-nakedness of the Masai had a different basis from her disapproval of the semi-nakedness of mini-skirts. In the case of the mini-skirts part of the disapproval stemmed from the allegation that this was a disreputable foreign intrusion into the dress culture of the country. On the other hand, getting the Masai to wear trousers was to impose on them a foreign mode of attire. For a further discussion of the politics of mini-skirts, see Ali A. Mazrui, 'Mini-skirts and Political Puritanism', *Africa Report* (Washington, D.C.) October 1968. See also *The Nationalist* (Dar-es-Salaam) and *East African Standard* (Nairobi) 8th and 9th October, 1968.

A related instance of Tanzania's political puritanism was the country's decision to abolish in 1968 the beauty contest for Miss Tanzania.

[2] See Diop's poem, 'The Renegade', translated and published in *Modern Poetry from Africa*, edited by Gerald Moore and Ulli Beier (Penguin African Library, 1963), p. 57.

his identity. After all, when everyone strips they are reducing themselves to their basic commonalty. If a Yoruba woman from Nigeria and a Muganda from Uganda were both dressed in their national apparel you would have a basis for distinguishing the Nigerian from the Ugandan. But were the two women to strip themselves, the badge of nationality would immediately be seriously blurred. The girls would then have been reduced to their essential femininity. A stranger seeing them would know more about their personal bodies but less about their personal identities. The price of bodily revelation in this case is national obscurity.

In this regard one might say that complete nakedness on the one hand, and Western dress on the other, are having the same total effect on the problem of identity in the second half of the twentieth-century. The spread of Western dress and its acceptance by peoples vastly differing in cultural background and historical origin does itself have this consequence of blurring distinctions between peoples. A Nigerian man in a suit and a Ugandan in a suit might be as difficult to differentiate nationally as the naked Nigerian and Ugandan women we have discussed already. Identity as the ultimate basis of distinctiveness therefore stands to suffer whether Africa moves in the direction of total Westernization in dress or in the direction of total renunciation of dress.

Yet the Masai retains a feature of distinctiveness by falling short of total nakedness. The *Shuka* with which he covers part of his body, and the ochre with which he colours his body, together constitute a persistent claim to cultural uniqueness. The acquisition of trousers by the Masai would be a step away from this uniqueness.

NUDITY AND RELIGIOUS REBELLION

In the course of the press debate on Tanzania's policy about clothing the Masai, the Masai elders in Kenya were reported to have asked the following question:

If the Almighty God could stomach seeing the entire anatomies of Adam and Eve in their complete nudity, is it not a little prudish for an African government to have fits by merely viewing a casually exhibited Masai buttock?[1]

In reply a correspondent writing for an East African magazine said, 'It should be remembered that the Masai are not living before the fall of mankind as Adam and Eve did. When Adam and Eve disobeyed God, they were clothed by God before He drove them out of the Garden.'[2]

These remarks immediately dramatized the long-standing link between nakedness and certain forms of rebellion. The link goes back, as this correspondent has suggested, to Adam and Eve and their own act of disobedience to God. This human act of disobedience to God was itself connected with a prior act of rebellion by Satan and his followers. Milton in *Paradise Lost* begins by first presenting Satan and his followers as rebels against divine absolutism—believing as they did that it was 'better to reign in hell than serve in Heaven'. In Miltonic terms, this was, as it were, the first political rebellion ever. But it was a rebellion of angels—who were then deported from Heaven.

What could the fallen angels now do in revenge against God's punishment? The Miltonic version of this story was that Satan and his followers decided to have their own back by perverting God's purposes for man. God had just created a new creature and given him a companion in the Garden of Eden. The creature had in fact been forged in God's own image, and a place of distinction was intended for this creature in God's grand design for the universe. What better way could the fallen angels have of 'hitting back' for their deportation from Heaven, than by setting out to frustrate God's intentions for man? And so the Miltonic Satan makes the great journey towards the Garden of Eden intent on this ultimate subversion. On arrival there he sees the grandeur and richness of the habitat, and then finally casts his eyes on the two creatures whose destiny he was about to subvert. Adam and Eve were striking pieces of creation. In their very nakedness lay the glory of their innocence:

> God-like erect, with native honour clad
> In naked majesty seemed lords of all,

[1] This question is cited and discussed in a letter by 'Marko' in *Reporter* (Nairobi), February 23, 1968, p. 4.
[2] *Ibid.*

And worthy seemed, for in their looks divine
The image of their glorious Maker shone . . .
Nor those mysterious parts were then concealed;
Then was not guilty shame; dishonest shame
Of nature's work, honour dishonourable,
Sin-bred, how have ye troubled all mankind
With shows instead, mere shows of seeming pure,
And banished from man's life his happiest life,
Simplicity and spotless innocence.[1]

Obviously this was the time of human evolution when nakedness was not a symbol of sensuous desire, but was a symbol of
innocence:

So passed they naked on, nor shunned the sight
Of God or angel, for they thought no ill . . .[2]

There are theological difficulties as to what the Original Sin
consisted of. One major interpretation is that the Tree of
Knowledge was in fact carnal knowledge. Adam and Eve
took a step towards sinfulness when they became conscious
of their nakedness. And with their Original Sin death came to
mankind.

If this interpretation is correct, if the forbidden fruit was
indeed love-making, there is perhaps a touch of mystery that
Christianity should regard this original capitulation to lust as the
cause of all human death. In some sense it would seem more
plausible to argue that the moment of lust between Adam and
Eve was the guarantee of all human reproduction. It might even
be argued that to a certain extent it is sin which makes us
human—just as it is death which completes our definition as
mortals. A human being who is not mortal is almost a contradiction in terms. And it was Adam's sin which created human
mortality.

But there are other implications of sin too. In political philosophy government itself has sometimes been interpreted as the
political equivalent of dress. There was once a political Garden of
Eden where men lived happily in innocent abandon and naturalness. But this political Garden of Eden came to be lost in terms

[1] Milton, *Paradise Lost*, Book IV, lines 288–318.
[2] *Ibid.*, lines 319–20.

comparable to the loss of the personal Garden of Eden when Adam and Eve experienced a moment of intimacy. In the words of the Anglo-American philosopher, Thomas Paine, 'Government, like dress, is the badge of lost innocence'.

Sometimes political philosophy and theology have merged in this equation. To Augustine, the 'earthly city', in the sense of secular government, became necessary when man proved his capacity for lawlessness by disobeying God himself. In a way the first godly city was the Garden of Eden—though it consisted of the most primary of all societies, man and wife. But Augustine carries the argument further. He not only says it was sin which made government necessary. This is implied in the trend of his argument, but his more specific formulation is of the relationship between sin and servitude. He says: 'Sin, therefore, is the mother of servitude, and first cause of man's subjection to man.'[1]

The worst form of servitude, however, is servitude to sin itself. Augustine views subjection to evil as being worse than any form of slavery to man: 'It is a happier servitude to serve man than lust. . . . He that is good is free, though he be a slave, and he that is evil, a slave though he be king.'[2]

With the coming of lust to human life nudity ceased to be a pure symbol of innocence and began to acquire all the connotations of bodily temptation. As that correspondent in an East African magazine put it: 'When Adam and Eve disobeyed God, they were clothed by God before he drove them out of the Garden.'[3]

The very concept of 'flesh' came to imply sensuousness; and the very idea of 'the flesh is weak' connoted the frailty of human discipline.

And yet Christian theology, while rejecting some of the more literal forms of bodily symbolism, nevertheless used a good deal of metaphor based on flesh as something sacred. The relationship between Christ and the Church is sometimes portrayed in decisively sensuous terms: 'Husbands, love your wives, as Christ loved the Church and gave Himself up for her' (Ephesians 5:25) or 'Husbands should love their wives as their own bodies. He who

[1] See Augustine, *Civitas Dei*, Vol. XIX, 15.
[2] *Civitas Dei*, Vol. IV, 3, 4, 6.
[3] *East Africa's Reporter*, February 23, 1968, p. 4.

loves his wife loves himself. For no man ever hates his own flesh, but nourishes and cherishes it, as Christ does the Church, because we are members of His body' (Ephesians 5: 28–33). Such notions of the body and the flesh as characteristic of Christ's relation to the Church are recurrent in the language of Paul. In condemning prostitution, for example, Paul said to the Corinthians, 'Do you not know that your bodies are members of Christ? Shall I therefore take the members of Christ and make them members of a prostitute? Never! . . . Every other sin which a man commits is outside the body; but the immoral man sins against his own body. Do you not know that your body is a temple of the Holy Spirit within you, which you have from God? You are not your own; you were bought with a price. So glorify God in your body' (I Corinthians 6: 15–20).

PAIN AND THE BODY

But it was not merely in its original theological formulation that Christianity managed to establish a link between rebellion and the body. There were also other ways, including the very notion of naked pain inflicted on the body as a form of divine passion. In the case of Jesus himself the martyrdom, though self-willed, was not self-embraced. Jesus did not *revel* in the sentence which awaited him. He gave guarded or ambiguous answers to many of the crucial questions posed to him. He would not admit to his message or to his position in clear unequivocal terms, but shrouded them all in the shadows of multiple meanings: 'And Pilate asked him, saying, Art thou the King of the Jews? And he answered him and said, Thou sayest it' (St Luke 23: 3, 4).

To the extent then that Jesus was careful in what he said, he was not rushing headlong towards his martyrdom. And even when he was crucified there was still in him a sense of despair as he cried out, 'My God, my God, why hast Thou forsaken me?' Here again is a dignified reluctance to revel in affliction.

But this dignity was not always present in the martyrdom of Christians later on. Some of the enthusiasm with which Christian martyrs later awaited their sentences of torture led to a spate of psycho-analytical speculation as to the basic motives for their behaviour. As Theodore Reik has pointed out, the study of psychological and psycho-analytical literature shows that many scientists in these fields are inclined to hold that religious martyrdom is a form of sexual masochism. A host of references have been offered to prove that the sexual element unconsciously determined the psychic life of many Christian martyrs. Reik himself describes the equation as excessive. Such scholars had an inadequate appreciation of an important difference. To dramatize this difference Reik presents two typical attitudes towards sexuality which have a common starting point. He cites the case of a 25-year-old man who whips himself to obtain sexual satisfaction from the sight, in a mirror, of his own blood.

For his other example Reik cites a Catholic legend which illustrates the counterpart of this conduct. One of the kindest of all Christian Saints passed many years of his manhood in sacred contemplation in the Chapel next to the Church San Marie near Assisi. One day he felt an intense and almost overpowering sexual desire. Reik continues:

> It was winter at its hardest; Nature seemed asleep under the snow that covered the little garden of the monastery, but the Evil One was awake. When St Francis was tortured by this thorn in his flesh so that he was in danger of succumbing to the temptation, he rushed into the snow and rolled himself in a thorn bush of wild roses. And then and there a miracle happened and the dew of his blood made the green sprout and in the snow roses blossomed whose petals were sprinkled blood-red. Up to this day the nuns of Assisi sell pressed roses the white petals of which bear the stigmata of the Saint in memory of his victory over the impure spirit.[1]

This psycho-analyst then proceeds to draw the distinctive features of each of these two cases. In the experience of the 25-year-old man in front of the mirror the pain constitutes an access to the otherwise forbidden satisfaction. In the experience of St Francis the pain served as defence against the sinful desire. In the first case it means a promotion of the sensual excitement, in the second its counter-weight. Reik goes on to argue that both do

[1] See Theodore Reik, *Masochism in Sex and Society*, translated by Margaret H. Beigel and Gertrude M. Kurth (New York: Grove Press Inc., 1962 edition), pp. 349–50. For a discussion of related issues see Chapter XVI following.

approximately the same thing, but the meaning of each act is different as it is performed under different psychic conditions. 'In the first case the affliction of severe punishment brings forth the enjoyment, in the second the self-punishment has to prevent gratification.'[1]

What matters from the point of view of our analysis here is that both in masochism and in martyrdom the body provides the means to a higher plane of experience. Even the most spiritual of the martyrs needs the body as the foundation of his martyrdom. There would have been no Passion in the Crucifixion had Jesus not possessed a human body.

In Sunni Islam martyrdom is a peripheral phenomenon. There is little glorification of self-willed suffering, but in Shi'a Islam there is an important masochistic theme. For example, the murder of Hussein, the prophet's grandson, is celebrated every year by one Shi'ite School with wailing and a passionate beating of the chest. The Ithnasharis sometimes go to the extent of making their chests bleed in ferocious sympathy with the martyrdom of Hussein. Here again the body of the believer is needed to provide access to physical suffering.

In some of the more simple religious movements the body is used not so much to provide access to pain as to provide access to ecstasy. The dance that leads on to a trance and to spiritual elevation becomes part of a total religious experience. R. R. Marett has even gone as far as to assert that primitive religion is 'not so much thought out as danced out'.[2]

African writers have often used the symbol of the African dance and the response to the drum as intimations of the ancestral spirit of Africa. In the words of David Diop:

> Negress my warm rumour of Africa
> My land of mystery and my fruit of reason
> You are the dance by the naked joy of your smile
> By the offering of your breasts and secret powers
> You are the dance by the golden tales of marriage nights
> By new tempos and more secular rhythms . . .

---

[1] Reik, *op. cit.*, p. 350.
[2] Harett, *Threshold of Religion* (London, 1909), p. xxxi. See also B. G. M. Sundkler, *Bantu Prophets in South Africa* (London: Oxford University Press, 1961 edition), p. 198.

> You are the idea of All and the voice of the Ancient
> Gravely rocketed against our fears
> You are the Word which explodes
> In showers of light upon the shores of oblivion.[1]

And Senghor has sometimes sung about 'the leader of the dance [making] fast his vigour to the prow of his sex'.[2]

The half-naked body, bleeding in places, has at times symbolized the agony of martyrdom in Christian history; the half-naked body, sweating in places, has at times symbolized the ecstasy of a religious trance in the history of African rhythmic experience.

NUDITY AND POLITICAL REBELLION

But it is not simply in the religious sphere that the issues of nakedness and dress has been interlinked with problems of rebellion and assertion. The realm of politics has, as we intimated, also sensed the relevance of apparel for human sensibilities.

Political rebellion can sometimes take the form simply of an obstinate refusal to change. To some extent this theme was discerned quite early in the attitude of the Masai when the new Tanzanian policy on their attire was proclaimed. One member of the tribe wrote an article to a Dar es Salaam newspaper pointing out that the policy was having the effect of forcing the tribe in the remoter places back into itself. The tribe was becoming more defensive than ever. The members that lived nearer the towns, and who had to establish contact with the towns, might feel the brunt of coercion and make concessions to it. But others who might at one time have been tempted to seek greater social intercourse with the urban areas might now be forced to reject these areas more completely.

> These people have resolved to ignore any force that is out to
> destroy their traditional outlook whatever the cost might be
> . . . Since they value their traditions more than all those things

---

[1] Diop, 'To a Black Dancer' in *Modern Poetry from Africa, op. cit.*, pp. 59–60.
[2] 'Congo', *Prose and Poetry*, p. 141.

they can get from the so-called 'civilized' society they will do whatever they can to keep away from it.[1]

If this was the correct interpretation of the Masai response to the new policies in the days ahead, it constituted rebellion by withdrawal, a cultural assertion by a quiet defiance.

A second form of assertiveness is that of *residual* cultural distinctiveness. In this latter case a person may have been basically de-culturated away from his ancient civilization, and might have adopted a new way of life in many respects. But he then decides to retain a residue of this former cultural identity. This is the case of a highly Westernized person whose main literary interest is in Shakespeare, whose favourite composer is Beethoven, who eats with a knife and fork at home, uses a flush lavatory, and has the rest of his house furnished in exquisite Western standards, but who nevertheless then decides to dress himself not in a suit but in an African or Oriental national garment. Pandit Nehru often made this assertion of residual cultural distinctiveness—permitting himself to be Indian by dress and by general sympathy yet Western by the totality of his intellectual and even domestic behaviour.

This form of assertion can sometimes invite ridicule from critics. Gandhi's determination to move around simply with a Dhoti, naked from the waist upwards, even when he was having an audience with British Royalty, was a striking case of cultural assertiveness. But it did provoke from Winston Churchill the taunt that India could not be entrusted to 'a naked fakir'.

Yet Indians have often been admired by nationalists elsewhere for their determination to retain at least these residual trappings of their ancient culture. Even in the course of the controversy over the Masai early in 1968 in East Africa one African correspondent, as has already been noted, had occasion to note, 'Indians and Pakistanis have been acquainted with Western civilization for centuries, yet they proudly use their traditional dress.'[2]

A third type of cultural assertion is that of ritualized rejection

[1] L. M. Ole Paraipuny, 'The Masai: One Tribesman's Views on a Complex Problem', *Sunday News* (Dar es Salaam), February 25, 1968, p. 4.
[2] Letter from O. N. Njau, 'Masai and Their Fashions', *East African Standard*, February 17, 1968. See p. 326, *n.* 14.

of a foreign dress that had already been adopted. This is somewhat different from the former case, where the residual trapping may never have been adopted. Moreover, in the case of ritualized rejection of Western dress, for example, the rejection may be only on special occasions or in the course of political demonstrations. The rest of the time the nationalists might still go about in their neckties.

Ritualized rejection of Western dress of this kind happened in the history of Kenya's nationalism, for example. Eliud Mathu, the first African member of the Kenya Legislative Council in the colonial period, once tore his jacket off at a public meeting in a dramatic gesture of rejecting Western civilization—if the price was the loss of land for the African. 'Take back your civilization —and give back my land!'

In the course of the Mau Mau rebellion there were similar moments of ritualized rejection of Western dress. Perhaps even more interesting was the utilization of nakedness as a method of adding solemnity to an oath. Josiah Kariuki tells us of the ritual which constituted the Mau Mau *Batuni* oath.

We sat down and Biniathi then told us to take all our clothes off except our trousers, and we stood patiently waiting to be called by him. I was called second after Kanyoi and there was no disobeying the summons. I took off my trousers and squatted facing Biniathi. He told me to take the thorax of the goat which had been skinned, to put my penis through a hole that had been made in it and to hold the rest of it in my left hand in front of me.

This was part of the ritual which culminated in this undertaking:

I speak the truth and vow before God
And by this *Batuni* oath of our movement
Which is called the movement of fighting
That if I am called on to kill for our soil
If I am called on to shed my blood for it
I shall obey . . .
I speak the truth and vow before God
That I shall never take away the woman of another man

> That I shall never walk with prostitutes
> That I shall never steal anything belonging to another
>   person in the movement
> Nor shall I hate any other member for his actions
> And if I do any of these things
> May this oath kill me . . .[1]

There was in this oath a commitment to fight the enemy, a commitment to collective solidarity among the 'Mau Mau' fighters, and a commitment to frugality and self-denial, especially in the all too dangerous sensuous area of relations with women. But to give the whole *Batuni* oath the overpowering air of binding force, it was deemed necessary to strip the man who was taking it. Nudity in this case was the requisite atmosphere for ominous awe.

A fourth form of political assertiveness connected with dress is itself a form of imitation. In some of the previous cases what was being dramatized was the rejection of a blind imitation of Western ways, but under this other category there is an imitation not necessarily of Westerners, but of those who have already come to symbolize a prior anti-Westernism. The adoption of Chinese attire among revolutionaries in countries like Tanzania is one case of revolutionary imitativeness. The Chinese style of dress becomes a symbol of solidarity worthy of adoption by African radicals as well.

Perhaps even more dramatic was the case of Cuban styles of attire as manifested among revolutionaries on the island of Zanzibar. Soon after the revolution which overthrew the Sultan's regime in January 1964 there was a widely publicized report that Cuban militiamen were among the revolutionaries. But Michael Lofchie's theory about the source of the confusion is persuasive. It is probable that the Cuban rumour was due to the presence of several trade union leaders who had joined the revolutionaries early on the first day of the New Era. Lofchie points out that:

> Many members of these groups had adopted the Cuban style
> of dress and appearance, and even employed the Cuban cry
> 'Venceremos' (We Shall Conquer) as a political symbol. Their

[1] Josiah Mwangi Kariuki, *'Mau Mau' Detainee* (London: Oxford University Press, 1963), pp. 29–30.

Cuban type of uniform set them off clearly from the [Afro-Shirazi Youth League] members and was probably the basis of the report that the revolutionary army contained Cuban soldiers.[1]

In this case imitation of the dress of others, far from being a detraction from nationalism, was in fact an ally of it. 'For the apparel oft proclaims the man', Polonius had said. And Zanzibaris in Cuban apparel proclaimed their revolutionary affiliations.

The fifth form of revolutionary assertion in politics, in-so-far as it is connected with the issue of dress and nakedness, comes as a response to the indignity of being compulsorily undressed or re-clothed by a conquering power. The conqueror lays down the law about a new mode of dress or against an old item of attire. The nationalist then responds to this with the militancy of offended pride.

A striking example of this kind of phenomenon in revolutionary Africa was the veil in Algeria. Franz Fanon, the West Indian psycho-philosopher who fought in the Algerian Insurrection, had time to analyse before his death the symbol of 'Algeria unveiled'. Fanon saw the veil of the Algerian woman both as a badge of identity and as a basis of solidarity:

In the Arab Maghreb, the veil belongs to the clothing traditions of the Tunisian, Algerian, Moroccan and Libyan national societies. For the tourist and the foreigner, the veil demarcates both Algerian society and its feminine component. . . . The woman seen in her white veil unifies the perception that one has of Algerian feminine society. Obviously what we have here is a uniform which tolerates no modification, nor variant.[2]

Fanon goes on to discuss the policy of the French authorities in its attempts to eliminate the veil from Algerian society. The French formula was 'Let's win over the women, and the rest will follow'. It was assumed that beneath the patrilineal pattern of Algerian society there was a matrilineal essence.

The success of the French assimilationist policy therefore

---

[1] Michael F. Lofchie, *Zanzibar: Background to Revolution* (Princeton: Princeton University Press, 1965), p. 276.

[2] *Studies in a Dying Colonialism, op. cit.*, pp. 35–6.

depended in part on an adequate awareness of the importance of the Algerian mother, the Algerian grandmother, the aunt and the 'old woman'. The colonial administration was, according to Fanon, convinced of this doctrine:

> If we want to destroy the structure of the Algerian society, its capacity for resistance, we must first of all conquer the women; we must go and find them behind the veil where they hide themselves and in the houses where the men keep them out of sight.

But in the heat of the Algerian War, it was not simple propaganda which was used. The occupying forces resorted at times to the personal aggression of forceful unveiling of women in the streets. The situation got worse when Algerian women became more systematically committed to revolution. They were unveiled in the streets partly out of the French soldiers' desire to subject the Arab woman to indignity, but also at times out of suspicion that behind the veil was a Stengun. Fanon discerned in European behaviour deeper psychological reasons as well. He had himself served as a medical psycho-analyst in Algeria and had treated both French soldiers and some prisoners of the Algerian War. Fanon notes: 'The rape of the Algerian woman in the dream of the European is always preceded by a rending of the veil.'

The French soldiers were sometimes influenced by a rape complex at the sub-conscious level if not in complete awareness.

> Unveiling this woman is revealing her beauty; it is baring her secret, breaking her resistance, making her available for adventure. Hiding the face is also disguising a secret; it is also creating a world of mystery, of the hidden. In a confused way, the European experiences his relation with the Algerian woman at a highly complex level. There is in it the will to bring this woman within his reach, to make her a possible object of possession.[1]

But in fact this is the time when the Algerian woman converted the veil more fully into a military camouflage. A technique was

[1] *Studies in a Dying Colonialism, op. cit.*, pp. 42–4.

evolved of carrying a rather heavy object dangerous to handle under the veil, and still give the impression of having one's hands free, of there being nothing under this *hiak* except a poor woman or an insignificant young girl. It was not enough to be veiled. One had to look so much like a 'fatma' that the soldier would be convinced that this woman was quite harmless. Fanon goes on to say that this technique was in fact extremely difficult.

Three metres ahead of you the police challenge a veiled woman who does not look particularly suspect. From the anguished expression of the unit leader you have guessed that she is carrying a bomb, or a sack of grenades, bound to her body by a whole system of strings and straps. For the hands must be free, exhibited bare, humbly and abjectly presented to the soldiers so that they will look no further.

But with the conversion of the veil into a military camouflage the enemy gradually became extra alerted.

In the streets one witnessed what became a commonplace spectacle of Algerian women glued to the wall, over whose bodies the famous magnetic detectors, the 'frying pans' would be passed. Every veiled woman, every Algerian woman became suspect. There was no discrimination. This was the period during which men, women, children, the whole Algerian people, experienced at one and the same time their national vocation and the recasting of the new Algerian society.[1]

But the Algerian woman sometimes *abandoned* the veil as an exercise in military camouflage. There were occasions when it was important that the feminine Algerian soldier should walk the streets looking as Europeanized as possible. For some of these girls it took a lot to escape the sense of awkwardness which came with the act of walking in the street unveiled. A newly unveiled feminine revolutionary 'has an impression of being improperly dressed, even of being naked. She experiences a sense of incompleteness with great intensity. She has the anxious feeling that something is unfinished, and along with this a frightful sensation

[1] *Ibid.*, pp. 61–2.

of disintegrating. . . . The Algerian woman who walks stark-naked in the European city relearns her body, re-establishes it in a totally revolutionary fashion.' Fanon describes this as 'a new dialectic of the body and of the world'. The newly unveiled must overcome all timidity and awkwardness 'for she must pass for a European'.[1]

In the case of the Zanzibari rebels in January 1964 the adoption of a foreign dress was an exercise in imitating admired revolutionaries elsewhere. The Zanzibaris embraced the Cuban style of attire. But in the case of the unveiled Algerian woman the idea was to embrace the French mode of attire and pass for a Frenchwoman. It will be seen that both exercises were in fact forms of revolutionary imitation. In the Zanzibari case it was an act of emulating comrades in arms on the international stage. In the case of the unveiled Algerian woman it was a case of imitating the enemy. Yet both remained acts of symbolic combat.

CONCLUSION

We have tried to demonstrate in this paper that dress and nakedness are factors in human existence which have had important connections with diverse forms of assertiveness and rebellion. The policy of the Government of Tanzania to try and revolutionize the lives of the Masai by making them wear trousers fell into line with a long stream of human experience in which dress, culture and social transformation have been intimately linked. Sometimes two acts can be the same but the meaning might be different. A French attempt to abolish the veil in Algeria and the campaign by Kamal Ataturk to abolish the Fez in Turkey do, at one level, appear to be comparable types of phenomena. And yet Ataturk's quest to abolish the Fez (and the veil) in Turkey following the disintegration of the Ottoman empire was in a large measure an act of cultural defensiveness. It was a quest for the kind of modernized status which would make the new Turkey survive. But the French attempt to unveil Algeria was by contrast an exercise in cultural aggression, compounded in the Algerian War by considerations of military precautions and tactical subterfuge.

[1] *Ibid.*, p. 59.

The place of dress and nakedness in relation to rebellion goes back, as we have indicated, at least to Adam and Eve. In Christian mythology one long-term consequence of the Original Sin was the evolution of the concept of 'private parts'. Until then these were not private. It was the consciousness of their role in sensuality, and the attempt to cover this up, which gave rise to the aura of intimacy surrounding the parts. In short, private parts became private when God sentenced Adam and Eve to eternal clothing. In the words once again of that correspondent in an East African magazine, 'It should be remembered that the Masai are not living before the fall of mankind. . . . When Adam and Eve disobeyed God, they were clothed by God before he drove them out of the Garden'.[1]

But nudity and dress have political as well as theological implications. In Africa the political implications have sometimes touched the whole movement of Negritude as a glorification of African naturalness. The emotive sensibilities of African culture, and the glistening response of the African body to rhythm and to the demands of the ancestral dance, have all become relevant.

But there have been other manifestations of the political meaning of dress and nudity in Africa's experience, ranging from the Mau Mau *Batuni* oath taken naked before the thorax of a goat, to the adoption of a Chinese style of dress in Tanzania as an act of identification with Mao Tse-tung.

'For the apparel oft proclaims the man', the voice of Polonius might once again remind us. Yet so does the lack of apparel. The song of nationalism in Africa has sometimes included a vow of nudity; the trumpet of revolution has at other times awakened radicalism to its uniform; and the world of social issues has often had to touch the revealed parts of personal intimacy. The problem of the Masai in Tanzania early in 1968 belonged to a whole universe of human experience. Here once again was one of the tense meeting points between the garment of culture and the body of man in history.

[1] *Reporter* (Nairobi), February 23, 1968, *op. cit.*

15 Political Sex[1]

Sex is a vital part of the life of an individual. Politics is often a vital aspect of the life of a society. Society consists of individuals. To what extent does the sex-life of the individual, and his ideas about sex, intrude into the politics of his society?

The question is much too big to be attempted in a short essay, but it needs to be asked in order to provide the context within which this small venture is to be placed.

The ambition of this short piece is not, however, all that modest. It seeks to draw attention to a possible correlation between the ethic of monogamy and the politics of racialism. But the extreme antithesis of monogamy is sexual communism. After all, monogamy is an ethic of sexual monopoly—and communism in this sphere would seek to ensure that no one man either monopolizes or is monopolized by any one woman.

Before we come to grips then with the racial and political consequences of sexual monopoly, let us therefore first digress to view its ultimate antithesis as discussed within two major schools of communism.

PLATO, MARX AND SEX

Modern Western civilization has essentially two fountains from which it flows—the fountain of pagan Greece and the fountain of Christianity. It was Christianity which came to emphasize the principle of monogamy—and neither Marx nor the Soviet Russians ever managed to escape the consequences of being post-Christian.[2] They never quite managed to repudiate the

---

[1] This first appeared in *Transition*, Vol. IV, No. 17, 1964 and is reprinted with permission.

[2] Marx himself was, of course, Jewish by racial extraction. He was born a

principle of monopoly as the ethical base of sex. But pre-Christian Plato had fewer inhibitions in his revolutionary fervour.

Plato has bequeathed to Western thought a particular concept of love—the concept of 'Platonic love'. The idea of Platonic love encompasses a number of attributes. But what should concern us here is a negative attribute—Platonic love is love without sex. But there is such a thing as 'Platonic sex' as well as sex without love. For this latter concept one looks not to the *Phaedrus* of Plato but to the *Republic*. The love which comes with sex is an enemy to justice—for it has a tendency to impair one's capacity for impartiality. Sexual possessiveness militates against objectivity. And so the rulers of the Republic are to have wives in common.

One point which arises here is whether in a situation where no woman belongs to a single man and no man to a single woman the language of 'wife' and 'husband' is applicable at all. Societies which are not monogamous are normally upholders of either polygamy or polyandry. But a society like Plato's which combines both poses the question whether the term 'marriage' is a meaningful concept at all. Double polygamy is perhaps not *gamos* at all.

Be that as it may, the idea of sexual communism as prescribed by Plato remains the most daring philosophical attempt ever made to come with grips with some of the political implications of sex.[1]

Many centuries later Karl Marx and his followers were to be accused of having embraced the principle of sexual communism and included it in their ideology. The *Communist Manifesto's* denial of this charge is not without equivocation. The Manifesto says that the whole bourgeoisie in chorus screams 'But you communists would introduce community of women!'

In reply the Manifesto sarcastically says that the bourgeois sees in his wife a mere instrument of production. He hears that the instruments of production are to be exploited in common. He can therefore come to no other conclusion than that women are to be exploited in common. The Manifesto declares: 'The

---

Jew by religion as well, but his parents were converted to Christianity while Karl was still a child. Karl himself was later to take a Hegelian route to atheism, but some Judeo-Christian inhibitions remained with him.

[1] For a critical analysis of the implications of Plato's position see K. R. Popper, *The Open Society and Its Enemies*, Vol. I (London: Routledge & Kegan Paul, 1962 edition), especially Chapters 4 and 8.

communists have no need to introduce community of women; it has existed from time immemorial . . . Bourgeois marriage is in reality a system of wives in common and thus, at the most, what the Communists might possibly be reproached with is that they desire to introduce, in substitution for a hypocritically concealed, an open legalized community of women.'

Here we think we are back to a Platonic communism of sex. But the Marxist *Manifesto* goes on to say: '.. . it is self-evident that the abolition of the present system of production must bring with it the abolition of the community of women springing from that system—i.e. prostitution, both public and private.'[1]

Plato had envisaged sexual communism as a way of ensuring that the rulers were just. But Marx sees a kind of sexual communism in bourgeois society itself—and takes it simply for one more symptom that the rulers are depraved and unjust. The Russian Revolution was later to see itself as the agent not only of an economic transformation but also of a revolution in sexual life. A very intelligent Russian post-graduate student whom I knew in Oxford was sincerely convinced that communism had wiped out prostitution in his country. But an eminent Soviet physician, Dr T. S. Atarov, has apparently pointed out elsewhere that it would be a mistake to imagine that the transformation of the sexual ethics of the Soviet Union had as yet been completed. The Russian doctor is quoted as saying:

> There are still in our present society plenty of old ideological survivals. Many of our men still think nothing of being unfaithful to their wives . . . Worse still, among our young people, there are some who tend to reduce their relations with the opposite sex to a mere satisfaction of their physical urge without any spiritual or moral connection with the person concerned.[2]

Dr Atarov's book then refers to a 'peculiar' philosophy which

---

[1] *Manifesto of the Communist Party* (1848). The edition consulted is the one in *Marx and Engels: Basic Writings on Politics and Philosophy* (ed. L. S. Feuer), (New York: Doubleday, 1959), pp. 24–6.

[2] *Problems of Sexual Education*, Moscow, 1959. Cited in *Russia under Khrushchev*, by Alexander Werth (New York: Fawcett World Library, 1962), p. 147. The official title of Dr. T. S. Atarov was Physician of Merit of the RSFSR, coupled with the high academic degree of Candidate of Medical Sciences.

was discernible in some quarters. This is the claim that promiscuity is an inevitable substitute for the prostitution which
communism had abolished. Monogamy, according to this school
of Russian sexual thought, is an artificial restraint on man's
natural impulses.

Dr Atarov's rejoinder is that this school is wholly contrary to
Lenin's view that 'free love' is *not* among the freedoms of a
socialist society.[1]

As for sexual perversions, a Soviet textbook on psychiatry has
been quoted as saying that 'phenomena like homosexuality
(which are acquired and not innate) have nothing in our environment to encourage them'. The book goes on to say that in pre-
war Berlin there were three newspapers for homosexuals, and
120 widely advertised clubs, besides numerous cafes where
people sharing this tendency met.

> The healthy atmosphere in which Soviet youth is brought up
> provides no conditions which would encourage the develop-
> ment of such perversions, the Soviet book asserts.[2]

The proletarian revolution had apparently reasserted Russian
manhood all over. And neither Socrates nor Plato are permitted
to compromise the heterosexuality of the toiling youth.

MONOGAMY AND RACIALISM

It is not merely with sexual communism and homosexual love
that Plato's name is associated. It is also linked with ideas about
the division of humanity into natural rulers and natural subjects—
and the application of rational principles of breeding to human
reproduction. 'God . . . has put gold into those who are capable
of ruling, silver into the auxiliaries, and iron and copper into the
peasants and other producing classes.'[3]

In essence Plato's division is a class division. But because he
links it to biological characteristics, a theory of class prejudice

---

[1] *Ibid.*, pp. 147–8.
[2] *Uchebnik Psychiatriyi*, by O. V. Kerbikov and others, (Moscow 1958), p. 313.
Cited in Alexander Werth, *ibid.*, p. 162.
[3] *Republic*, 415 *a*.

expands into a theory of racial prejudice. And a warning against miscegenation is formulated. 'The first and chief injunction laid by heaven upon the Rulers is that, among all the things of which they must show themselves good guardians, there is none that needs to be so carefully watched as the mixture of metals in the souls of the children.'[1]

Starting from these Platonic notions one sometimes discerns a curious relationship between the horror of miscegenation and the ethic of monogamy. The horror of miscegenation can sometimes destroy the ethic of monogamy or be indifferent to its demands. This is certainly the case when appeal is made to eugenics in order to avert miscegenation. Hitler's Germany and Plato's Republic share a common adventure in the application of the principles of animal breeding to experimental human reproduction. Such an application cannot be consistent with the implicit precepts of Christian monogamy.

But there are times when Christian monogamy itself can be a breeding ground of racialism in relations between the sexes. This has a lot to do with the *spiritualization of sex* in Christianity. Extra-marital sexual relations are regarded as sin. This is not unusual—it is common to a good many other religions and codes of conduct as well. But he who regards extra-marital relations as sinful does not have to go to the extent of regarding *marital* sexual relations as sacred. Yet the Christian in history has tended to do precisely this, though not always consistently. In general the Christian has not been satisfied with saying that marriage is a device for avoiding sin. He has gone further and invested the institution with sacredness. And the sexual act within marriage is sometimes too closely identified with the fulfilment of God's will.

And what is God to the Christian? God is a good many things— but God is also Love. And an unconscious equation emerges within the universe of the Christian mind: 'Sex is Sacred; God is Love; Sex is Love'. For Christianity itself the sex that is sacred is, of course, sex within marriage. But although the hold of Christianity has been loosening in the Western world, its influence on Western ways of thought and modes of behaviour is stronger than might appear from statistics about Church attendance in Europe. And the influence of Christianity is not always manifested

1 *Republic*, 546a. Also related is 434c.

in ways which Christianity itself would approve. The equation between sex and love gets extended in the West beyond the sacred boundaries of Christian marriage. So intimate becomes the logical relationship between the *idea* of sex and the *idea* of love in the Western mind that the sexual act itself becomes characterized as an act of 'making love'.

Why should sex and love be wedded together in this way? If you ran into a couple in a sexual embrace, and your mind was using Western concepts, the conclusion you are likely to reach is that these two strangers are two 'lovers' enjoying themselves. It would certainly be odd if you started off with the hypothesis that the two figures engaged in a sexual act were not 'lovers' but mutual 'haters'.

To a certain extent all this is not peculiar to a Western frame of reasoning. Whatever the frame of reasoning, love and lust are both emotions of *attraction* serving to draw people together in the typical course of their inherent tendencies. Hate, on the other hand, is usually an emotion of *repulsion*—serving to keep people apart. We therefore do not consider it normal that two people who are repelled by mutual hate should at the same time be brought together by mutual sexual desire. Normal human behaviour does not make us think of 'hate' when we stumble onto a couple in a sexual embrace.

But if it is true of any human society that sex and hate would normally make very strange bed-fellows, why then did we single out the Euro-Christian frame of reference? The reason is that the Euro-Christian frame of reference not only dissociates hate from sex but goes a step further and associates spiritualized love with sex. The idea of sex as an act of love is by no means universal. There are societies which regard the sexual act essentially as an act of masculine assertion; or as Nature's way of saying that the male of the species is superior and ought normally to be 'on top'. Or a society might just regard sex as Nature's insurance against perpetual boredom—one additional method of breaking the monotony and having a bit of fun. None of these attitudes to sex equate it with love. And none of them would be readily acceptable to the typical Westerner.

But what has all this specifically to do with Christian monogamy as such? The answer lies in the fact that Euro-Christian culture has tried to spiritualize 'physical love' by *dualizing* it.

God can love all his creatures; a mother can love all her children—
but 'a man can really love only one woman'. Love between a man
and woman, in their capacities as such, must be *dual* if it is to be
'love' at all.

Duality as part of the definition of 'love' encourages more than
ever Love's equation with Sex within the Western frame of
reference. Such an equation would be untenable within a
polygamous society. Love and sexual desire can indeed coincide
in a relationship between two people—but the two feelings do
not entail each other. A person from a polygamous society might
therefore say to a Westerner:

> You surely must know from concrete experience that you can
> desire a woman and not love her; love her and not desire her;
> both love and desire her—or be completely indifferent
> towards her. Surely even in your own Western society, if you
> were to stumble on to two people in a sexual embrace, the
> statistical chances would be that they were *not* in love. All that
> the act would tell you is that at least one of the two figures
> before you was engaged in a quest for sexual satisfaction. If
> your experience confirms this, why does your theory insist on
> maintaining a logical intimacy between the concept of love
> and the idea of sex?

If love is dual, and sex is plural or promiscuous in a polygamous
society, then sex does not even logically imply love in such a
society. A polygamous society might therefore be said to recognize
in logic what even a Western society knows in practice—that only
in a minority of cases is the sexual act an expression of love.

But does it matter what the different words imply in different
languages? The answer must be that it *does*—because the multiple
associations of words are an important factor in the way people's
attitudes are conditioned. And people's attitudes to sex or marriage might have important implications in wider social and
political terms. By definition a polygamous attitude to marriage
is significantly different from a monogamous one. What are apt
to be overlooked are indeed those wider social and political consequences of this simple difference.

One area of life which can all too easily be affected by this
difference is the area of race relations. It is probably a fact that

polygamy is more conducive to toleration of mixed marriages then monogamy is. The classic case of a polygamous 'race' which is at the same time culturally homogeneous is perhaps the Arab race. And the Arabs also 'happened to be' that most mongrel race on earth. In skin-colour the range is from the white Arabs of Syria and the Lebanon, the brown Arabs of the Hadhramout and the Yemen, to the black Arabs of parts of Saudi Arabia, Oman and, of course, the Sudan. If the father is Arab the offspring is Arab without qualification—the idea of a half-caste being virtually alien to the relational universe of this mongrel race. We see those Arabs scattered across both sides of the Red Sea, neither completely African nor completely Asian—and certainly impossible to classify neatly in pigmentation. Historically they were sexually promiscuous—and out of promiscuity grew relative toleration of mixed marriages and a complete absence of horror at the idea of miscegenation. What after all is the Arab race but Miscegenation Incarnate?

But does this really mean that Arabs are less racialistic than others? Not necessarily. It might merely mean that their particular brand of racialism does not express itself in attitudes to intermarriage. It might indeed be true that Arabs are more tolerant of mixed marriages than Europeans have tended to be. And yet this might *not* be because the Arabs think more highly of other races. The real reason might be that they think less highly of the institution of marriage. The Arabs made marriage less of a sacred mission and more of a simple social convention; and they made sex within marriage less divine and more human. By thus reducing the spirituality of marriage, they made *inter*-marriage less of an issue. 'My second wife is Turkish. She is a good wife. For how long are we Arabs going to tolerate the arrogant tyranny of those Turkish dogs?'—so has an Arab in history been known to say. His domestic contentment was untouched by the racial prejudices of his politics. He had married across the race boundary not because he thought more highly of the Turks, but because he thought differently of marriage.

And yet there is an element of oversimplification in all this. To remove intermarriage from the sphere of racial prejudice is, in a sense, to reduce the area of prejudice itself. Sex can be the most sensitive issue in race relations. And to reduce the scope of sexual prejudice is perhaps a major mitigation of racial tension in its own right. It might even be true after all that polygamous attitudes to marriage tend to promote greater racial intercourse and greater tolerance at large.

By thus examining the nature of polygamy we should have derived some insights into the tendencies of monogamy. The Germanic Europeans are among the most monogamous of the Westerners. In the more literal meaning of the word, all Westerners are, of course, equally monogamous. The laws of their countries do not permit more than one *wife*. But when we talk of monogamous *attitudes*, we are referring to inclinations even outside marriage. In general, the Germanic-speaking Europeans are more monogamous in their sexual moralism than the Latin-speakers are known to be. The French, the Italians and the Latin Americans are, in other words, less moralistic in their attitude to promiscuity than are the Anglo-Saxons. The case of the Iberian peninsula is complicated by the direct massive influence of the Church. Were the Church as weak in the peninsula as it is in Latin America, France and Italy it is probable that Spain and Portugal would also have shared the sexual broad-mindedness of their fellow Latins.

Given then that the Germanic peoples are more monogamous in their attitudes, is it merely a coincidence that they also happen to be more racialistic in their attitudes to intermarriage? Perhaps no Latin country could have produced a racist maniac like Hitler dedicated to 'the purity of the blood'. Perhaps only the Germans proper could have worked themselves up into such a frenzy about miscegenation. But theirs was an extreme case of something shared by other Germanic peoples. As Margery Perham put it in her Reith Lectures, 'The Germanic-speaking Europeans—the British, the Germans, the Americans, the Dutch—share a deep bias against inter-marriage with the Negro race . . . This conscious, or sometimes subconscious, fear of race mixture accounts both for the [Germanic] white man's innermost ring of defence and also for all his outer ring of political, social and economic ramparts.'[1] Miss Perham does not go on to say it, but it is not entirely a coincidence that Hitler and Verwoerd belong to the same Germanic stock.

The experience of the two Americas offers tempting conclusions in this respect. If the white citizens of the United States had,

[1] *The Colonial Reckoning* (Collins Fontana Library, 1963), pp. 64–5.

in fact, been Arab, most of the coloured citizens would have become Arab too. It has been estimated that over seventy per cent of the Negro population in the United States has some 'white' blood. And the 'white' blood was much more often than not derived from a white *father*. Now, given the Arab principle that if the father is Arab the child is Arab, most of the Negroes of the United States would have been Arab had the white people of America been Arab too. But the white Americans are Caucasians and the dominant culture is Germanic. And so if either of the parents is non-Germanic, the offspring cannot be Germanic either. In fact, the law of white-dominated Florida defines a Negro as a person with 'one eighth or more of African or Negro blood'. And the laws of Florida, like the laws of eighteen other states in the American Union, specifically prohibit 'miscegenation'.[1]

To complicate the situation further, the old Western equation of love and sex becomes all mixed up with such prejudices in the United States. And the phrase 'Nigger-*Lover*' becomes an expression of racial *hatred*.

THE ATHLETICS OF SEX

But the United States is part of a whole hemispheric melting pot of race. It has been estimated that one sixth of the population of the new world consists of 'half-castes'—different 'mixtures' of white, Indian, and Negro. In Paraguay up to 97 per cent of the population is Mestizo; in Venezuela from 70 per cent to 90 per cent of the population is mixed.[2] The population of Negroes in Brazil is about the size of the population of Uganda as a whole. They constitute eleven per cent of the population of Brazil. The brown sector of Brazil is 27 per cent, and the white or 'of white descent' is 62 per cent.[3]

[1] For quite a while the United States Supreme Court had avoided a direct ruling on the constitutionality of laws which forbade mixed marriage. But such a ruling by the Court is now being demanded. For a useful background article see Arthur Krock, 'Miscegenation Debate', *The New York Times* (Review of the Week), September 8, 1963. See also the more recent article by Charlotte G. Moulton published in *The Nationalist* (Dar es Salaam), November 11, 1964.

[2] These estimates were given by Charles Winick in his *Dictionary of Anthropology* (London: Peter Owen Ltd., 1957). The percentages are not likely to have changed significantly.

[3] See Florence Elliott and Michael Summerskill, *A Dictionary of Politics* (Penguin, 1959 issue), p. 43.

But is there no form of race prejudice in Latin America? That would be an absurd claim. There is indeed a good deal of prejudice—but the Germanic horror of 'mixing blood' is nowhere as acute. Here we must, in fact, distinguish between race prejudice and colour prejudice. Very often the two coincide, but they need not. And even where they coincide a difference in emphasis can sometimes be discerned. One might even distinguish between a race prejudice which is essentially based on colour and a race prejudice which is obsessed with the myth of blood. Among north American whites the emphasis is on purity of blood. A person might have a skin which is indisputably white. But if the Legal Calculators of Florida were to discover that one eighth of this white man's blood was 'African or Negro blood', the white-skinned man becomes classified as a Negro.

The prejudice of Latin America, however, seems to be based ultimately on colour. Class stratification in Brazil follows faithfully the shades of skin-colour—the fairer your child is the better are its chances of social success in the future.

If we go back north and look at canons of social evaluation among the Afro-Americans themselves we might again discern differences in social status according to shade of skin-colour. That is to say, American Negroes between themselves are like Latin Americans—they sometimes classify each other socially on a basis of varying pigmentation. Until fairly recently it was a case of rising in respectability the paler you became. But now there is a distinct school of Afro-American aesthetic thought which would award you more credit points if you manage to get any darker. Sociologically all this is essentially an example of colour prejudice without race prejudice—assuming that you accept the thesis that the Negroes of the United States constitute a single race. One thing ought to be emphasized—that colour prejudice within the American Negro community itself is of limited significance. On the one hand, it is an effect of white racism in the country. On the other hand, it is now being squeezed out of existence by that very racism of the white sector of America—as the Negroes acquire a greater sense of common purpose; a greater consciousness of a shared predicament.

A more significant case of colour prejudice without race prejudice is to be found in India. Between Indians themselves this can be a straightforward problem of the aesthetics of sex—

whereby fairness of skin is deemed more attractive than darkness of skin. The colour-criterion of beauty is, I understand, an important factor in the sociology of marital selectivity in India. But this is not entirely unrelated to the multifarious implications of the caste-system itself. India is a monogamous subcontinent independently of the Christian tradition. But Indian monogamy is certainly no more tolerant of mixed marriages than is the extreme Germanic expression of Euro-Christian sexual monopoly. The caste-boundary, sometimes even the linguistic one, are India's equivalents of the race-barrier in marriage.

CONCLUSION

There is something about monogamy which encourages endogamy—that is the persistent intimation we get from looking at these different groups. This endogamous tendency does not always prevail—it might be diluted by other considerations or even be completely neutralized. But as a generalization we can say that an attitude which permits a person to acquire a number of wives is at the same time an attitude which permits him to look beyond his own group for some of those wives. This permissive attitude towards polygamous intermarriages is then extended to the phenomenon of intermarriage generally. Only a small minority of Arabs in the world do, in fact, have more than one wife. When we refer to them as 'polygamous' we are referring to their *toleration* of polygamy rather than their practice of it. It is the attitude which is crucial in this analysis. And the attitude which is tolerant of polygamy has a *tendency* to tolerate exogamous adventures as well.

But the relationship of this marital toleration to racial tolerance at large is by no means a neat one. A complete acceptance of intermarriage does not necessarily denote a complete absence of racial prejudice. The Arabs are not without racial dislikes in spite of their exogamous broadmindedness.[1] And the Latin Americans are

[1] Arab acceptance of intermarriage is far from 'complete'. There are hardly any reservations about Arab males marrying into other races, but there are definite inhibitions about Arab girls becoming wives of non-Arabs. From the point of view of the thesis of this article, this difference is not surprising. Arab polygamy is, in fact, only *polygyny* and never polyandry. The male is permitted more than one wife—therefore the male is also permitted to cross

not without *colour* prejudice in spite of their assimilationist achievements and promiscuous liberalism.

But untidy as the correlation might be between inter-marriage and racial tolerance at large, there can be no doubt that a connection exists. Sex—in or out of wedlock—is a major area of possible inter-group tension. And inter-group relations are bound to be less emotionally charged where this area of tension is narrowed. The politics of sexual inhibitions and sexual rivalry bedevil many a plural society, openly or at the level of the subconscious. And the very idea of sex becomes not only divorced from love but actually tied to the keg of communal hate. Need we ask for whom those wedding bells toll?

---

the racial frontier. But the woman is not permitted to have more than one husband—therefore she is not easily permitted to cross the racial frontier either.

16 Sacred Suicide[1]

DID JESUS CHRIST COMMIT SUICIDE?

A startling question! A question which, to Christians and Muslims alike, verges on blasphemy. Some might even assert that it *is* blasphemy. But that would be an exaggeration. There is a spiritual impotence in *inquiry* which saves it from sinning. Only *answers* have the capacity to blaspheme. And we have yet to answer the question 'Did Jesus Christ commit suicide?'

The question is important because the death of Jesus dramatizes the difficulties of disentangling martyrdom from self-embraced death. Those difficulties are partly logical and partly moral. This paper hopes to outline the main problem involved in them. But an even more ambitious undertaking of the paper is to draw attention to a possible correlation between suicidal tendencies and doctrinal non-violence. In other words, *a creed which over-emphasizes a non-violent approach to human disagreement tends to sharpen suicidal inclinations in its fanatics—That is the main thesis of this article.* The creeds which spring to mind include certain schools of Hinduism, Buddhism and Christianity. It is not belief in these religions which sharpens suicidal inclinations; it is *fanatical* belief which does so. Islam, on the other hand, does not overglorify the virtues of non-violence. Fanaticism in Islam has therefore tended to produce aggression against others, rather than self-destruction. The depressing moral of all this is that ultimate heights of dedication to a cause are violent in nature. The point at issue is simply whether the violence is self-regarding or other-regarding. And so even passive resistance is often just an instance of suppressed violence, capable of erupting into acts of heroic suicide. Modern examples of such eruptions must include the political suicides by fire which Buddhists in South East Asia have

[1] Reprinted with permission from *Transition*, Vol. V, No. 21, 1965.

repeatedly demonstrated to the world in recent months. A more controversial case concerns the death of Dag Hammarskjöld. Here again we are on the brinks of blasphemy—this time diplomatic rather than religious. But did Dag Hammarskjöld commit suicide?

MARTYRDOM AND SUICIDE

Before we take a closer look at these enquiries about Jesus and Hammarskjöld let us first examine the relationship between suicide and martyrdom at large. Suicide is self-destruction; martyrdom is often self-exposure to destruction by another. The Christian tradition in the West has tended to condemn suicide while admiring martyrdom in its own cause. And yet there are occasions when martyrdom should, in fact, be deemed to be the most reprehensible form of suicide. After all, a person who kills himself with his own hand is doing his own dirty work; whereas the martyr often revels in letting someone else take the guilt of his destruction. It is like the war hero who undertakes a task for which his enemy, as his enemy, has to kill him. If the hero's death was absolutely predictable before he started, the greater would his heroism be in the eyes of his countrymen. But the same countrymen would have despised their man if he had pulled the fatal trigger himself. This kind of attitude was best illustrated in Fascist thought, but it is characteristic of the ethics of warfare at large. As Mussolini put it:

> War alone brings all human energies to their highest tension and sets a seal of nobility on the peoples who have the virtue to face it. All other tests are but substitutes which never make a man face himself in the alternative of life or death . . . It is thus that the Fascist loves and accepts life, ignores and disdains suicide.[1]

That is the whole paradox of the ethics of war. The American equivalent of this bravado is the immortal line, 'Give me liberty

---

[1] 'The Doctrine of Fascism: Fundamental Principles', *Encyclopedia Italiana*, Vol. XIV. See I. S. Munro, *From Fascism to World Power* (London: Alexander Maclehose, 1933).

or give me death.'[1] And yet there is a further irony in this—and it concerns the bounds of that liberty. Liberty for the individual implies some kind of choice. The ultimate physical events for the individual are his own birth and his own death. No individual chooses to be born—barring accidents of passion, the choice was at best made by his parents on a night nine months previously. But the same person who could not choose whether to be born will one day be able to choose whether to die. 'To be or not to be'—Hamlet was in the typical agony of someone contemplating suicide. But an important point in the dilemma of this Danish prince was obscured by the way it was formulated. The choice before Hamlet was not really between 'being and not being'. In logic, only an unborn babe could have such a choice. The real question before Hamlet was negative; it was 'To die or not to die.' Entry into a state of being is not, in practice, a matter of choice. Only *exit* out of being can be optional. And even that option has definite limits.

If then freedom of the individual postulates choice, and death is the ultimate optional physical event for the individual, cool self-destruction is the ultimate exercise of individual freedom. But the normal ethics of heroism in the West outside existentialism do not concede this point. A war hero is permitted to give his life for the sake of freedom, but he is not permitted to take his life as an act of freedom. The morality of 'Give me liberty or give me death' does indeed regard death as an escape from tyranny; but it does not regard death as freedom itself when self-embraced.

One of the few occasions when direct suicide is dignified in the ethics of warfare is in the case of abject failure after heroic pretensions. That is the difference between Mussolini and Hitler. By the nature of his death Mussolini 'lived' up to his claim that Fascism 'disdains suicide'. He was executed. But by that very execution Mussolini died without dignity. Contrast this with the account of Hitler's death as given by Erik Kempka, Hitler's private chauffeur. About half an hour or more before his death Hitler called his chauffeur and pilot and said he wanted to say goodbye as well as to give him his last orders. Hitler proposed to shoot himself—but he wanted his pilot to try out one more exercise in dispatching. 'I make you personally responsible for

---

[1] It served as a militant slogan for both American liberalism and American nationalism.

burning the corpses of my wife and me,' Hitler gave his last orders.[1]

On that thirtieth day of April, 1945, Hitler shot himself. But shooting was a little too masculine for Eva, Hitler's wife. She used poison instead for her own exit. Theirs was an end which had greater dignity than that of Mussolini. Suicide becomes respectable when the life which it ends at once aspired to great heights and descended to such depths. That was the suicide of Brutus when his grand Roman designs crumbled at the final battlefield. It was the suicide of Hitler when his own Caesarian ambitions dissolved in ignominy a generation ago.

THE BUDDHIST IN FLAMES

But occasions for dignified suicide are not always as few in the Orient as they have been in the West. One of the striking things about the first half of this decade in Asia is the use of self-inflammation as a form of political protest. There are indeed precedents in that part of the world for this kind of indignation, but the flames of self-immolation have assumed greater global conspicuousness in the last few years. Christianity, which is itself based on the martyrdom of Jesus, was challenged in its own language in South Vietnam in 1964. Buddhist monks set themselves on fire in protest against religious persecution from a Christian regime. The fact that these suicides were by priests lent a halo of Buddhist sacredness to the flames of self-destruction.

And yet Buddhism is the creed of non-violence par excellence—attaching greater value to life than even Jesus did. Buddhism seeks to spare not just human life but animal life at large. As the great Teacher said: 'A man is not of the Noble (*Ariya*) because he injures living creatures; he is so called because he refrains from injuring *all* living creatures.'[2] Buddha was also aware of the dangers of precipitate indignation, for he warned: 'Beware of bodily anger, and control thy body! . . . Beware of the anger of the mind, and control thy mind!'[3] And yet we have seen the

[1] WPIX Inc., *The Secret Life of Adolf Hitler* (New York: The Citadel Press, 1960). There are alternative accounts of Hitler's death.

[2] See *The Dhammapada*, translated by Irving Babbitt (New York: New Directions Publishing Corporation, 1965), p. 42.

[3] *Ibid.*, p. 37.

spectacular indignation of Buddhist monks as they set themselves aflame in our own time.

But perhaps Buddhism heightens the suicidal urge not only because of its doctrinal non-violence but also because of the whole idea of Nirvana as the extinction of fundamental human desires. The Buddhist seeks this extinction in a way similar to the Christian aspiration for admission into Heaven. Some scholars have argued that 'the Buddhist Nirvanic quest is at bottom not for mere cessation but for the eternal'.[1] This is a persuasive interpretation of the quest. But the great majority of adherents of any religion follow a mere vulgarized form of that religion. Followers of the Buddha are no exception. If Nirvana is the extinction of earthly human desires one desire which could easily be included is the desire to live. It might then be assumed that this desire, too, needs to be conquered in the here and now— provided the cause is right. And Nirvana vulgarized then becomes a call to suicide.

But just as Buddhism was born out of Hinduism, Nirvana was possibly born out of the Yoga tradition and of the whole ascetic impulse of Hindu thought. Doctrinally, Hinduism is not quite as non-violent as Buddhism—though the immense variations in Hinduism ought to be born in mind. Vegetarianism among Hindus is not as comprehensive as among Buddhists nor is the definition of 'vegetarianism' quite as strict.[2] To the extent that Hinduism is thus less inhibited in 'injuring other creatures' its followers are less spectacular in destroying themselves than some Buddhists have been.

There is little Buddhism now left in India, but some degree of mutual influence between Buddhism and Hinduism is sometimes discernible in Ceylon and South India. And it was in South India in 1965 that linguistic nationalism expressed itself in self-ignition in true Buddhist style. On February 12, for example, the headmaster of an elementary school burned himself to death as a protest against the introduction of Hindi as the official language. That was already the fourth reported case of self-immolation in the heat of the agitation against the introduction of Hindi as the official language of India.

---

[1] See Irving Babbitt's essay 'Buddha and the Occident', *ibid.*, p. 96.
[2] This is perhaps more true of Theravada Buddhism than of some of the other denominations.

Further North in India Hinduism becomes more clearly unaffected by its Buddhist offspring. Spectacular suicides are less in evidence, but the tradition of asceticism retains its hold. Asceticism is self-denial; it becomes a life of self-imposed hardship; then a life of self-inflicted suffering. From this doctrine is an easy transition to the slow suicide of the passive fanatic.

The relevance of this to the success of Gandhism in India is not difficult to see. Tom Mboya put this in a different way when he said 'Even those leaders who accept Gandhi's philosophy find that there are limitations to its use in Africa.'[1] What limitations? One limitation we might include is that Africa has no ascetic tradition of the Hindu kind. The idea of lying across a railway line as a form of passive resistance would fire few imaginations on the African continent. As for the idea of 'fasting unto death', this has become almost uniquely Indian. These are instances where the spirit of non-violent resistance needs a certain suicidal resignation to work effectively. In Hindu movements of protest in modern times martyrdom and a suicidal inclination are once again impossible to separate. In this particular respect, if in no other, Hinduism is perhaps in an intermediate stage between Buddhist self-sacrifice and the tradition of martyrdom in Christianity.[2]

ADAM AND SOCRATES

But death in Christianity is related not only to sacrifice and salvation but also to sin and punishment. And it all goes back to Genesis.

[1] *Freedom and After* (London: Deutsch, 1963).

[2] For a discussion of some aspects of Hindu asceticism see G. S. Ghurye, *Indian Sadhus* (Bombay: The Popular Book Depot, 1953). E. W. F. Tomlin has noted: 'If a half-naked or wholly naked Hindu . . . persists in holding his arm in the air until, deprived of circulation, it begins to wither and atrophy . . . or, if the better to demonstrate his indifference to material wants, he starves himself to within an ace of death or nearly buries himself alive—or actually does so—we tend to dismiss these acts as mere wanton aberrations, the product of ascetic high spirits. Such a judgement is superficial. . . . The Yogi is simply a man who takes the Hindu philosophy to its logical conclusion.' See Tomlin, *The Oriental Philosophers* (New York: Harper Colophon Books, 1963), p. 231.

For background about religion and politics in Burma, the Philippines and Indonesia see Fred R. von der Mehden, *Religion and Nationalism in Southeast Asia* (Madison: University of Wisconsin Press, 1963).

In the Garden of Eden something approaching suicide took place. Mankind virtually committed suicide when the first man, Adam, sinned his way to Death. This relationship between sin, suicide and punishment was later to find some kind of echo in the fate of Socrates. Socrates was sentenced to suicide on charges of corrupting the youth of Athens with his teaching. There were several occasions when, pending the execution of the sentence, the sage could have escaped from jail, but he decided to respect the sentence even though he disagreed with it. He had the suicidal dignity to wait for the hemlock—and drink it.

The analogy between the fate of Adam and the fate of Socrates is, in some ways, powerfully imaginative. Socrates had described himself as a midwife of philosophy—helping pregnant minds to deliver their own thoughts. But another metaphor is to regard Socrates as a Tree of Knowledge, bearing philosophical fruit which was soon forbidden to the youth of Athens. There are two ways of dealing with a situation in which forbidden fruit is partaken. One is to punish the one who partakes of the fruit—which is what happened to Adam. The other is to destroy the fruit itself or the tree which bears it—which was the fate suffered by Socrates. In both stories we find insinuations of sexual disobedience too. Adam and Eve 'corrupted' themselves, while Socrates allegedly 'corrupted' young Athenians. Self-awareness, sin and suicide find parts to play within the two dramas. The fate of Adam is the most momentous punishment in theology; the fate of Socrates the most momentous one in intellectual history. Both cases have raised basic questions about the nature of justice. The case of Socrates raised questions about justice in the state and the limits of freedom in educating the youth. The case of Adam raised questions about justice before God and the limits of man in educating himself. Was Athens just to Socrates? Posterity has tended to say No! Was God just to Adam? Posterity can say Yes. But was He just to Mankind following Adam's sin? That is more difficult to answer.

> As by one sole man sin entered the world,
>   and death by sin.
> And thus death passed to all men,
>   because all have sinned.[1]

[1] Romans 5: 12, 18–19.

If we decide to say that God was just in this matter, and mankind must bear full responsibility, it is difficult to escape the suicidal implications of this. If man sinned with complete deliberation, then mankind inflicted Death on itself that fatal day in the Garden of Eden. But a more limited way of putting it is to say that Adam made all future suicides possible. There could be no suicide without a capacity to die; and no death without Adam's sin.

But this is a minimal claim. A more ambitious one would take us right back to the brink of blasphemy. Our defence can only be that we are still in the realm of hypothesizing. All hypotheses are questions and, until answered, all questions fall short of blasphemy.

The hypothesis this time is that Christianity in its original formulation rested on two Pillars of Suicide. Paradise was both lost and regained by acts verging on the suicidal. It was lost, as we have seen, because of Adam's sinful passport to the domain of human demise. Paradise was later to be regained because Jesus gave his life for man's redemption.

A SUICIDE ON THE CROSS?

There is a dialectic which is almost Hegelian in the implications of this redemption of man. Death came when Adam sinned. Death is a negation. Man was redeemed when Jesus was crucified. Jesus's death thus negated the death which came with Adam's sin. This is the Divine Dialectic—the ultimate negation of the negation.

> As by one sole man sin entered the world,
>   and death by sin.
> And thus death passed to all men,
>   because all have sinned . . .
>
> As from one sole transgression
>   there followed condemnation for all,
> So from one sole deed of justice
>   there followed justification for life . . .[1]

[1] *Ibid.*

In the Divine Dialectic Jesus and Adam became two Adams—
two men who determined the whole course of human history.
The fifteenth chapter of the First Corinthians is more explicit
about this doctrine of two Adams:

> Thus is it written:
> There was made the first man, Adam,
>   living soul
> The last Adam
>   lifegiving Spirit.

In *Paradise Lost* Milton was later to capture the essential
voluntariness and premeditation of the death of Jesus. This
comes out more effectively in Milton's masterpiece that it does in
his sequel of *Paradise Regained*. The conversation in Book XI of
Paradise Lost between the Son of God and His father thousands
of years before Jesus became Son of Man heightens the cool
premeditation of it all. Adam's sin did not have to be redeemed
by a crucifixion. It was up to God himself to determine the price
of atonement. That the price was the death of Jesus was something agreed between God and his Son. As a former Professor of
Sacred Scriptures at the *Institut Catholique* in Paris put it,

> Jesus was not condemned because he had been misunderstood.
> He had exposed himself to suspicion by the attitude he had
> openly adopted and by the tenor of his message. Only by his
> death did he triumph over his accusers. Had Pilate, *per
> impossible*, decided to keep him in prison, the Christian
> religion would not have owed its birth to him.[1]

And yet his death was to give rise to a doctrine of *deicide* against
the Jews. It is perhaps in such cases that martyrdom gives the
impression of being less self-regarding than suicide—since the

---

[1] Alfred Firmin Loisy, *The Birth of the Christian Religion and the Origins of
the New Testament* (New York: University Books, 1962. Translated from the
French by L. P. Jacks), p. 84. Alfred Loisy was born in 1857 and died in 1940.
From his appointment in 1889 to the professorship of Sacred Scriptures at the
Institut Catholique in Paris until his excommunication in 1908, he was one of
the acknowledged leaders of that movement in the Roman Catholic Church
known as 'Catholic Modernism'. See W. Norman Pittenger's introduction to
Loisy's book cited above.

martyrdom is made possible by an assumed guilt in others. Again the year of 1965 was historic from the point of view of the doctrine of deicide. It marked an attempt at the Vatican to reintroduce the doctrine after its abolition the previous year. At its fourth session in 1964 the Ecumenical Council adopted, by an overwhelming majority, a statement absolving the Jews of the Crucifixion. But in the course of the first few months of 1965 there were reports from Rome indicating that modifications of the text absolving the Jews were being considered to meet theological objections from Catholic conservatives.

The Rome report evoked criticism from such Jewish leaders as Morris B. Avram, President of the American Jewish Committee, and the Rev. Dr Joachim Prinz, President of the American Jewish Congress. Some secular Jewish groups apparently went as far as to lobby Catholic clergy at the Ecumenical Council in an attempt to secure theological changes and doctrinal amendments. But these groups were criticized by Moses I. Feuerstein, President of the Union of Orthodox Congregations of America. Mr Feuerstein said that the Roman Catholic Church alone must determine whether it wishes to change its theology, dogmas and principles. He asserted that Jews had 'suffered the evils of hatred, persecution and bloodshed for centuries, due to the viciousness of the label of deicide'. He added

This is a blot on the historical record of Christianity. Its eradication is not the task of the Jewish community and not a problem of the Jewish conscience.[1]

It seems reasonable to suppose that the doctrine of deicide was a misunderstanding of the real implications of the sacrifice of Jesus. And the abolition of the doctrine by an overwhelming majority of the Ecumenical Council in 1964 was a measure of the more tolerant majority opinion of Catholics in the world. But if that is the case we have in the sacrifice of Jesus an eternal martyr without an eternal culprit. If we take 'deicide' out of the Crucifixion, does not Crucifixion become more clearly than ever a case of divine suicide?

In the Gospel according to St John suicide and deicide become a dialogue of suspicion between Jesus and the Jews. Jesus knows that

[1] See *New York Times*, May 10, 1965.

the Jews are about to contrive his death—and thus commit deicide.
The Jews in turn think that Jesus is about to commit suicide.

> Then said Jesus again unto them, I go my way, and ye shall
> seek me and shall die in your sins; whither I go you cannot
> come.
> Then said the Jews, will he kill himself? because he saith,
> whither I go, ye cannot come.[1]

In this dialogue of mutual suspicion, perhaps both divinations
were true in their different ways. The particular Jews who contrived to have Jesus crucified according to the Gospels were
themselves guilty of deicide—but not their posterity. Yet this
guilt is purely symbolic, for Jesus died because he wanted to.

As for the effect of all this symbolism on doctrinal non-
violence in Christianity, direct suicide remains a 'mortal' sin in
much of Christian thought. Christian priests in spectacular
flames would be a rare sight. Moreover, Christianity is more
permissive of violence against living creatures than either
Buddhism or Hinduism. Christianity does indeed highly respect
human life, but it does permit itself a concept of 'crusade' or, in
a more modern guise, a 'just war'. It has no strong protective
umbrella for the animal kingdom to compare with that of Hindus
or Buddhists. To the extent that the instinct to violence in man
is permitted by Christianity to shed the blood of other creatures
under certain conditions, that instinct is less tempted to turn itself
against itself. And so the *blatant* suicidal impulse that one sometimes finds in Hindus and Buddhists is not quite as active in the
Christian.

What is more usual in Christian idealism is the more disguised suicidal trend of martyrdom. Early in the second century
Ignatius, a Christian leader in Asia, revelled in the expectation
of being flung to the lions in the Colosseum by the Romans.
As he was being transported to Rome Ignatius wrote:

> Suffer me to become food for the wild beasts through whose
> instrumentality it will be granted to me to attain God . . .
> Permit me to be an imitator of the passion of my God.[2]

---

[1] St. John 8: 21, 22.
[2] Ignatius: *Epistles to the Romans*, iv, V, trans. by A. Roberts and J. Donaldson.

This revelling in imitating the martyrdom of Jesus is an enduring theme in the universe of Christian aspirations at their most idealized. It is like the cry of St Peter when, years after Jesus, he too was sentenced to crucifixion:

'To die as the Lord died? It is more than I deserve!'

THE MYSTERY OF HAMMARSKJÖLD

But what place have all these themes in the modern world? We know that spectacular suicides by fire are part of the recent political picture of the Orient. But does the Christian theme of martyrdom also manifest itself in modern politics?

As a step towards answering this question, let us once again quote:

For the sacrificed—in the hour of sacrifice—only one thing counts: faith—alone among enemies and skeptics. Faith, in spite of the humiliation which is both the necessary precondition and the consequence of faith, faith without any hope of compensation other than he can find in a faith which reality seems so thoroughly to refute.

Would the Crucifixion have had any sublimity or meaning if Jesus had seen Himself crowned with the halo of martyrdom? What we have later added was not there for Him.[1]

These were the words of Dag Hammarskjöld. They were written four years before he was killed in a plane crash near Ndola, Zambia, in the course of United Nations involvement in the chaos of the Congo. They constitute only part of the theme of self-sacrifice which keeps on recurring in the record of his thoughts. In our discussion of Buddhism and Christianity we have so far focused our attention on the doctrine of non-violence. This doctrine has, of course, an intimate relationship with *Peace* as a human aspiration. In our own day the United Nations Organization is mankind's most specific instrument for the pursuit of peace. And the Secretary-General of that Organization

[1] Dag Hammarskjöld, *Markings*, trans. from the Swedish by Leif Sjoberg and W. H. Auden (New York: Alfred A. Knopf, 1965), p. 151. (In UK, Faber.)

becomes the diplomatic equivalent of a religious teacher—a servant of peace and of the salvation of states.

But what connection does this really have with religion in the more literal sense? We might first note the coincidence of religious affiliation. The first two Secretaries-General, Trygve Lie and Dag Hammarkjöld, happened to come to their peace missions via the Christian ethic of their Scandinavian homes. With the election of U Thant the Buddhist tradition, too, came to contribute its own servant to world peace.

But have these people been genuinely influenced by their religious backgrounds in their international activities? And if they have, has there been a theme of martyrdom or suicide in the roles which they have played?

During the years that U Thant has held office no great issue has as yet shaken the status of the Secretary-General. As for Trygve Lie, he was, at the most, a martyr only in a figurative sense. Nominated by the Russians themselves for the post of Secretary-General in 1946 he later became a victim of intense Russian hostility—and was forced to resign in 1952.

It is on the fate of Dag Hammarskjöld that the possibilities of a more literal martyrdom might really hinge. His friend, W. H. Auden, tells us that two themes came to preoccupy Hammarskjöld's thoughts. First, the conviction that no man could properly do what he is called upon to do in this life unless he can learn to forget his ego and act as instrument of God. Second, that for Hammarskjöld himself, the way to which he was called would lead to the Cross, i.e. to suffering, worldly humiliation, and the physical sacrifice of his life. Auden goes on to ask himself:

> Just how did Hammarskjöld envisage his end?
> Did he expect to be assassinated like Count Bernadotte?
> To be lynched by an infuriated General Assembly?
> Or simply to drop dead from a heart attack brought on by hard work?[1]

Auden then goes on to note that Hammarskjöld did indeed come to be killed in the course of duty—but to Auden 'it is difficult to think of an airplane crash as an "act of sacrifice" in the sense in

[1] W. H. Auden's Introduction to *Markings, op. cit.*, p. xvii.

which Hammarskjöld uses the term. It could happen to any of us, regardless of any "commitment".'[1]

But, in fact, Hammarskjöld's death was not regarded as devoid of 'commitment'. On September 29, 1961, many world figures assembled in Sweden to honour him. Among those who stood in silent respect were King Gustav and Queen Louise of Sweden, Vice-President Lyndon B. Johnson of the United States, and Trygve Lie, Hammarskjöld's predecessor in the post. Resting on Dag Hammarskjöld's coffin was his family's wreath with a single word for an inscription—'Why?'

To many the answer was that Hammarskjöld had died in the service of a divided mankind. And for those who suspected sabotage by his enemies, the martyrdom was more literal still.

But now there is a school of thought which is putting forward a thesis that Hammarskjöld actually committed suicide. In the United States this theory is espoused by a small radical wing of American intellectuals. The claim is that never had Hammarskjöld felt as lonely internationally as he must have felt that autumn. Not only the Soviet bloc with its demands for a *troika* but also Britain, France, Portugal and Belgium were arrayed against him. Although he was leaving on yet another peace mission for the Congo, prospects for a durable success seemed more remote than ever. Was this the kind of situation which would turn the thoughts of a man like Hammarskjöld to suicide? Was he indeed that kind of man?

Fatigue dulls the pain, but awakes enticing thoughts of death. So! *that* is the way in which you are tempted to overcome your loneliness—by making the ultimate escape from life . . . I dare not believe, I do not see how I shall ever be able to believe: that I am not alone . . . Loneliness is not the sickness unto death. No, but can it be cured except by death?[2]

These were Hammarskjöld's words. They were written nearly a decade before his actual death, but they at least help to bear out W. H. Auden's statement that 'the thought of suicide was not strange to Hammarskjöld'.[3]

[1] *Ibid.*
[2] Dag Hammarskjöld, *Markings, op. cit.*, pp. 86–7.
[3] Auden, *op. cit.*, p. xv.

But did he kill himself on that plane in September 1961? Auden does not consider this possibility. But those who have done so claim that Hammarskjöld was mystically involved with an obsessive image of himself as a Christ figure who must follow Christ's path. 'His suicidal drives were no longer a private affair— they became God's demand for sacrificial death which would redeem the world, a crucifixion.' He then contrived the plane crash at Ndola.

The trouble with this theory so far is not that it is implausible but that it is being championed by people who are hostile to the memory of Hammarskjöld for other reasons. And so the theory is expressed in words of bitter polemics and condemnation. This is certainly the case in regard to Eric Norden's article in the militant American magazine *Fact*. Norden cites in support of his theory of suicide Dr John Lindberg, 'the prominent Swedish economist, philosopher, international-law expert, and one of the world's foremost social theorists'. Apparently Lindberg had taught Dag Hammarskjöld and had been an associate of his for many years.

But one need not be a John Lindberg to reach the shocking conclusion that Hammarskjöld became a schizophrenic megalomaniac towards the end of his life, that his death was neither accident nor political plot, that he committed suicide in a tortured, twisted and brutal manner, and that he murdered 15 innocent people in the process. In his last act Hammarskjöld was no better than the scourge of the commercial lines: the suicidal maniac who takes out an astronomical insurance policy on himself and then blows up the plane in flight. The only difference was that Hammarskjöld's insurance was not a million dollars. It was—or he hoped it would be—immortality.[1]

These are words of hostility, but one need not be hostile to the memory of Hammarskjöld to regard suicide as a possibility. Was the balance of his mind upset by the loneliness of the Congo crisis? And did he want a suicide which looked like sabotage? We shall never know for certain. A certain mystery surrounds some of the decisions he took in regard to his flight on the *Albertina*. In his book *The Last Days of Dag Hammarskjöld*

---

[1] Eric Norden, 'The Strange Death of Dag Hammarskjöld', *Fact*, Vol. II, No. 2, March–April, 1965, pp. 4–5.

Arthur Gavshon draws attention to some of these. He says:
'Hammarskjöld arranged his flight in conditions which looked
absurd to cautious men.'[1] The *Albertina* was a damaged plane;
it had no escort; it was out of radio contact with base; it flew
unnecessarily at night; it remained in the air surprisingly long;
it changed its mind suddenly about where to land. There was one
survivor of the crash—Sergeant Harold M. Julien, acting Chief
Security Officer for the UN Congo Command and a former
American Marine. Julien died later, but not before he had said
that Hammarskjöld had suddenly 'changed his mind' about
landing at Ndola and that he had told the pilot to alter course for
another destination. Moments later, according to the injured man,
there was a series of explosions aboard the plane.

Two days before flying to the Congo Hammarskjöld had
dictated a letter to an old friend of his at the Swedish Foreign
Office. He asked him to take charge of all his personal documents
in case he should die. In the course of the preceding three months
Hammarskjöld had had occasion to write the following lines:

> Do I fear a compulsion in me
> To be so destroyed?
> Or is there someone
> In the depths of my being,
> Waiting for permission to
> pull the trigger?
> Tired
> And lonely,
> So tired
> The heart aches . . .[2]

CONCLUSION

With the violent death of every great man there is a great
temptation to look for reasons other than the obvious. Thus it was
that Bertrand Russell headed a 'Who Killed Kennedy?' committee
in Britain, sincerely dissatisfied with the official explanation of

---

[1] Arthur L. Gavshon, *The Last Days of Dag Hammarskjöld* (London:
Barrie and Rockliff with Pall Mall, 1963), pp. 63–4.

[2] *Markings*, June 18, 1961 and July 6, 1961, pp. 212–13.

the Warren Report. And thus it is that others are seeking alternative explanations for the plane crash which killed Dag Hammarskjold.

But from the point of view of this particular essay what matters is not whether Hammarskjöld actually did finally arrange to kill himself but that he had gone through life combining a quest for martyrdom, and a desire to serve God with a suicidal instinct.

In Adam mankind had committed a suicidal sin. In Jesus Christ mankind was redeemed by an act of martyrdom on the Cross. And then the United Nations Organization came to be formed for a different kind of man's redemption.

Was the *Albertina* a Cross in the sky?

Index